Supporting
Microsoft®
Windows® 95 Volume Two

Hands-On, Self-Paced Training for Supporting Windows 95

PUBLISHED BY
Microsoft Press
A Division of Microsoft Corporation
One Microsoft Way
Redmond, Washington 98052-6399

Library of Congress Cataloging-in-Publication Data
Microsoft Windows 95 training : hands-on, self-paced training for
    supporting Windows 95 / Microsoft Corporation.
        p.   cm.
    Includes index.
    ISBN 1-55615-931-5
    1. Microsoft Windows 95.   2. Operating systems (Computers)
I. Microsoft Corporation.
QA76.76.O63M524213 1995
005.4'469--dc20   95-36241
                                              CIP

Printed and bound in the United States of America.

1 2 3 4 5 6 7 8 9 MLML 0 9 8 7 6 5

Distributed to the book trade in Canada by Macmillan of Canada, a division of Canada Publishing Corporation.

A CIP catalogue record for this book is available from the British Library.

Microsoft Press books are available through booksellers and distributors worldwide. For further information about international editions, contact your local Microsoft Corporation office. Or contact Microsoft Press International directly at fax (206) 936-7329.

3Com and EtherLink are registered trademarks of 3Com Corporation. Adobe and PostScript are trademarks of Adobe Systems, Inc. AT&T is a registered trademark of American Telephone and Telegraph Company. Apple, Macintosh, and TrueType are registered trademarks and Power Macintosh is a trademark of Apple Computer, Inc. Banyan and VINES are registered trademarks and StreetTalk is a trademark of Banyan Systems, Inc. Compaq is a registered trademark of Compaq Computer Corporation. CompuServe is a registered trademark of CompuServe, Inc. ArcNet is a registered trademark of Datapoint Corporation. DEC, DECnet, and PATHWORKS are trademarks of Digital Equipment Corporation. Truespeech is a trademark of DSP Group, Inc. Kodak is a registered trademark of Eastman Kodak Company. FTP Software is a registered trademark of FTP Software, Inc. DeskJet, Hewlett-Packard, HP, JetDirect, and LaserJet are registered trademarks of Hewlett-Packard Company. Intel and Pentium are registered trademarks of Intel Corporation. AT, IBM, Micro Channel, OS/2, PS/2, and XGA are registered trademarks and PowerPC and POWERstation are trademarks of International Business Machines Corporation. Helvetica is a registered trademark of Linotype AG and its subsidiaries. Logitech is a trademark of Logitech, Inc. 1-2-3 and Lotus are registered trademarks of Lotus Development Corporation. Matrox is a registered trademark of Matrox Electronic Systems, Inc. Panasonic is a registered trademark of Matsushita Electric Co., Ltd. DoubleSpace, FoxBASE, FoxPro, Microsoft, Microsoft Press, MS, MS-DOS, PowerPoint, Visual Basic, Win32, Windows, and the Windows logo are registered trademarks and BackOffice, DriveSpace, Microsoft At Work, Natural Keyboard, Visual C++, and Windows NT are trademarks of Microsoft Corporation. NetScape is a trademark of NetScape Communications Corporation. DR DOS, NetWare, and Novell are registered trademarks of Novell, Inc. Epson is a registered trademark of Seiko Epson Corporation, Inc. Shiva is a registered trademark of Shiva Microsystems Corporation. SONY is a registered trademark of Sony Corporation. Stacker is a registered trademark of STAC Electronics. PC-NFS is a registered trademark and SunSoft is a trademark of Sun Microsystems, Inc. Western Digital is a trademark of Western Digital Corporation. XEROX is a registered trademark and XNS is a trademark of Xerox Corporation. UNIX is a registered trademark in the United States and other countries, licensed exclusively through X/Open Company, Ltd.

Project Lead/Instructional Designer: Jeff Madden
Principal Subject Matter Expert: Mike Galos
Subject Matter Experts: Robert Laws, Jeff Clark,
   Richard Wallace
Network Concepts CBT: Nicole McCormick
Technical Contributors: Jonas Roco, Autumn Womack
Editor: Shari G. Smith

Indexer: Jane Dow
Production Support: Irene Barnett, Barnett Communications
Graphic Artists: Julie Stone, Kirsten Larson
Manufacturing Support: Bo Galford
Product Managers: Robert Stewart, Elaine Stovall,
   Steve Thues
Multimedia Production: Digital Post & Graphics

Contents

Volume 1

Volume 2

CHAPTER 13

Communications

Before You Begin

To complete the lessons in this chapter, you must have:

- Completed Chapter 1 and installed Microsoft Windows 95.

Lesson 1: Communications Architecture

Windows 95 communications architecture uses one main virtual device driver to manage access to communication resources. This lesson provides you with an overview of the communications architecture.

After this lesson you will be able to:

- Explain the purpose of VCOMM.VXD.

Estimated lesson time 10 minutes

A communications resource is a physical or logical device that provides a single asynchronous data stream. Serial ports, parallel ports, fax machines, and modems are examples of communications resources.

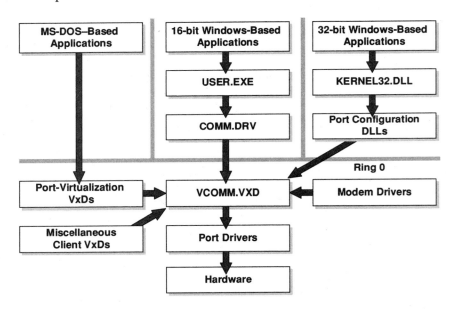

Figure 13.1 Windows 95 communications architecture

The central communications component in Microsoft Windows 95 is the virtual communications driver (VCOMM), a virtual device driver (VxD) that manages all access to communications resources. VCOMM relies on separate VxDs, or port drivers, to access communications resources. This design makes VCOMM easily extensible. If another vendor wants to support a nonstandard communications port, it can create a port driver.

The following briefly describes the components of the architecture.

Component	Description
VCOMM.VXD	The virtual communications driver. VCOMM is a nonreplaceable system component that manages all access to communications resources.
COMM.DRV	The Windows communications driver. COMM.DRV provides a set of exported functions, used for thunking, that USER.EXE calls to implement the Windows communications API. The COMM.DRV file and its functions are used to maintain compatibility with programs designed for Windows 3.*x* communications architecture.
	COMM.DRV uses the VCOMM protected-mode API and is not tied to any specific communications hardware. Hardware vendors should not replace COMM.DRV, as was done in previous versions of Windows, but should create a port driver instead.
Client VxDs	Any VxDs that use the VCOMM client VxD services to access communications resources. Port-virtualization VxDs can be VCOMM client VxDs. Also, certain programs might install VCOMM client VxDs, bypassing the Windows communications API.
Port drivers	Installable VxDs that VCOMM uses to access communications devices. Hardware vendors create port drivers to enable Windows-based programs and VxDs to use their communications ports.
Port-virtualization VxDs	Installable VxDs that virtualize communications hardware for programs running in non-system virtual machines (VMs). Communications hardware vendors can create port-virtualization VxDs to virtualize their devices for Microsoft MS-DOS–based programs.

Because the architecture is virtualized, there is no architectural limit on COM and LPT ports, but there may be hardware limits. If the hardware is available, the computer may have as many COM and LPT ports as wanted.

Sharing Ports and Serial Devices

The actual port is not what is shared but rather the device connected to that port. For example, a user can share serial printers because the printer driver can allow its device to be shared on the network.

Printing for Windows 95 is intercepted and handled by print services.

Port Contention

The default for 16-bit Windows- and MS-DOS–based programs is that only one program can open the same COM port at a time. However, the default behavior can be changed to allow 16-bit Windows- and MS-DOS–based programs to be able to open a COM port already opened by a program if the COM port has been inactive for more than a specified number of seconds. To change the default behavior, add the following entry to the SYSTEM.INI file.

```
[386enh]
COM1AutoAssign=2
```

The actual COM port is identified on the left side of the entry (COM*x*); the amount of idle time is listed on the right side of the entry. In this example, two seconds have been specified.

The default behavior was designed to reduce any possible support problems with programs that wait for calls in the background, such as fax or dial-up servers.

32-bit Windows-based programs have no such limit with programs that access the COM ports because the new communications API calls do not make the same assumptions about port availability.

Lesson Summary

VCOMM.VXD manages access to communications resources. There is no architectural limit on the number of COM and LPT ports present on a computer, only hardware limits.

Lesson 2: Modems

More and more computers include modems as part of their standard equipment. While installation of modems in Windows 95 is usually automated, there may be times when you have a specific configuration that you want to use. This lesson demonstrates how to configure and diagnose modems using Windows 95.

After this lesson you will be able to:

- Install and configure a modem to meet a specific set of user requirements.

Estimated lesson time 20 minutes

Modems are treated as virtualized devices in Windows 95. As such, they have an architecture in the same way print services have an architecture.

There is a main device driver—called Unimodem and provided by Microsoft—and mini-drivers for each modem. A mini-driver is used to make it easier for modem manufacturers to create device-specific functions. The Unimodem driver provided by Windows 95 contains most of the functionality needed by a modem. The modem manufacturers provide the specifics for their hardware in the mini-driver.

Modem Installation

Modems are installed by using the interface provided under the Modems icon in the Controls folder.

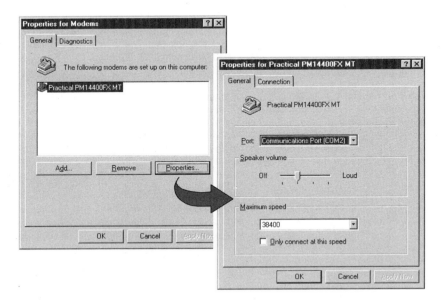

Figure 13.2 Installing a modem

If you install The Microsoft Network, Dial-Up Networking, or other 32-bit Windows-based communications programs without a modem installed, these programs start the Install New Modem wizard.

▶ **To manually install a modem**

1. In the Control Panel, double-click the Modems icon.

   The Modems property sheet appears. It lists the modems installed on the computer.

   If a modem has not been installed, the Install New Modem wizard starts.

2. If you have a modem installed, click the Add button.

The Install New Modem wizard starts.

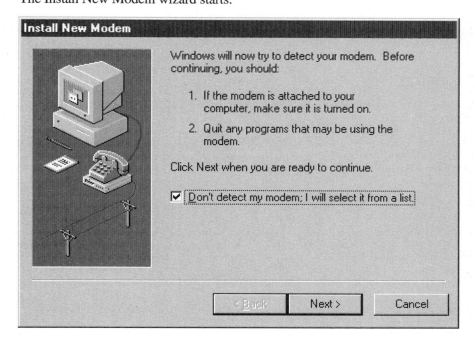

Figure 13.3 Install New Modem wizard with manual installation selected

In this dialog box, you may have the option of automatically or manually installing the modem by using the Detect and Select options.

Leave the check box blank—Windows 95 automatically detects and configures the modem. You will be asked to confirm the configuration.

Click the check box—You manually step through the Install New Modem wizard and make selections.

3. Click the check box, and then click Next.

The Select Device dialog box appears.

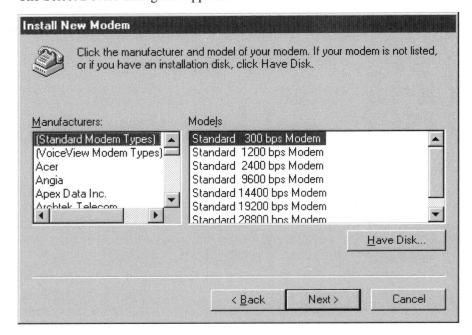

Figure 13.4 Install New Modem wizard with modem selected

4. Click the manufacturer of the modem you want to install. (The manufacturer's name should be located somewhere on the modem.)

The known models by the selected manufacturer appear in the Models list.

5. Click the appropriate modem model, and then click Next.

The Modem Setup dialog box appears.

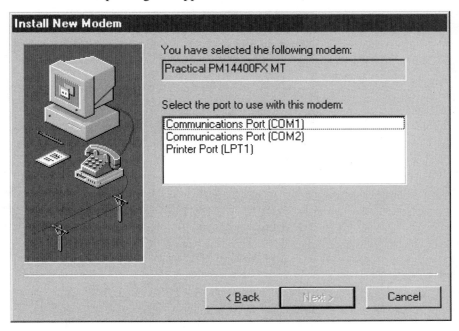

Figure 13.5 Install New Modem wizard with port selected

6. Select the port where the modem is connected. You may also change the model name to something that is more relevant to your computer. Click the Next button.

7. Click the Finish button when the modem has been set up successfully.

The Modems property sheet appears when the installation is complete.

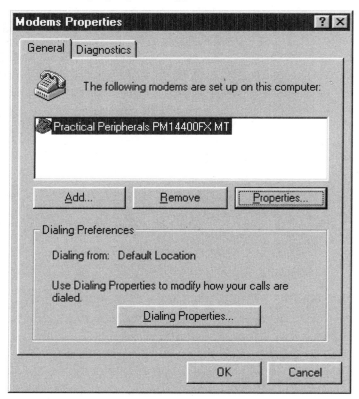

Figure 13.6 General tab on the Modems property sheet

▶ **To change the configuration of a modem**

1. In the Control Panel, double-click the Modems icon.

The Modems property sheet appears.

2. Select a modem.

3. Click the Properties button.

The property sheet of the selected modem appears.

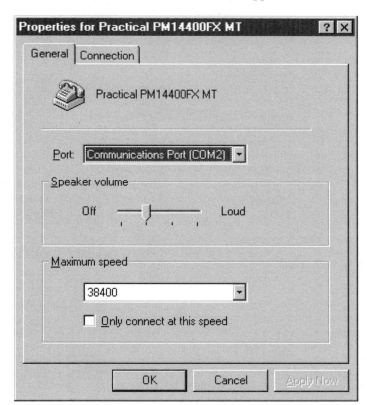

Figure 13.7 Property sheet for a specific modem

On the General tab on the Modems property sheet, the port may be changed or configured, and the maximum speed may be set, but this is not necessarily the speed of the modem. Speaker volume may be adjusted on some models of modems.

4. Click the Connection tab.

The Connection tab on the Modems property sheet of the selected modem appears.

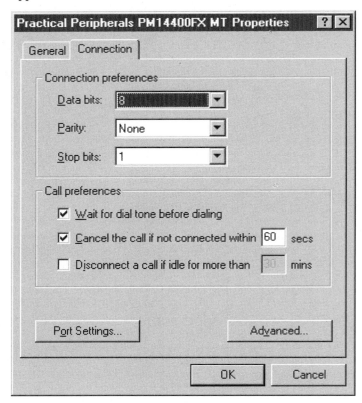

Figure 13.8 Connection tab on the Modems property sheet

The options that appear on this property sheet depend on the type of modem you are using. Options generally include settings for connection and call preferences. If there are additional settings, they would be accessed by clicking the Advanced button.

Clicking the Advanced button displays a dialog box with options to adjust error control, flow control, and set the modulation standard used. It also contains options to enable call logging and to add additional command strings for the modem.

Clicking the Port Settings button displays a dialog box with the option to enable or disable FIFO buffering on a 16550-compatible Universal Asynchronous Receiver Transmitter (UART). You can also adjust the size of the individual transmit and receive buffers in this dialog box.

5. Click the OK or Cancel button to return to the list of installed modems.

6. Click the Close button to close this process.

Modem Diagnostics

The Diagnostics tab on the Modems property sheet allows you to troubleshoot the modem.

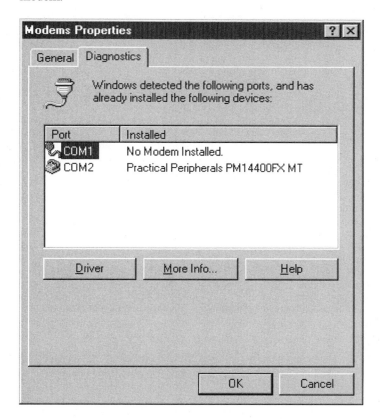

Figure 13.9 Diagnostics tab on the Modems property sheet

When you click the Diagnostics tab, a list of installed serial ports and modems appears. You can choose a given port or modem and receive information about the device selected.

If there is no modem or mouse on a selected port, you will receive information about the port name, interrupt, port address, and universal asynchronous receiver transmitter (UART) chip used. If a mouse is present on the port, the UART information is not shown because the UART test may cause the mouse to stop responding.

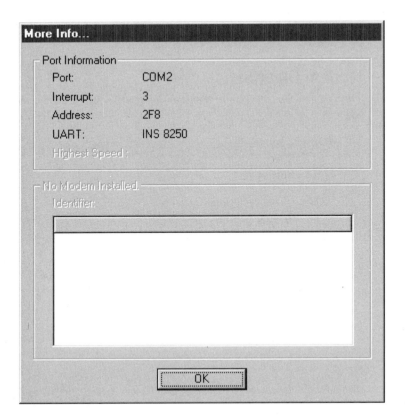

Figure 13.10 Results of modem diagnostic test when no modem is present

If a modem is found on the port, the modem's responses to the ATI1–ATI7 commands, the response to the AT+FCLASS=? fax capabilities test, and the maximum speed of the modem are shown. This data can be used to isolate problems caused by the modem.

The exact meanings of the responses to the ATI1–ATI7 commands, while generally standardized, should be confirmed with the technical reference material for the specific modem. The response to AT+FCLASS=? will be a list of fax modem classes that are supported by the modem.

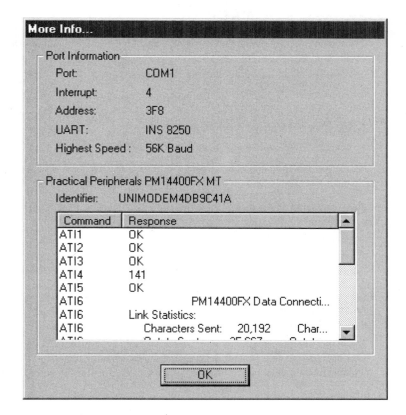

Figure 13.11 Results of modem diagnostic test

Lesson Summary

Modem installation is usually automatic, either as part of the initial installation
process or by using the modem installation function in the Control Panel. However,
you can install and configure a modem manually by walking through the Install
New Modem wizard. Windows 95 also includes modem diagnostic functions which
can be used to determine if a modem is functioning properly.

Lesson 3: Telephony API (TAPI)

Telephony Application Programming Interface (TAPI) is a set of commands and codes that programmers can use when developing programs using telecommunication devices. This lesson introduces some of the TAPI functions that are included with Windows 95.

After this lesson you will be able to:

- Define TAPI and explain how it is used.
- Implement the various telephony options to meet a specific set of user requirements.

Estimated lesson time 25 minutes

The Windows Telephony Application Programming Interface (TAPI) provides a standard way for programs to control telephony functions. TAPI virtualizes the telephone system by acting as a device driver for a telephone network.

Dialing Properties

The basic TAPI settings for the computer are set up from the Install New Modem wizard. Additional details can be set using the Dialing Preferences section of the General tab on the Modems property sheet. In addition, any program that uses TAPI should have a way to access the TAPI Dialing property sheet.

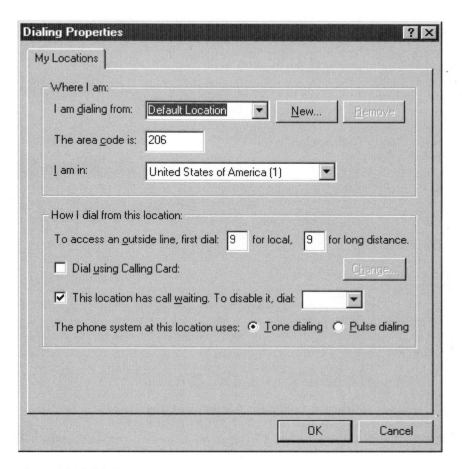

Figure 13.12 Dialing property sheet

One way to access this screen is from Phone Dialer. From the Phone Dialer Tools menu, click Dialing Properties.

The Dialing Properties dialog box allows you to set up locations, calling cards, and drivers.

Location Setup

A *location* in Windows 95 is a set of information which Windows 95 telephony uses to analyze telephone numbers in an international number format that you dial, and to determine the correct sequence of numbers to be dialed. A location does not need to correspond to a particular geographic location, but it usually does. A location could be the numbers needed to dial from your office or the numbers required from a particular hotel room. You can name locations anything you want to help you remember them and select them later.

The information included in a location includes:

- Area (or city) code
- Country code
- Outside line access codes (for both local and long distance calls)
- Preferred calling card

Calling Card

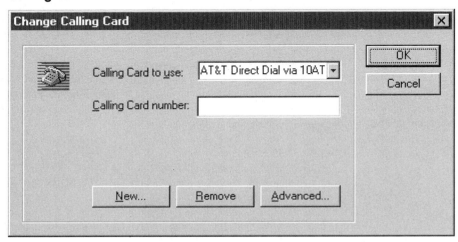

Figure 13.13 Change Calling Card dialog box

A *calling card* in Windows 95 is a set of information which Windows 95 telephony uses to create the sequence of numbers to be dialed for a particular card. A calling card definition may have a calling card number which can be dialed at a specific time during the call placement, without the need to specify the actual number being called. Multiple calling cards may be defined.

Drivers

A Windows 95 telephony driver, also known as a telephony service provider, is software that controls your telephony hardware, for example, a modem, voice mail card, telephone, or other equipment, as directed by your telephony application programs through the Windows TAPI. Usually, the driver is included with your hardware and automatically installed as part of the setup procedure for the hardware.

Using TAPI Functions

In this exercise, you will use the Phone Dialer program to demonstrate the use of the TAPI functions.

▶ **To start the Phone Dialer**

- On the Start menu, point to Programs, Accessories, and then click Phone Dialer.

Note For this exercise, the examples use the 206 area code. Please use your own area code where 206 is shown.

Before continuing, make sure that your modem is *not* connected to the telephone line to prevent making unwanted telephone calls.

If you travel with your computer, you may need to dial from hotels. Generally, each hotel has a different telephone system with different dialing rules. In this exercise, you will set up a hotel location.

▶ **To dial a call in your home area**

1. On the Phone Dialer Tools menu, click Dialing Properties, and then click Default Location in the I am dialing from text box.
2. Click OK to close the dialog box.
3. Type 1 (206) 555-1234 as the number to dial.

   (Remember to substitute your area code for 206.)
4. Click the Dial button.

   What number was used to dial?

   _____

   You will get an error message after a few seconds because your modem is not connected to the telephone lines. If you didn't write down the number dialed, close the error message dialog box and dial again.

▶ **To set up a second location**

1. On the Phone Dialer Tools menu, click Dialing Properties.

   The Dialing Properties dialog box appears.
2. Click the New... button.
3. Type **hotel** in the text box as the new location name, and then click OK.
4. Use Dialing Properties to configure the second location according to the following scenario.

   This example assumes the hotel is in New York City, so the area code is 212. (If your normal location is in the 212 area code, substitute Los Angeles (213) for 212 in the examples.)

To access an outside line, you must dial 9 for a local call and 8 for long distance.

You use an AT&T calling card; its number is 20655512349876. Make sure to select AT&T via 1-800-321-0228 in the Change Calling Card dialog box.

The hotel has call waiting that can be disabled by dialing 70#.

5. When you have made these changes, click OK to close the Dialing Properties dialog box.

6. Type 1 (206) 555-1234 as the number to dial.

   (Remember to substitute your area code for 206.)

7. Click the Dial button.

   What number was used to dial?

   _____

▶ **To dial an extension**

1. On the Phone Dialer Tools menu, click Dialing Properties. In the I am dialing from text box, click Default Location.

2. Click OK to close the Dialing Properties dialog box.

3. Enter 5551 as the Number to dial. Assume that this is a valid internal extension in your company.

4. Click the Dial button.

   What number was used to dial?

   _____

5. Exit Phone Dialer.

Lesson Summary

Telephony functions of Windows 95 are supported in a variety of programs. These programs, such as Phone Dialer, HyperTerminal, and others, allow you to use your computer to make telephone connections from various locations without having to reconfigure the program.

Review

The following questions are intended to reinforce key information presented in this chapter. If you are unable to answer a question, review the appropriate lesson and then try the question again.

1. What is the central communications component in Windows 95?

_____

_____

2. Name the two types of device drivers needed for modems and describe the function of each.

_____

_____

3. What is TAPI?

_____

_____

C H A P T E R   1 4

Printing

Before You Begin

To complete the lessons in this chapter, you must have:

• Completed Chapter 1 and installed Microsoft Windows 95.

Lesson 1: Windows 95 Printing Features

Windows 95 supports several enhancements to the printing process. This lesson introduces these printing features.

After this lesson you will be able to:

- Explain the concept of mini-drivers.
- List the advantages of metafile spooling.

Estimated lesson time 10 minutes

Plug and Play

For printers that recognize Plug and Play, printer installation becomes as simple as plugging in the printer and confirming the printer configuration.

Bidirectional Communications

Bidirectional communications in Windows 95 supports Nibble mode, which provides an asynchronous identification channel between printers and computers. Printers supporting this communication system use this channel to report the device identification on its ROM to the computer. Nibble mode works with Plug and Play.

Extended Capabilities Port

The Extended Capabilities port (ECP) support in Windows 95 allows the use of hardware add-on port cards. ECP features data compression to increase the transfer efficiency of the print job to the printer. This can make spooling about four times faster. Printer support is in the firmware on the card.

Image Color Matching

Image Color Matching allows for color WYSIWYG with device independent-color for color that is consistent across all devices. It supports both universal drivers and PostScript™ mini-drivers which render the printer's colors and images. The Kodak® image color matching software is used for color matching.

Printer Drivers

Windows 95 features two types of drivers designed to solve printer problems caused by larger, more complex printer drivers.

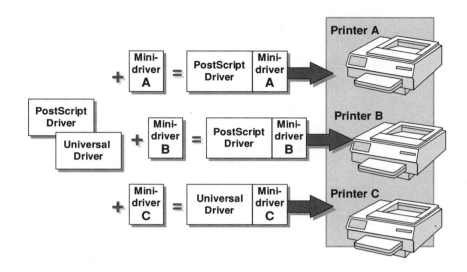

Figure 14.1 The Windows 95 printer driver model

- Universal drivers—Generic drivers used for all printers. There are two types:
  - Regular—Used for all printers except PostScript and some Hewlett-Packard InkJet printers. This is used with a mini-driver which gives the characteristics of the specific printer.
  - PostScript—The PostScript universal driver is used with a PostScript mini-driver which gives the characteristics of the specific printer. PostScript mini-drivers use the Adobe™ PDD and SPD printer description format.

- Mini-drivers—Smaller chunks of code specifically for certain printers. They contain information on specific printer models.

There is one exception to the generic drivers. The HP Color InkJet requires a monolithic driver. This is a unique category that does not follow the mini-driver model.

Universal Drivers Plus Mini-Drivers

With the combination of universal drivers written by Microsoft and the mini-drivers supplied by printer companies, printer vendors only need to supply small blocks of 'exception' code rather than large blocks of printer-driver code.

Metafile vs. Raw

Printing in Windows 95 uses two data formats:

- Enhanced MetaFile (EMF)—The Windows 95 internal graphics language. A metafile is a collection of internal commands that Windows 95 uses to create images.

- Raw—The printer's natural language such as HPPCL, PostScript, escape codes, and so on. The raw format tends to be printer-specific. Raw format of data for one type of printer may require conversion before it can be printed on a different type of printer.

Metafile Spooling in Windows 95

Windows uses Enhanced Metafile (EMF) printing because EMF files are generally not device-specific. Therefore, EMF files can be rendered and printed in the background or sent across the network to a variety of devices without having to worry about device-particular drivers.

Metafile printing appears faster than other printing methods because metafiles are produced by the program directly and do not need rendering by the driver. Metafile spooling, therefore, can return control to the user faster than conventional printing can. All Windows 95 print jobs except PostScript are spooled as EMFs rather than printed directly.

Enhanced metafile printing is enabled by default. With metafile printing activated, the computer sends a print job to the metafile spool and returns to the program nearly four times faster than without metafile printing activated.

Problems in EMF Printing

If there are problems printing in Windows 95, the first step should be to disable enhanced metafile spooling to determine if it is causing the problem.

Lesson Summary

Windows 95 supports the use of universal drivers and mini-drivers, allowing the computer to interface easily with complex printers. Windows 95 also supports enhanced metafile printing for faster printing.

For more information on	See
Bidirectional communication support for printing	The *Windows 95 Resource Kit*

Lesson 2: The Windows 95 Printing Process

The Windows 95 printing process supports both enhanced metafile and raw print spooling. This lesson explains the printing process, including the advantages of enhanced metafile and raw print spooling.

After this lesson you will be able to:

- Outline the major steps in the Windows 95 printing process.

Estimated lesson time 10 minutes

Non-PostScript printers spool enhanced metafiles instead of raw printer data. When you direct a program to print, it prints more quickly by as much as twice as fast.

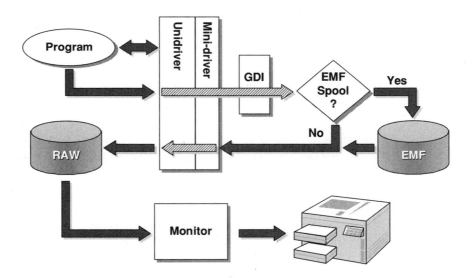

Figure 14.2 Windows 95 print process

The printing model, like other parts of Windows 95, is modular. The model in Figure 14.2 assumes that the workstation and the server are separate computers, and that both are running Windows 95.

When you instruct a Windows 95-based program to print to a remote printer, you initiate the following sequence of events:

1. The printer driver for the specified printer is copied from the printer server to the workstation's disk and then loaded into RAM. If the workstation already has a current version of the driver on disk, the driver is not be copied. If the printer server has a later version, the server's version is copied. This enables the program to query the driver for current printer settings such as resolution, color, fonts, and so on, and to produce a WYSIWYG image of the document. The program communicates with the printer driver through the graphics engine.

2. Next, the Windows-based only program generates a description of the requested output by using graphical device interface (GDI) commands. These commands specify everything Windows 95 needs to know about the content and formatting of the document, but do not tell the printer how to print the document.

3. The Windows 95 graphics engine translates these GDI calls into enhanced metafile (EMF) format.

4. What happens next depends on whether or not the EMF spooler is used.

   If the EMF spooler is used, the graphics engine writes these calls to the EMF spool. This method frees up the program to process the next set of commands.

   If the format type does not use the EMF spooler, the program waits until the print job completes before continuing.

5. The spooler passes the document back into the driver, with a pass through the mini-driver. The mini-driver converts the data type to Raw, the format required for the specific printer. The document is then sent to the print spooler.

6. The spooler on the client workstation passes the document to the spooler on the printer server through the Windows 95 router software. If the client and server are the same computer, this step is skipped. If the router software fails, you never see an error message or symptom.

7. On the print server, the spooler passes the document to the monitor. The monitor writes the data to the appropriate print destination, such as LPT1, COM1, *\\server\sharename*, or the address of a network interface printer's network adapter card.

8. The print device receives the information and produces printed output, and the monitor displays a message letting the user know the document is printed.

Where Printing Components Are Stored

Windows 95 stores printing components on both the hard disk and in the registry.

Hard Disk Locations

Windows 95 stores printing components on the hard disk in the following directories:

- Drivers are stored in \WINDOWS\SYSTEM
- Queued print jobs are stored in \WINDOWS\SPOOL\PRINTERS

Registry Locations

Windows 95 printing components are stored in the registry.

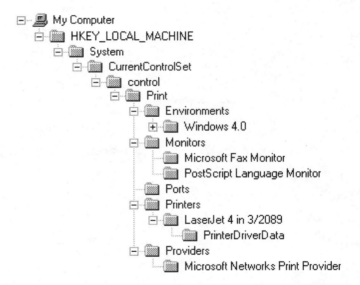

Figure 14.3 Location of Windows 95 printing components in the registry

The registry location of HKEY_Local_Machine\System\CurrentControlSet\
Control\Print contains printer configuration parameters. The subtrees below this point contain the configuration data for all the installed printers and the system-wide configuration information.

Printers Folder

The Printers folder is where you perform all printer administration tasks.

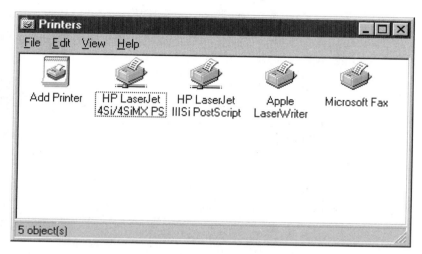

Figure 14.4 The Printers folder is used for printer administration tasks

The Printers Folder

The Print Manager familiar to Windows 3.1 users has been replaced in Windows 95 by the Printers folder.

You can use the Printers folder to:

- Install a printer.
- Share a printer.
- Set permissions for printer access.
- Redirect output to a printer over the network.
- Administer printers from a remote location.
- Control printer characteristics, such as fonts and paper size.
- Set up auditing of printer use.

Lesson Summary

Using enhanced metafile spooling frees programs sooner than using no spooling at all.

Lesson 3: Installing and Managing Printers

Printer installation is automated in Windows 95, however, you can manually configure a printer when necessary. This lesson explains the installation and configuration process and explains how you can use the Printers folder to manage print queues.

After this lesson you will be able to:

- Implement Microsoft Windows 95 printing from stand-alone computers.
- Create and reorder a Windows 95 print queue.
- Delete a document from the Windows 95 print queue.
- Set up and remove printer drivers in a Windows 95-based computer.

Estimated lesson time 30 minutes

Installation

Printers may be installed during the initial Setup process or at any time after Windows 95 is set up.

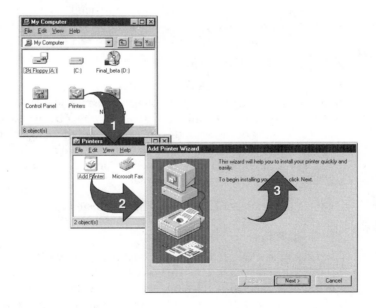

Figure 14.5 Printer installation procedure

To install a printer in Windows 95, you need to specify whether it is local or remote.

Local Printers

The Add Printer icon in the Printers folder is used to install printer drivers on a Windows 95-based computer for a printer that is physically attached to the computer.

You need to specify the type of printer and indicate to which local port it is attached.

If the printer is Plug and Play-compatible, Windows 95 automatically configures the printer correctly.

Remote Printers

Remote printer installation is covered in Chapter 15, "Network Printing."

Friendly Names

Printer names in Windows 95 can be up to 31 characters long, including null characters. For example, you could name a printer "New LaserJet® on second floor." This is known as the *friendly* printer name. Each friendly name, however, must be unique.

Printers may always be referred to by their friendly names as opposed to their model names. For example, programs running on Windows 95 recognize the printer in the example above, as "New LaserJet® on second floor" instead of HP LaserJet III.

Friendly Name Issues

Some programs display a warning when a document that was created under a previous version of Windows is used and a printer by the same name cannot be found. This may occur when the program stored the actual printer string from the previous version of Windows. In this case either change the friendly name to the one that was used previously, or select the new name for the printer. In either case, documents should not require reformatting.

Tools in the Printers folder can be used to change a printer's friendly name.

The Test Page

As part of the final printer installation step, Windows 95 prints a test page on the newly installed printer to verify that the installation was successful. This page lists the printer drivers installed along with their versions, and prints sample graphics and text. On color printers, the Microsoft Windows logo graphic will be in color.

Creating a Local Shared Printer

In this exercise, you will create a shared printer on your computer. It does not matter if you actually have a printer attached or not. You need to be using share-level security.

▶   **To create a new printer on your computer**

1. In the Control Panel, double-click the Network icon, and then click the Access Control tab.

2. Verify that your Access Control is set to Share-level access control, and then click OK.

3. On the Network property sheet, click the Configuration tab, and then click Client for Microsoft Networks.

4. Click the File and Print Sharing button, and then enable both options in the File and Print Sharing dialog box.

5. Click OK. If prompted to restart you computer, click Yes.

Note   If Share-level security and File and Print Sharing are already enabled, you will not have to restart your computer.

---

6. Open the Printers folder located in the My Computer icon, or on the Start menu in the Settings item.

7. Double-click the Add Printer icon to start the Add Printer wizard.

8. Click Next to continue.

9. Click Local printer, and then click Next.

10. Click the manufacturer and brand of the printer you are installing, and then click Next.

11. Click the physical port on the computer where the printer is attached, or any unused port if a printer is not attached, and then click Next.

12. Type a friendly name for the printer, and then click Next.

    The printer drivers are now copied from a source location and the printer is installed.

13. When prompted, click No in response to Would you like to print a test page, and then click Finish.

14. Use the secondary mouse button to select Properties to open the properties sheet for the printer just created.

15. Click the Sharing tab, and then click Share As to share the printer.

16. Assign the password PASSWORD to the share, and then click OK.

    When you created the printer, you specified a password which was associated with the printer. This password is used for share-level protection. To set user-level protections, you need to establish user-level security from the Network property sheet. You then see a different user interface that allows you to select the various users which have the ability to print to your printer.

Printer Configuration

To change a printer's configuration, use the printer's property sheet.

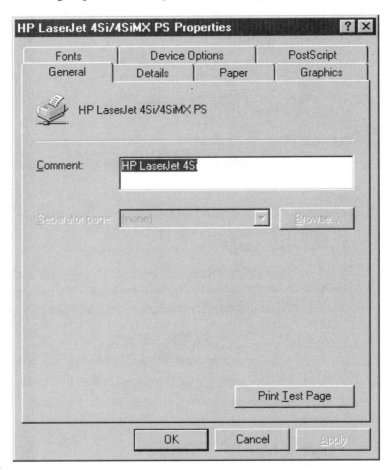

Figure 14.6 General tab on the Printer property sheet

All printers have a General and Details tab. A local printer may also have a tab for sharing the printer. Other property tabs may be present, however they are associated with a specific printer.

General

The General tab lists the printer's name. You can add a comment, specify a separator page (separator pages print between print jobs), or send a test page to the printer.

Details

The Details tab specifies the location of the printer, what driver to use, details and configuration of the printer port, and the settings for spooling print jobs. Any additional settings that are displayed depend on the type of printer.

Paper

Information on this tab varies by printer. It may contain configuration settings for some of the following.

- Paper size—Size of paper to use. This may be listed as letter, legal, envelopes, or by inches (8.5 by 11, 8.5 by 15, and so on).
- Orientation of the print job—How the print job looks in reference to the paper. Portrait and landscape are the most common settings.
- Layout—1, 2, 4, or more versions of the print job on a single sheet of paper.
- Paper Source—Paper tray or bin to use when printing.
- Copies—Number of copies of the print job to print. This only appears on printers that support multiple copies.

Additional configuration settings such as duplex printing may be included on Advanced or Option buttons.

Graphics

Information on this tab varies by printer. The following are some of the more common configuration settings.

- Resolution—Detail (dots per inch) of the default print job.
- Color control—Configures how the color calibration is performed if the printer supports color printing.
- Halftoning—Determines how the graphics are rendered and printed.

Other settings may include reversing the image (as a mirror or a negative image), scaling, and so on.

Fonts

Many PostScript printers print faster when the fonts used in the print job are the same as the fonts that are built-in to the printer. However, you may not have those fonts installed on your computer. Windows 95 includes some TrueType® fonts for its programs.

This section may be used to determine how TrueType fonts are printed. There are three basic ways to print TrueType fonts:

- Send TrueType fonts to printer according to the font substitution table—This method uses a table to convert a specific TrueType font into a specific PostScript font. You may configure this table to get the best overall results (speed and appearance) for a specific printer.

- Always use built-in printer fonts instead of TrueType fonts—This method simply uses the closest match between the TrueType font and the built-in font. The results may not appear the same as when you created the document, but this is the fastest method of printing.

- Always use TrueType fonts—This method guarantees that the document always appears exactly as you created it, however, it may take considerably longer to print.

Other printers may have additional settings for configuring fonts.

Device Options

These options are specific to a printer, not just to a class of printers. The settings may involve memory, specific printer features, installable options, or whatever the printer manufacturer wants to include.

PostScript

The information on this tab involves configuring PostScript data. This includes the following:

- Output format—May be selected if specific file compatibility is required.

- Header—Every PostScript print job normally includes a header file that contains information to configure the printer. If you have a dedicated, local printer that does not change configuration, print jobs are sent faster by not including the header with every print job. If anyone else can access the printer, you should include the header information to guarantee the proper configuration.

- Error information—Allows print errors to be printed out by the printer. This does increase the size of the header file, but you are guaranteed to receive feedback in case of a printing error.

- Advanced information may include specifying the PostScript language level (levels 1 and 2 are supported by Windows 95), bitmap compression, and data format.

Management and Administration

When you want to print to a Windows 95-compatible printer, you can drag the files to be printed to printer icons on your desktop and the documents will be printed, providing the correct permissions and associations are in place. Existing methods of printing still can be used; the ability to drag and drop to a printer object is a Windows 95 functionality.

Printers may be managed from several locations. From the Printers folder, select a printer and click the secondary mouse button. The menu that appears allows you to pause the printer or purge (remove) any current print jobs.

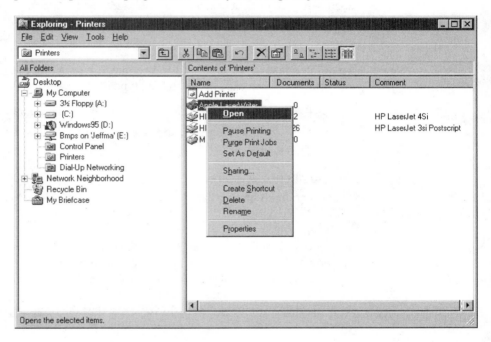

Figure 14.7   Opening a print queue for a printer

If you click Open, the print queue for that specific printer appears. From this dialog box, you can control the printing of specific documents.

You may also accomplish the same functions from Windows Explorer.

Print Queues

Windows Explorer also makes each printer's queue available so you can monitor jobs that are printing or waiting to print. A Windows 95 print queue lists documents sent by you and other users on the network.

Pausing and Resuming a Print Job

You can pause the printing of another user's document on the list for a printer you are sharing or you can pause your local printer. In the print queue on a network printer, you can pause only the printing of your own document—you cannot pause the printer or anyone else's document unless you have administrative privileges for that server.

Canceling a Print Job

You can cancel the printing of a document by deleting it on the list of documents waiting to print. When using a network printer, you can delete only your own document, and only before it starts printing. On a local printer, you can delete any document at any time.

Separator Pages

To differentiate between print jobs, you may use separator pages. A separator page is inserted between each print job. The type of separator pages are:

- Full—The separator page may use various fonts and graphics.
- Simple—The separator page uses a Courier font. This is useful for dot matrix or slower printers.

The Number of Printers

There is no fixed limit to the number of printers available in Windows 95.

Working Offline

Working offline gives you the ability to print to the spooler without being attached to a printer. This can be useful in several situations. For example, if your network is not functioning, you can start print jobs which will print on the network printer when the network becomes available. Another example is using deferred printing with a portable computer, as it allows you to start the printing process without being attached to a printer. The documents complete printing when a printer is detected.

Designating Default Printer

When you choose the Print command in many Windows-based programs, the print job is sent to the designated default printer. Because of this, you should designate the default printer to be the one you use most often.

The Print Queue

To access a printer's queue, double-click the printer's icon.

In the following exercise, you will be managing a print queue. A printer does not need to be physically attached to your computer. For this exercise, you can use the printer installed in the previous exercise or one previously installed.

▶ **To manage a print queue**

1. Open the Printers folder.

   The Printers folder can be accessed through the My Computer icon, or on the Start menu in the Settings item.

2. Use the secondary mouse button and click the printer you want to use.

3. From the Context menu, click Pause Printing to pause the printer.

4. Start WordPad.

   WordPad can be started from the Start menu by pointing to Programs, Accessories, and then clicking WordPad.

5. Create a document by typing some text in and saving the file as DOC1.

6. From the File menu, click Save As, and then create a document named DOC2.

7. Repeat step 6 and create documents named DOC3 and DOC4.

8. Print each of these documents in numerical order.

9. Open the Printers folder and click the secondary mouse button on the printer you are using.

10. On the File menu, click Open to see the print queue.

11. Click DOC3.

12. On the Document menu, click Cancel Printing.

    Notice that DOC3 is removed from the print queue.

13. Drag and drop DOC1 to the last entry in the print queue.

14. Drag and drop DOC4 so that it is the first print job in the print queue.

15. From the Printer menu, click Purge Print Jobs to clear the print queue.

Lesson Summary

The Add Printer wizard helps you install printers. Once a printer is installed, you can configure it to meet specific needs. The actual configuration options depend on the printer.

When you print jobs, you can manage the print queue from your desktop. You can pause and start the printer, and pause, reorder, and cancel specific print jobs.

Lesson 4: Common Printing Problems

There are some basic steps you can take to isolate and diagnose printer problems. This lesson explains these basic troubleshooting procedures.

After this lesson you will be able to:

• Diagnose and identify problems that may occur from time to time.

Estimated lesson time 10 minutes

If you have problems installing a printer, you can use the Print Troubleshooter in Help. The troubleshooter can walk you through most common printing problems.

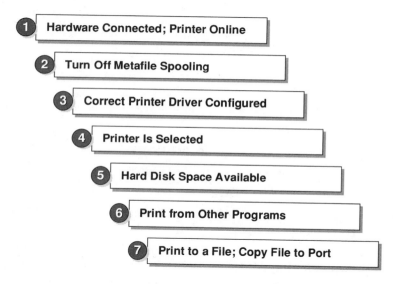

Figure 14.8 Basic printer troubleshooting steps

Many of the printing troubleshooting techniques used in Windows version 3.1 can apply to Windows 95.

1. Check the cable connections and the printer port, and verify that the printing device is online.
2. Turn off metafile spooling. Metafile spooling is a relatively new process and may be causing problems with a computer or printer that does not recognize it.
3. Verify that the printer settings are correct in Printer property sheet.

4. Verify that the correct printer driver is installed and configured properly.

   If necessary, reinstall the printer driver. If a printer driver needs updating, install and configure the new printer driver through the Printers folder.

   If you are using a PostScript printer and the problem is intermittent, download a PostScript error handler to the printer.

5. Verify that enough hard disk space is available to generate the print job.

6. Verify that printing can occur from other programs within Windows 95.

   If the user is experiencing trouble when printing from a Microsoft MS-DOS– or 16-bit Windows-based program, but the user can print from a 32-bit Windows-based program, the problem may be isolated to a computer or to the specific program from which the user is printing.

7. Print a file or to a file, and then copy the output file to a printer port.

If this works, then the problem is spooler- or data transmission-related. If this doesn't work, then the problem is program- or driver-related.

▶ **To disable enhanced metafile spooling (optional)**

1. From the Start menu, point to Settings, and then click Printers.

2. Click the icon for your printer with the secondary mouse button, and then click Properties.

3. Click the Details tab, and then click Spool Settings.

4. In the Spool Settings dialog box, click RAW on the Spool Data Format list. Click OK.

Lesson Summary

Print problems can usually be isolated and identified if you take a logical approach to solving the problem.

Review

The following questions are intended to reinforce key information presented in this chapter. If you are unable to answer a question, review the appropriate lesson and then try the question again.

1. Describe the different types of printer driver combinations used in Windows 95.

2. How do you check the status of the print queue in Windows 95?

C H A P T E R   1 5

Network Printing

Before You Begin

To complete the lessons in this chapter, you must have:

- Completed Chapter 1 and installed Microsoft Windows 95.
- A network server with a shared printer.

Lesson 1: Network Printing Architecture

The Windows 95 printing architecture is both compatible with existing printing processes and provides an open, modular 32-bit print interface. This lesson describes the network printing architecture.

After this lesson you will be able to:

- Describe the network printing features of Microsoft Windows 95.

Estimated lesson time 10 minutes

Windows 95 has a number of new features to facilitate network printing:

- Network Printer Shortcuts on the Desktop—These can be placed on the desktop for easy drag and drop printing of files.

- Multiple Print Provider Architecture—Windows 95 print architecture allows for multiple print providers to print to local printers and multiple types of network printers.

- Point and Print Installation—Windows 95 supports the automatic installation of printer drivers over the network from a properly configured network server.

- Microsoft Print Server for NetWare—A Windows 95 machine can be configured to act as a NetWare print server, despooling print jobs from NetWare print queues.

- JetAdmin Program—A Windows 95 machine can administrate HP JetDirect printers or print to them directly.

- DEC PrintServer Support—A Windows 95 machine can print directly to a DEC PrintServer printer on the network using TCP/IP.

The architecture of Windows 95 printing consists of a series of interfaces and layers to support local printing and network printing.

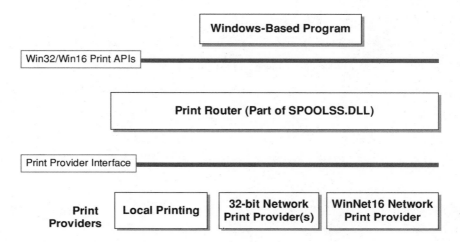

Figure 15.1 Windows 95 network printing architecture

Win32/Win16 Print APIs

The Microsoft Win32/Win16 Print APIs are used by programs. Win32/Win16 printing functions include the ability to open, write, and close print jobs and perform print queue management.

Print Router

The print router, part of SPOOLSS.DLL, routes printing requests to a driver that can complete the request on the basis of the print destination. The driver that can complete a printing request is called a print provider. If the printing request is for a locally connected printer, the print router routes the request to the local printing print provider, also part of SPOOLSS.DLL. If the printing request is for a network printer, the print router routes the request to any number of installed 32-bit network print providers.

Print Provider Interface

Like the Windows 95 Service Provider Interface, the Print Provider Interface (PPI) is an open, modular interface to allow multiple 32-bit print providers to be installed in Windows 95 simultaneously. The Print Provider Interface is a set of APIs used by the Windows 95 print router to submit print jobs and manage print queues. The Print Provider Interface sits below the WinNet 32 API and provides the needed network services to complete a Windows 95 request for printing services. These requests are then passed to the appropriate print providers.

The Print Provider Interface enables Microsoft or any other network vendor to integrate network printing services seamlessly into Windows 95.

Print Providers

The print providers provide the following functions:

- Accessing network printers (Open Printer, Close Printer)
- Submitting a print job (Open, Write, and Close Print Jobs)
- Print queue management (View Queue, Pause Queue, Continue Queue, Delete Queue Job, and so on)

There are three kinds of print providers:

- Local
- Network
- WinNet16 Network

Local Printing

The Local Printing print provider is part of SPOOLSS.DLL. This print provider handles sending print jobs to local ports and local print queue management.

Network Print Providers

The network print providers convert the PPI call to a Win32 WinNet call or to an instruction for the network redirector. These print providers are specific to the networks they support.

WinNet16 Network Print Provider

The WinNet16 Network Print Provider is provided for backwards compatibility with Windows version 3.x WinNet16 network drivers. The WinNet16 Network Print Provider converts a 32-bit PPI call to a WinNet16 API call so that the printing request can be serviced by a WinNet16 network driver.

Example of Print Provider Support: The Network Printer Designation String

When performing a network printer installation from Add Printer in the Printers folder, the printer path string used to identify the print share is passed to the installed print providers. If a print provider understands the syntax, it attempts a Win32 WinNet call, through WNetAddConnection, using the printer path string to create a connection to the network printer share.

The syntax supported here is entirely dependent on what the print provider has been programmed to understand and may not match the syntax supported by the corresponding network provider. As an example, the Banyan VINES network provider may support both UNC and StreetTalk™ server name strings, but the Banyan VINES print provider may only support UNC server name strings.

Lesson Summary

The Windows 95 network printing architecture is a 32-bit printing interface that also supports legacy printing processes.

Lesson 2: Print Providers

Windows 95 provides support for a variety of print providers. This lesson introduces the various print providers and explains their functions.

After this lesson you will be able to:

- Describe print provider support for Microsoft networks, Novell NetWare networks, other vendor networks, and WinNet16 networks.

Estimated lesson time   15 minutes

Microsoft Network Print Provider (MSPP32.DLL)

The Microsoft network print provider is a 32-bit DLL that allows the Print Provider Interface (PPI) and the Print Router to communicate.

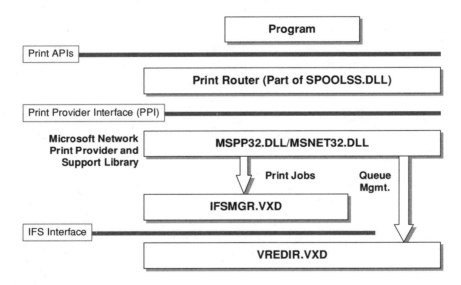

Figure 15.2 Microsoft network print provider in Windows 95

The Microsoft Network Print Provider (MSPP32.DLL) interacts with the Microsoft Network support library (MSNET32.DLL) and the Installable File System Manager (IFSMGR). In Figure 15.2, note that there are two arrows from the print provider, one going to IFSMGR.VXD and one going to VREDIR.VXD.

When a print function is for printing over the network, for example, open a print job, write to a print job, or close a print job, the call is submitted to IFSMGR. Open/Write/Close print job operations are the same as file I/O operations in the Win32 API. IFSMGR hands the request to the SMB redirector, VREDIR.VXD.

When a print function is for queue management, for example, view a network printing queue, delete a job in the network printing queue, reorder a job in the network printing queue, the call is submitted directly to VREDIR.VXD.

Note that when sending a print job, VREDIR does not copy the print job to VCACHE.

Print Queue Management

Windows 95 has full capabilities to manage print jobs on another Windows 95-based computer.

Registry Settings

HKEY_LOCAL_MACHINE

   \System

      \CurrentControlSet

        \Control

          \Print

            \Providers

              \Microsoft Networks Print Provider

NetWare Network Print Provider (NWPP32.DLL)

Windows 95 currently supports only bindery-based NetWare print queues and does not support NetWare 4.*x* NDS printer objects. NetWare 4.*x* NDS print queue objects are supported through bindery emulation which is enabled by default on NetWare 4.*x* servers.

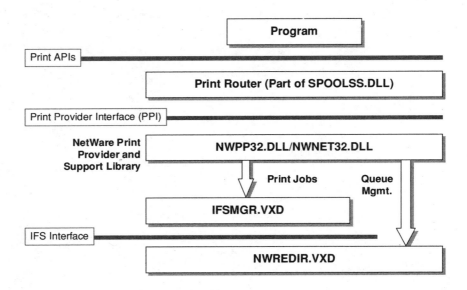

Figure 15.3 NetWare network print provider in Windows 95

Microsoft Client for NetWare Networks (NWREDIR)

The NetWare Network Print Provider (NWPP32.DLL) interacts with the NetWare Network support library (NWNET32.DLL) and the Installable File System Manager (IFSMGR). The two data paths—one going to NWREDIR.VXD and one going to IFSMGR—and VCACHE behavior is functionally identical to the Microsoft Print Provider.

Real-Mode NetWare Client (NETX/VLM)

When the real-mode Novell NetWare client is installed, the instructions that are handed to the redirector must be thunked, or converted to 16-bit, and transferred to the real-mode NetWare redirector, NETX or VLM.

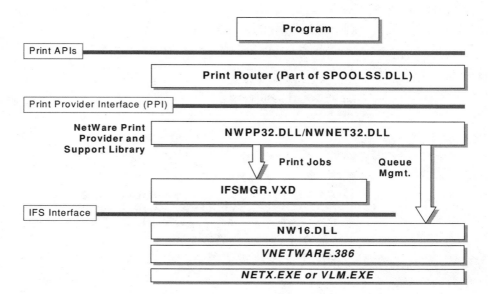

Figure 15.4 Real-mode NetWare components in Windows 95

NW16.DLL provides the thunking and translation a real-mode NetWare client needs when a 32-bit network DLL, NWPP32.DLL or NWNET32.DLL, accesses NetWare services. NW16.DLL thunks and translates the call and transfers the call to NETX or VLM through VNETWARE.386.

Registry Settings
HKEY_LOCAL_MACHINE

   +System

      +CurrentControlSet

         +Control

            +Print

               +Providers

                  Microsoft Print Provider for NetWare

WinNet16 Print Provider

If a network client does not have 32-bit network and print providers, then network printing can be accomplished by installing and using the Windows version 3.x WinNet16 driver. The WinNet16 driver from Windows version 3.x understands only WinNet16 calls and does not understand the 32-bit PPI calls made by the print router.

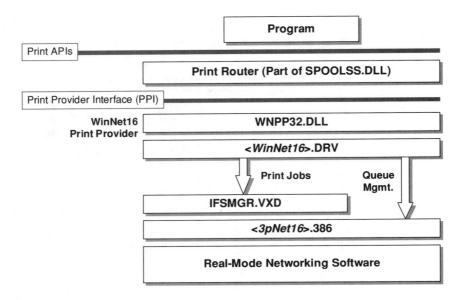

Figure 15.5 WinNet16 network print provider in Windows 95

WNPP32.DLL takes the 32-bit PPI call from the print router and translates or thunks it to a 16-bit call that the WinNet16 driver can understand. The WinNet16 driver then calls the real-mode network client through the VxD (*3pNet16.386* in Figure 15.5). If a print job is being submitted through the use of OpenFile operations, it is first trapped by IFSMGR.VXD which passes it on to the real-mode networking software by means of *<otherpartynetwork>.386*.

Print Queue Management

The functionality of print queue management is wholly dependent on what functionality is implemented in the other vendor WinNet16 driver. Print queue management options that are not available are grayed.

Registry Settings

HKEY_LOCAL_MACHINE

+System

+CurrentControlSet

+Control

+Print

+Providers

WinNet Print Provider

Other Print Providers

Windows 95 supports any number of additional print providers written by other vendors.

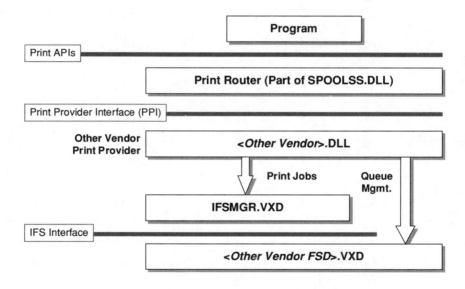

Figure 15.6 Other vendor network print provider in Windows 95

Other vendors may make print providers available to you. A print provider must be written to allow the print router PPI to communicate and to submit networking requests to an appropriate network file system driver. Additional print providers are installed using the Control Panel Network option.

Print Queue Management

The functionality of print queue management is wholly dependent on what functionality is implemented in the print provider. Print queue management options that are not available will be grayed.

Lesson Summary

Windows 95 provides print providers for Microsoft networks, NetWare networks, and WinNet16. Additional print providers written by other vendors are supported as long as they follow the network printing architecture.

Lesson 3: Network Printer Installation

Network printers may be installed using the Add Printer wizard or by using a technique called Point and Print. This lesson demonstrates both methods of installing a network printer.

After this lesson you will be able to:

- Install a network printer using the Add Printer wizard.
- Install a network printer using Point and Print.

Estimated lesson time 30 minutes

Manual Installation

A network printer can be installed in Windows 95 two different ways:

- From Add Printer in the Printers folder
- Through Point and Print installation

▶ **To install from Add Printer in the Printers folder**

1. To install support for a network printer in Windows 95, double-click the Add Printer icon in the Printers folder.

2. Click Network Printer for the printer type.

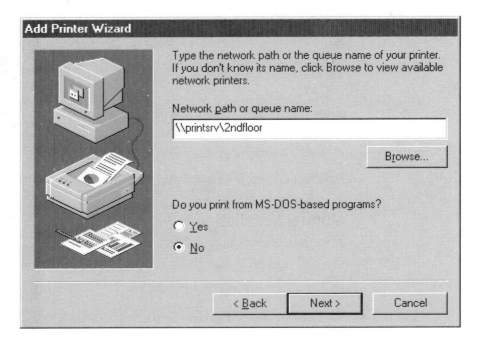

Figure 15.7 Adding a network printer using the Add Printer wizard

3. Type the network path to the printer share.

4. Specify whether or not this printer will be used for Microsoft MS-DOS–based programs. MS-DOS–based programs must print to a port name such as LPT1:. MS-DOS–based programs cannot print to a network path designation.

5. If Yes is selected, you are prompted to associate an LPT port to the network path previously specified.

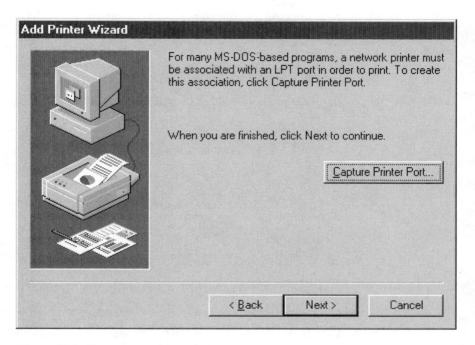

Figure 15.8 Capturing a printer port

6. To associate an LPT port, click the Capture Printer Port button.

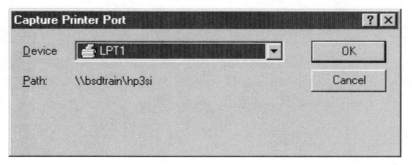

Figure 15.9 Associating a printer port of MS-DOS–based programs

7. Click the correct port on the drop-down list.
8. Click the printer manufacturer and model names.
9. Type a friendly name in the Printer name text box.
10. Windows 95 will copy the appropriate printer driver files to the \WINDOWS\SYSTEM directory.

11. Print a test page.

The new network printer icon appears in the Printers folder.

Figure 15.10 Printers folder with new network printer icon

Point and Print Network Printer Installation

Windows 95 simplifies network printing with Point and Print installation of networked printers.

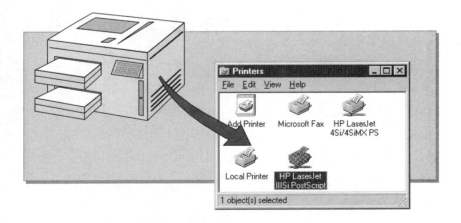

Figure 15.11 Point and Print network printer installation

Point and Print works two ways:

- To install the driver files for a network printer driver, drag the Point and Print-enabled network printer icon from the server's shared resource window to the Printer folder. Alternatively, click Install on the Point and Print-enabled network printer's context menu, or double-click the network printer icon.

- To print to a networked printer, drop a document on the Point and Print-enabled network printer icon. Windows 95 determines the printer name and automatically loads the driver files across the network to the local hard disk, configures the printer on the user's computer, loads the program, and then sends the print job to the newly created network printer.

For Windows 95 point and print servers, Point and Print is automatically supported and requires no setup. For NetWare and Microsoft Windows NT servers, extra steps need to be performed on the server by a network administrator to enable this functionality. There is no way to tell by a network printer's icon appearance or properties whether it is point and print-enabled.

▶   **To install a printer using Point and Print**

This exercise requires access to another computer.

Note   It does not matter whether or not you actually have a printer attached to your computer. You will pause the printing process before anything is actually sent to a printer.

---

1. Click the secondary mouse button on a local printer that you previously installed.
2. Click Properties.
3. Click the Sharing tab and make sure the Shared As option is selected.

   If you need to add a name, you can use the default name for the printer, the same one you gave it when you installed the printer.
4. Click OK.

   The printer icon appears with a hand, indicating it is shared.
5. Click the printer icon, and on the File menu, click Open.
6. On the Printer menu, click Pause Printing.
7. On the second Windows 95-based computer, open WordPad, and create a small document containing this text: **This is a test print document.**
8. Save the document as TEST.DOC, and then exit WordPad.
9. In Network Neighborhood, open the first computer and locate the shared printer.
10. Drag the shared printer to the Printers folder.

11. The following prompt appears:

    ```
    Do you print from MS-DOS-based programs?
    ```

    The default is No. Click Next.

12. Assign the printer the name Point and Print, and make it your default printer.

13. Do not print a test page. Click the Finish button.

14. Drag TEST.DOC to the Printer Shortcut icon.

15. Check the queue for the printer and make sure the TEST.DOC is queued to print.

    Because the printer is paused, TEST.DOC should appear in the print queue, but will not be printing.

Windows 95 copies the appropriate files across the network from the server to the \WINDOWS\SYSTEM directory.

The network printer icon shows up in the Printers folder.

Lesson Summary

Printers may be installed by using the Add Printer wizard or by dragging and dropping the network printer to your desktop using Point and Print.

Lesson 4: Setting Up Point and Print Servers

For a printer to be point and print-enabled, the appropriate drivers need to be installed on the printer server. This lesson explains how to set up various servers for Point and Print.

After this lesson you will be able to:
- Describe how to set up Point and Print on a Windows 95, Windows NT, and Novell NetWare server.
- Configure and use Windows 95 as a NetWare-compatible print server.

Estimated lesson time 30 minutes

Point and Print Setup for Windows 95 Servers

If your computer is running File and Printer Sharing for Microsoft Networks or File and Printer Sharing for NetWare Networks, you don't need to do anything other than share your printer and grant appropriate permissions to configure Point and Print on your Windows 95 print server.

Because the printer and the drivers are already installed on the Windows 95 server, the Windows 95 server knows:

1. The printer name and configuration.
2. Which printer driver files to provide to a client from the printer .INF files.
3. The location of the printer driver files, the \WINDOWS\SYSTEM directory.

When sharing a printer on a Windows 95-based computer, the \WINDOWS\SYSTEM directory is automatically shared as a Read Only share. The share name is PRINTER$ and there is no password. If the computer named \\JOHNDOE shares its local printer, the share \\JOHNDOE\PRINTER$ is created. It is a hidden share, but can be mapped through a Map Network Drive dialog box or the **net use** command. The \SYSTEM directory does not appear to be shared in Windows Explorer, which means that there is no hand sharing icon for the \SYSTEM directory.

The hidden PRINTER$ share is needed for Point and Print support so that the printer driver files can be made available over the network.

For Point and Print from a Windows 95-based server, all communication of printer information occurs between VREDIR on the Windows 95-based client and VSERVER on the Windows 95-based server.

1. VREDIR sends a request for Point and Print printer setup.

2. VSERVER sends the friendly name of the printer to VREDIR.

3. The user on Client for Microsoft Networks is prompted with a friendly printer name dialog box.

4. VREDIR asks VSERVER which files need to be copied and where the printer files are located.

5. VSERVER tells VREDIR which files need to be copied, and that they can be found on \\<*server name*>\PRINTER$.

6. VREDIR makes a connection to \\<*server name*>\PRINTER$ and copies printer driver files.

7. VREDIR terminates the connection to \\<*server name*>\PRINTER$.

8. The icon for the network printer is created in the Printers folder.

Point and Print Setup for Windows NT Servers

Point and Print installation from a Windows 95-based client to a Windows NT 3.1 or 3.5x server is supported in the following way:

- Printer driver files are copied from the client's installation point, rather than directly from the Windows NT server. Because the driver is not downloaded from the print server, the settings are not inherited from the print server. For example, the user may need to make adjustments to paper size and memory.

- If the name of the printer driver on the Windows NT server has the same filename and .INF file as the one used by Windows 95, the user will not be prompted for the printer model. Otherwise, if the filenames are different, the user will be prompted for the printer model.

If your computer is running File and Printer Sharing for Microsoft Networks or File and Printer Sharing for NetWare Networks, nothing must be done other than share your printer and grant appropriate permissions to configure Point and Print on your Windows 95 print server.

Point and Print from a Windows 95 server to a Windows NT client is not supported.

Point and Print Setup for NetWare Bindery-Based Servers

NetWare servers have no concept of a Point and Print setup for Windows 95. To enable Point and Print on a NetWare server, Windows 95 must write some configuration information to the NetWare server that is accessible from any Windows 95 client.

Windows 95 writes to the NetWare server's bindery. More specifically, Windows 95 adds properties and values to the NetWare print queue object in the NetWare server bindery so that any Windows 95-based client can read those properties for the printer name and configuration information, the list of printer driver files, and where the printer driver files are located.

Bindery Overview

The bindery on a Novell NetWare server is a three-tiered database composed of objects, properties, and values.

- **Object**
- **Properties**
- **Values**

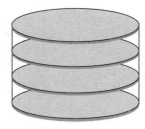

Figure 15.12 NetWare bindery components

An *object* is identified by its name and its type. An object type can be a user, group, file server, print queue, print server, or anything else the NetWare developer wants it to be.

Properties are attributes of an object. In the case of the user object, properties are the user's full name, groups that the user belongs to, the user's password, and so forth.

Values are the actual value of the property. For example, in the case of the user object JOHNDOE, the value of the Full Name property is "John Doe," the value of the Groups Belonged To property is "EVERYONE, MISC," and so forth.

Note The user must be logged in as a supervisor or supervisor equivalent to set up Point and Print on a NetWare server. You must have supervisor privileges in order to write to the NetWare server bindery.

▶ **To set up Point and Print on a NetWare bindery-based server**

1. Log on to the NetWare server as the supervisor or a supervisor equivalent.

2. Highlight a NetWare print queue on a NetWare server, and then open the context menu. Click Point and Print Setup. Note that the Point and Print Setup menu option will only appear if you have logged in to the NetWare server as the supervisor or as a supervisor equivalent.

Figure 15.13 Point and Print Setup on the NetWare Print Queue context menu

3. Click Set Printer Model.

4. Click the printer manufacturer and model in the Standard Print Setup dialog box. For example, the Epson® LQ-800.

5. Click Set Printer Path.

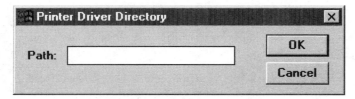

Figure 15.14 Specifying a printer driver location

6. Type the UNC path to where the driver files for the above printer model will be located.

For NetWare, the user would enter \\<*server*>\<*volume*>\<*path*>

A NetWare administrator might enter \\NW312\SYS\PUBLIC

7. Manually copy the appropriate printer driver files, as indicated for the printer manufacturer and model from MSPRINT.INF, to the printer path indicated above.

   A NetWare administrator copies the driver files for the Epson LQ-800 to \\NW312\SYS\PUBLIC.

8. Grant NetWare users rights—Read and File Scan at a minimum—to the directory specified in Step 6.

   Because the files were copied to the SYS:\PUBLIC directory, the network administrator does not need to grant any additional rights. If the network administrator wanted to keep all the Windows 95 printer driver files in a separate directory (SYS:\WIN95DRV), the network administrator would have to use the SYSCON program and grant the Everyone group Read and File Scan rights to the \WIN95DRV directory on the SYS: volume.

Changes to the NetWare Server Bindery

As an example of how the NetWare bindery gets modified to support Windows 95 Point and Print installation, refer to the previous example of setting up the Epson LQ-800 printer driver to \\NW312\SYS\PUBLIC.

The print queue QUEUE2 was set up on the NetWare server NW312. The bindery information for QUEUE2 is:

Object: QUEUE2

    Property: Q_DIRECTORY

    (Directory under SYS:\SYSTEM where print jobs are spooled)

        Value: B009203F

    Property: Q_OPERATORS

    (List of Print Queue Operators)

        Value: SUPERVISOR

    Property: Q_SERVERS

    (List of Print Queue Servers servicing print queue)

        Value: PS1

    Property: Q_USERS

    (List of Print Queue Users)

        Value: EVERYONE

After completing the Windows 95 Point and Print setup, the bindery information for QUEUE2 now reads:

Object: QUEUE2

> Property: Q_DIRECTORY
>
> > Value: B009203F
>
> Property: Q_OPERATORS
>
> > Value: SUPERVISOR
>
> Property: Q_SERVERS
>
> > Value: PS1
>
> Property: Q_USERS
>
> > Value: EVERYONE
>
> Property: WIN_ENV_LIST
>
> *(Property indicating that the print queue is Point and Print-enabled)*
>
> > Value: Windows 4.0
>
> Property: DRV_0000
>
> *(Information on printer model and files to copy)*
>
> > Value: Epson LQ-800, EPSON24.DRV, UNIDRV.DLL,
> >
> > UNIDRV.HLP, DMCOLOR.DLL
>
> Property: DIR_0000
>
> *(UNC path to location of printer driver files)*
>
> > Value: \\NW312\SYS\PUBLIC

The Windows 95 Point and Print setup writes the WIN_ENV_LIST, DRV_0000, and DIR_0000 properties and values to the NetWare server print queue bindery object. A Windows 95 client can access these bindery properties and values and get the information needed for Point and Print setup.

For Point and Print from a NetWare server, all printer information is read from the NetWare server print queue bindery object.

1. The NCP client scans the NetWare server bindery for the print queue object.
2. The Windows 95 client reads the DRV_0000 print queue property and value, and gets the friendly printer name and list of files to copy.

3. Windows 95 client reads the DIR_0000 print queue property and gets the UNC location of where the files are located.

4. A user on Windows 95 client sees a friendly printer name dialog box and clicks OK.

5. Windows 95 client copies files from UNC location to the local \WINDOWS\SYSTEM directory.

6. The icon for the network printer is created in the Printers folder.

The bindery properties written to the print queue object can be removed with Bindery Editor programs available in the public domain.

Remote Print Queue Management

The capabilities for remote queue management will depend on:

- The capabilities of the network operating system. Microsoft networks print queue management differs from Novell NetWare networks print queue management, which differs from Banyan VINES networks print queue management, and so on.

- The capabilities of the network components installed in Windows 95. A specific vendor's network components—whether they are a Windows 95 32-bit driver or a WinNet16 driver—may not implement all the print queue management functionality of the network operating system.

- The user's level of access to the print queue, as specified by the network administrator.

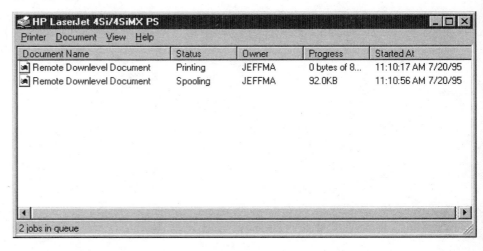

Figure 15.15 Print queue

Print Queue Management Capabilities

The following are the maximum capabilities available to manage remote print queues. The network operating system, security of the network operating system, and the capabilities of the network components available may make some of the options above unavailable. If they are unavailable for a particular configuration, the Printer and Document menu options will be grayed.

- View the queue. Double-click the printer in the Printers folder.
- Pause the current job. On the Document menu, click Pause Printing.
- Resume printing the current job. On the Document menu, click Pause Printing.
- Pause the print queue. On the Printer menu, click Pause Printing. A check mark indicates that the printer is paused.
- Resume the print queue. On the Printer menu, click Pause Printing. The absence of a check mark indicates printer is paused.
- Delete all print jobs in the queue. On the Printer menu, click Purge Print Jobs.

Lesson Summary

In order to enable Point and Print on a NetWare server, Windows 95 must add properties and values to the NetWare print queue object in the NetWare server bindery. Any Windows 95-based clients can then read these properties for the printer name and configuration information, the list of printer driver files and where the printer driver files are located. In order to be able to write to the NetWare server bindery, you must be logged in as a supervisor or supervisor equivalent.

Lesson 5: Microsoft Print Server for NetWare

Windows 95 can be configured to provide NetWare print server functions. This lesson explains how this is designed and how to install this service.

After this lesson you will be able to:

- Describe the installation and architecture of the Microsoft Print Server for NetWare.
- Install and configure Microsoft Print Server for NetWare.

Estimated lesson time 10 minutes

The Microsoft Print Server for NetWare (MSPSRV.EXE) is designed to run on a Windows 95-based computer configured with Microsoft Client for NetWare Networks. It provides a Windows 95-based computer NetWare Print Server machine functionality, allowing it to despool print jobs from a NetWare print server to a locally installed printer. MSPSRV.EXE is a 32-bit Windows-based program that can be enabled on the property sheet of any locally-attached printer.

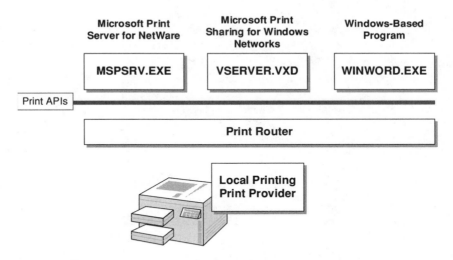

Figure 15.16 How Microsoft Print Server for NetWare functions

Using the Microsoft Print Server for NetWare does not prevent the user from printing to the locally attached printer, nor does it impair the user's ability to share that printer on the network. MSPSRV.EXE is simply another 32-bit Windows-based program submitting jobs to the local printer's print queue. The locally attached printer can service local print jobs from programs, such as WINWORD.EXE, from the network server (VSERVER.VXD or NWSERVER.VXD), and despooled print jobs from the NetWare print server (MSPSRV.EXE) all at the same time.

Setup of the Microsoft Print Server for NetWare

To enable the Microsoft Print Server for NetWare:

1. Verify that a print server object has been set up on the desired NetWare server and that the print queue is configured to print on Printer 0-Remote, LPT1:.

2. Bring up the printer properties of a locally installed printer.

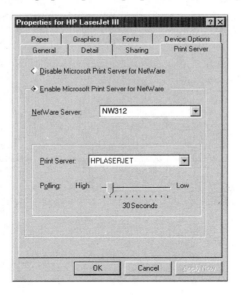

Figure 15.17 Enable Microsoft Print Server for NetWare on the Print Server tab

3. Click the Enable Microsoft Print Server for NetWare option on the Print Server property sheet. All NCP servers that are accessible on the network are listed on the NetWare Server drop-down list.

4. Click a NetWare server; the available Print Server object names configured on the NetWare server appear on the Print Server drop-down list.

5. Click a NetWare print server object name on the drop-down list.

In order to list the print servers on the NetWare server, you must successfully log in to the NetWare server. After selecting the NetWare server, click the print server name for which the Windows 95-based computer will be acting as the print server machine.

You can adjust the time interval for polling the print queue. This setting can be adjusted as high as 15 seconds for maximum Print Server performance, or as low as three minutes for increased local performance. The default is 30 seconds.

Administrative control over MSPSRV is coupled with the Printer Sharing control—the one option controlling the user's ability to both share a local printer and act as a Microsoft Print Server for NetWare. If the administrator for the Novell NetWare server has specified that print sharing is not allowed, MSPSRV will not load, and the user enable and disable options will be unavailable.

Lesson Summary

The Microsoft Print Server for NetWare is designed to run on a Windows 95-based computer configured with Microsoft Client for NetWare Networks. It allows a Windows 95-based computer to act as a NetWare Print Server and to despool print jobs from a NetWare print server to a locally installed printer. Using the Microsoft Print Server for NetWare (MSPSRV.EXE) does not prevent the user from printing to the locally attached printer, nor does it prevent sharing that printer on the network. MSPSRV.EXE is simply another 32-bit Windows-based program submitting jobs to the local printer's print queue.

Lesson 6: HP JetDirect

Windows 95 network printing supports the HP JetDirect product. This lesson explains how the HP JetDirect architecture fits into the Windows 95 architecture and how to install the HP JetAdmin program.

After this lesson you will be able to:

- Describe the installation and architecture of the HP JetAdmin tool for administrating an IPX/SPX configured HP JetDirect printer.

Estimated lesson time 20 minutes

HP JetDirect Architecture

The HP JetDirect product is a network adapter that is installed in HP LaserJet III and later laser printers. HP JetDirect allows a print job to be despooled from a network server print queue across the network, rather than having to be directly connected by means of a parallel or serial cables to a computer connected to the network. This allows the HP printer to be placed anywhere in the office where there is access to the network. Printer placement is not bound by length restrictions of serial and parallel cables.

Windows 95 network printing architecture is designed to work with the HP JetDirect architecture.

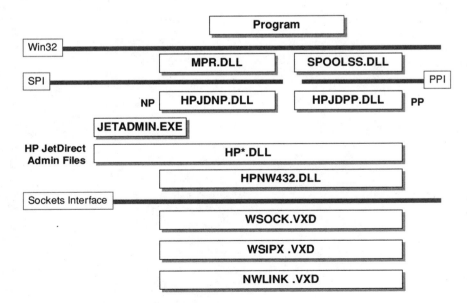

Figure 15.18 HP JetDirect network printing architecture

The HP JetDirect architecture fits into the Windows 95 network printing architecture in the following manner.

1. Calls from a program are handed to the HP JetDirect Network Provider (Network Neighborhood) or HP JetDirect Print Provider (Microsoft Word for Windows begins to print).

2. SPI and PPI calls from the network provider and print provider are handed down to the HP JetDirect DLLs (HP*.DLL).

3. The component HPNW432.DLL makes IPX/SPX socket calls to the 32-bit Windows Sockets interface.

4. The data is transmitted to the printer over IPX/SPX.

HP JetAdmin Program

The HP JetAdmin program is an administrative tool shipped with Windows 95 that is used to install and configure Hewlett-Packard printers connected to a network using printers with the HP JetDirect interface. The HP JetAdmin program uses IPX/SPX to configure a HP JetDirect printer which:

- Despools from a NetWare print server machine for a Novell NetWare Print Server object, which requires a Novell NetWare server on the network, using the HP Network Printer Service with NetWare.

- Despools from a network printer for a Novell NetWare Print Server object, which requires a Novell NetWare server on the network, using HP Network Printer Service with NetWare.

- Despools from a Windows 95 server print queue using the HP Network Printer Service without NetWare.

- Prints jobs directly from Windows 95-based computers using the HP Network Printer Service without NetWare.

Installing the HP JetAdmin Program

Installing the HP JetAdmin program is done through Control Panel, Network, Add Services, Hewlett-Packard.

Note In all of these configurations, the HP JetDirect printer is configured using the IPX/SPX protocol, not the DLC protocol. Windows 95 does not include support for HP JetDirect printers configured for the DLC protocol.

▶ **To install the HP JetAdmin program**

1. You must have the following Novell NetWare files available in order to use the HP JetAdmin program with NetWare: NWCALLS.DLL, NWIPXSPX.DLL, NWLOCALE.DLL, NWNET.DLL, and NWPSRV.DLL. These files are provided by Novell with its VLM client and various updates, and by Microsoft Windows for Workgroups version 3.11.

2. On the Start menu, point to Settings... and then click Control Panel. Double-click the Network icon.

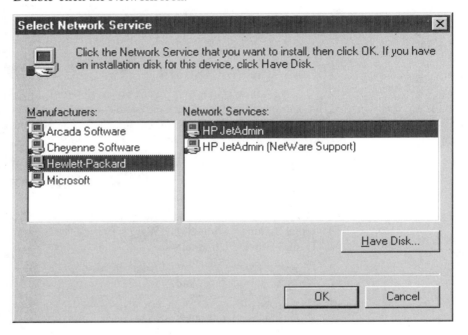

Figure 15.19 Selecting HP JetAdmin printer network services

3. On the Configuration property sheet, click the Add button.

4. In the Select Network Component Type dialog box, click Service, and then click Add.

5. In the Select Network Service dialog box, click Hewlett-Packard on the Manufacturers list. You will then see the HP JetAdmin network printer service or HP JetAdmin network printer service with NetWare on the Models list box.

6. Click Close in the Network Services dialog box.

7. Click OK in the Network dialog box, and provide the Novell NetWare files listed in step #1 when prompted, if using the HP Network Service with NetWare.

8. After all of the files have been copied, restart Windows 95 when prompted.

9. After restarting Windows 95, on the Start menu, point to "Settings..." and then click Control Panel. Double-click the HP JetAdmin icon.

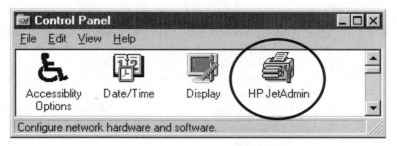

Figure 15.20 HP JetAdmin icon in the Control Panel

10. Use the HP JetAdmin program to configure the printer appropriately.

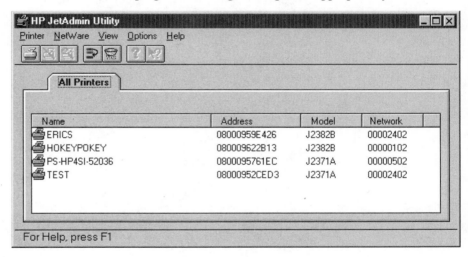

Figure 15.21 HP JetAdmin program

Lesson Summary

The HP JetAdmin program is an administrative tool shipped with Windows 95 that is used to install and configure Hewlett-Packard printers connected to a network using printers with the HP JetDirect interface. It is used with an HP JetDirect printer which despools from a NetWare print server machine, or from a network printer for a Novell NetWare Print Server object. Both situations require a Novell NetWare server on the network and HP Network Printer Service with NetWare. The HP JetAdmin program can also configure an HP JetDirect printer that despools from a Windows 95 server print queue using the HP Network Printer Service, or that prints jobs directly from Windows 95-based computers using the HP Network Printer Service.

In all of these configurations, the HP JetDirect printer is configured using the IPX/SPX protocol, not the DLC protocol. Windows 95 does not include support for HP JetDirect printers configured for the DLC protocol.

Lesson 7: Digital PrintServers

Digital's PrintServers are completely supported by Windows 95. This lesson explains the architecture and how to install support for Digital PrintServers.

After this lesson you will be able to:

- Describe the installation and architecture of DEC PrintServers.

Estimated lesson time 15 minutes

Printing to Digital PrintServers

Digital's PrintServer printers are a family of fully bidirectional, high-speed, high-capacity PostScript printers that connect directly to Ethernet networks and offer powerful remote management capabilities.

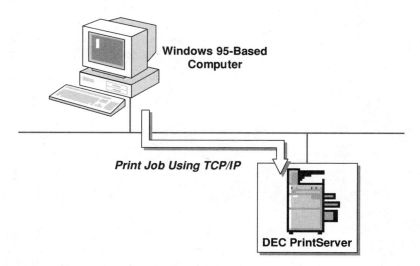

Figure 15.22 Print process with Digital PrintServer

When you print to a Digital PrintServer printer, you can print directly—without an intervening server or spooling host. This minimizes network traffic, eliminates the redundant existence of files on multiple computers during print time, and guarantees you the fastest possible job completion.

Windows 95 includes DEC PrintServer drivers and support files which allow a Windows 95-based computer to print directly to a DEC PrintServer connected to the network using the Windows 95 TCP/IP protocol.

Architecture of a Digital PrintServer

Windows 95 network printing supports the Digital PrintServer architecture.

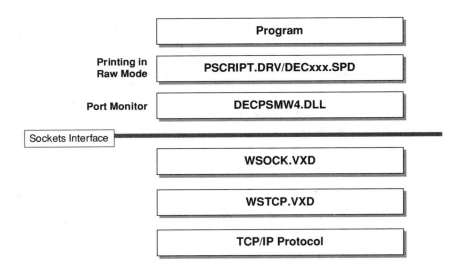

Figure 15.23 Digital PrintServer architecture

1. A program prints to a DEC PrintServer.
2. The PostScript printer driver and SPD file (PSCRIPT.DRV/DECxxx.SPD) process the print job in raw mode and sends it to the DEC PrintServer port name.
3. The DEC PrintServer port monitor (DECPSMW4.DLL) takes the raw print job from the PrintServer port and submits it as a streams-based 32-bit TCP/IP Windows socket request, which is then passed to the TCP/IP protocol.

Installing a Digital PrintServer

You must have TCP/IP network protocol support installed and working before performing any of the steps listed below.

1. On the Start menu, point to "Settings...", and then click Printers. The Printer folder will appear. Double-click the Add Printer icon. Click the Next button in the first dialog box. Click the Local printer option, and then click the Next button.

2. In the Add Printer wizard dialog box, click Digital on the list of manufacturers. Next, click the specific Digital PrintServer model—only printers with /Net after their name have PrintServer support—you want to install, and then click Next.

    The appropriate files are copied onto your local hard drive.

3. In the Add Printer wizard dialog box, click the Add Port button. Select the appropriate PrintServer Printer or if your printer is not listed, select Other PrintServer printer.

4. Type the name you wish to use for the port in the Name text box, and then enter the TCP/IP address of the printer in the Address text box. Click OK to close this dialog box.

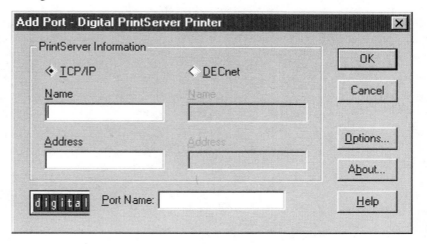

Figure 15.24 Adding ports to a Digital PrintServer printer

5. Type the friendly name you want to use for the printer, and then click Next button.

6. Restart your computer for these changes to take effect.

7. After restarting Windows 95, on the Start menu, point to "Settings..." and then click Printers. Click the DEC printer you just installed support for with the secondary mouse button, and then click Properties.

8. Click the Details property sheet page. In the Print To list box, scroll to the name of the port you created in step #3. Click the port name and then click the OK button on the lower-left side of the dialog box.

9. You can now print to the PrintServer at the TCP/IP address provided.

Note Use of DECnet as the protocol is currently not supported in Windows 95.

Lesson Summary

Windows 95 includes DEC PrintServer drivers and support files which allow a Windows 95-based computer to print directly to a DEC PrintServer connected to the network using the Windows 95 TCP/IP protocol.

Review

1. After installing a printer using the Point and Print method on your desktop, how is this printer referenced by Windows 95?

    A. Using a mapped letter, for example, P:

    B. Using a mapped port, for example, LPT3:

    C. Using the UNC name, for example, \\server\printer

    D. Using a dynamically loadable printer reference. This is possible because of the new dynamically loadable device drivers that come with Windows 95.

C H A P T E R   1 6

Programs and the Windows 95 Architecture

Before You Begin

To complete the lessons in this chapter, you must have:

- Completed Chapter 1 and installed Microsoft Windows 95.
- The following files located in the C:\LABS folder.

  BADAPP16.EXE

  BADAPP32.EXE

  SPINDIB16.EXE

  SPINDIB32.EXE

  BILLG.BMP

Lesson 1: Program Compatibility

This lesson demonstrates and explains how Windows 95 is compatible with Microsoft MS-DOS–based, 16-bit Windows-based, and 32-bit Windows-based programs.

After this lesson you will be able to:

- Explain the differences of running MS-DOS–based, 16-bit Windows-based, and 32-bit Windows-based programs under Microsoft Windows 95.

Estimated lesson time   10 minutes

Windows 95 has the capability to run a variety of existing programs. This includes:

- MS-DOS–based programs
- 16-bit Windows-based programs
- 32-bit Windows-based programs

This includes the capability to cut and paste data, use OLE, and dynamic data exchange (DDE) functions between all types of programs.

▶ **To verify that Windows 95 can run all three types of programs**

1. Open a command prompt window.
2. Change to your old MS-DOS directory, type **edit**, and then press ENTER.

   The MS-DOS Edit program starts.
3. Return to the Windows 95 desktop. From the Labs folder, start SPINDIB16.EXE.

   The 16-bit Windows-based program starts.
4. From the Labs folder, start SPINDIB32.EXE.

   The 32-bit Windows-based program starts.
5. Switch between the three programs to verify that all three operate in Windows 95.

Lesson Summary

You can operate MS-DOS–based, 16-bit Windows-based, and 32-bit Windows-based programs in Windows 95 without any changes to the computer.

Lesson 2: General Protection Faults

Poorly written programs may attempt processes that are not allowed by the operating system. Some of these may cause a general protection fault. The results of a general protection fault is different depending on the type of program. This lesson explains the different consequences between programs.

After this lesson you will be able to:

- Explain the consequences to the operating system when MS-DOS–based, 16-bit Windows-based, or 32-bit Windows-based programs cause a general protection fault while running under Windows 95.

Estimated lesson time 20 minutes

There are two basic ways a program can stop working. The program may attempt to violate system integrity, for example, a program may try write to the operating system's protected memory address, or a program may stop responding to system messages.

System Integrity Violations

If a program attempts to violate the integrity of the system, it is theoretically possible for the program to corrupt the entire virtual machine (VM). However, the architecture of the Windows 95 system offers certain protections, depending on the type of program that attempts to violate system integrity. If a program tries to write to a protected memory address, the Windows 95 system stops the program before it can do any damage and issues a general protection (GP) fault.

MS-DOS–Based Programs

If an MS-DOS–based program attempts to violate system integrity, only that program is affected; remember, each MS-DOS–based program runs in its own VM. When this occurs, the Windows 95 system issues a general protection (GP) fault. A GP fault message appears to identify the program that has tried to violate system integrity. When you click OK, the MS-DOS–based program is closed along with its virtual machine.

16-bit Windows-Based Programs

If a 16-bit Windows-based program attempts to violate system integrity, the system traps the attempt to prevent the program from damaging other programs. The result is a general protection (GP) fault identifying the program that attempted to violate system integrity. In addition, all other 16-bit Windows-based programs are stopped until the GP faulted program can be closed; remember, all 16-bit Windows-based programs are cooperatively multitasked. Once the GP faulted program is closed, the remaining 16-bit Windows-based programs continue to run.

32-bit Windows-Based Programs

If a 32-bit Windows-based program causes a GP fault, it does not affect any other program; remember, 32-bit Windows-based programs have separate memory addresses. The program is closed when the user responds to the GP fault message.

Driver Failures

As in any operating system, a GP fault in a device driver can affect the stability of the entire operating system. This is a result of the high privilege level granted to code needing to access hardware.

Examples of General Protection Faults

Now that you have an understanding of what should happen when a program causes a GP fault, you can observe the effects of a general protection fault error caused by programs by completing the following steps. You will then repair the Windows-based program that is causing system problems.

Description of Program Menus in BadApp16 and BadApp32

The following information describes the program menus you will encounter in the exercise.

Action Menu

- GP Fault—Causes the program to generate a general protection fault. This can demonstrate the error trapping functions of the operating system.

- Hang—Causes the program to go into a tight loop. The cursor changes to an hourglass when in the program, and the program does not respond to input.

Options

- Zoom Factor—Allows you to make the program larger. This can be used to make the projection more visible.

- Title—Allows you to change the title on the program title bar. Note that a change made here will change *all* copies run after this point—both 16-bit and 32-bit Windows-based programs.

Help Menu

- About—Displays a dialog box with version information about the program.

▶ **To test the functions of 16- and 32-bit Windows-based programs**

In this procedure, you verify that the 16- and 32-bit Windows-based programs are functioning properly.

1. From the Labs folder, double-click the SPIND16.EXE icon.

   The SPINDIB16.EXE program starts.

2. Click the Open button.

   A File Open dialog box appears.

3. Click the BILLG.BMP file, and then click the OK button.

   A bitmap of Bill Gates appears inside the SpinDIB16 window.

4. Click either the Spin or Flip button.

   The bitmap should spin or flip, respectively, and a return to the normal layout. A time appears on the right side of the toolbar.

5. Repeat steps 1 through 4 for the SPIND32.EXE program.

   Leave both programs active on your computer.

▶ **To cause a 16-bit general-protection fault**

1. With SPIND16.EXE and SPIND32.EXE active, start BADAPP16.EXE.

   These programs are located in the C:\LABS folder.

2. Arrange your desktop to view all of the programs. One easy method to do this is to click the taskbar with the secondary mouse button, then click Tile Horizontally or Tile Vertically. This automatically arranges all of the open programs on your desktop.

3. On the Action menu, click Options, and then turn off the sound.

4. On the Action menu, click the GP-Fault option.

   When the fuse burns down, the bomb explodes. At this point a general protection fault is triggered.

   Windows 95 displays a dialog box allowing you to close or ignore the GP fault.

5. Click the Close button. Do not click Close again.

6. Windows 95 displays a Program Error dialog box with details of the error and a Close button.

7. Click SPIND32. Is this program still active? _____

8. Click SPIND16. Is this program still active? _____

9. Click BADAPP (Program Error dialog box).

10. Click the Close button to close BADAPP.

11. Are the 16-bit Windows-based programs active now? _____

▶ **To cause a 32-bit general-protection fault**

1. Start BADAPP32.EXE and make sure that the SPIND programs are still active.

2. Arrange your desktop so that you can see all programs.

3. On the Action menu, click the GP-Fault option.

   When the fuse burns down, the bomb explodes. At this point a general fault is triggered.

   Windows 95 displays a dialog box with details of the error.

4. Select any of the programs to demonstrate that the system is active.

5. Switch back to the BADAPP32 program error dialog box.

6. Click the Close button to close the program.

Lesson Summary

If a 16-bit Windows-based program causes a GP fault, it may cause all other 16-bit Windows-based programs to halt until the offending program is closed. If MS-DOS–based or 32-bit Windows-based programs cause a GP fault, no other program is affected.

Lesson 3: Program Stops Responding to System

Similar to GP faults are instances when programs do not respond to the system. This lesson explains how these programs are handled by Windows 95.

After this lesson you will be able to:

- Explain the consequences to the operating system when MS-DOS–based, 16-bit Windows-based, and 32-bit Windows-based programs stop responding to the system while running under Windows 95.

Estimated lesson time 20 minutes

Programs may stop responding to the system. Depending on the type of program that stops responding, the rest of the system may not be affected.

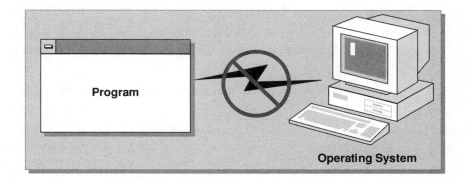

Figure 16.1 Program no longer responds to the system

MS-DOS–Based Programs

If an MS-DOS–based program stops responding to the system, you can terminate the program by performing a local reboot.

A local reboot accomplished by pressing the CTRL+ALT+DEL keys once. Windows 95 gives you the following three options, which is similar to Microsoft Windows NT when you perform a local reboot.

- End Task—Immediately shuts down the program.
- Shut Down
- Cancel—Does not end the task.

In addition, if the program was running in a window, it may be closed from the Properties window.

16-bit Windows-Based Programs

If a 16-bit Windows-based program stops responding in the foreground, it may never release control. All other 16-bit Windows-based programs are stopped at the same time because they cannot reach the message queue. If this happens, you need to perform a local reboot to terminate the program that has stopped responding. After terminating the non-responsive program, all other programs should resume.

32-bit Windows-Based Programs

If a 32-bit Windows-based program stops responding, you can terminate the program by performing a local reboot. Because 32-bit Windows-based programs have a separate message queue, no other programs are affected.

All Programs

If any program stops responding while using a critical resource, any program that needs that resource is stopped. The other programs may appear to have stopped responding, but a local reboot indicates what program is actually stopped. The stopped program needs to be closed. Resources used by the program are returned for system use when the virtual machine is closed.

In all these situations, you are not required to restart the entire Windows 95 system. A local reboot indicates which program has stopped, and the stopped program can be closed.

It is important to keep track of which programs actually cause the system to stop responding. By tracking these problems over a period of time, you can identify programs which cause problems.

Examples of Programs Hanging

The following exercise allows you to observe the effects of a program that stop responding. You will then repair the Windows-based program that is causing system problems.

▶ **To cause a 16-bit Windows-based program to stops responding**

1. With SPIND16.EXE and SPIND32.EXE active, start BADAPP16.EXE.

2. Arrange your desktop so that you can see all programs.

3. On the Action menu, click Hang.

   When the fuse burns down, the bomb explodes. At this point the program stop responding.

4. Verify that all programs, both 32-bit and 16-bit, on the system no longer respond.

5. Start the Close Hung Program dialog box by pressing CTRL+ALT+DEL.

6. Click the BadApp not responding line, and then click End Task.

   A dialog box appears prompting you to either End Task or Cancel.

7. Click End Task.

   The remaining programs become active.

▶   **To cause a 32-bit program to stop responding**

1. With the two SPIND programs active, start BADAPP32.EXE.

2. Arrange your desktop so that you can see all programs.

3. On the Action menu, click Hang.

   When the fuse burns down, the bomb explodes. At this point the program stops responding.

4. Move the mouse pointer out of the BADAPP window to show that BADAPP has stopped.

5. Select any other program to demonstrate that the system is active.

   This is evident because 16-bit Windows-based programs are already started.

6. Start the Close Hung Program dialog box by pressing CTRL+ALT+DEL.

7. Click BADAPP, and then click End Task.

   A dialog box appears prompting you to either End Task or Cancel.

8. Click End Task.

   BadApp is closed.

Program Resources

When an MS-DOS–based program is closed, its virtual machine and all resources used by that virtual machine are returned to the system.

16-bit Windows-based programs may use resources without the operating system being aware of that usage. 16-bit Windows-based programs may also use resources shared by other 16-bit Windows-based programs. Because of these issues, the resources used by 16-bit Windows-based programs are not returned to the system until there are no 16-bit Windows-based programs running. At this point, any orphaned resources from all the 16-bit Windows-based programs are returned.

Because resource usage by 32-bit Windows-based programs can be completely tracked, a closed 32-bit Windows-based program's resources are returned to the system as part of the termination process.

Although resources may be returned to the system, your resource counts may not return to their original points. This is due to Windows 95 caching of frequently shared resources. If resource usage becomes critical, these cached resources are unloaded if they are not needed.

Lesson Summary

When a program stops responding to the system, it can tie up the message queue. Because all 16-bit Windows-based programs share a single message queue, all 16-bit Windows based programs may be affected by the stopped program. All 32-bit Windows-based programs have their own message queue, preventing one program from blocking the others.

Lesson 4: 16-bit System Code

Windows 95 still contains 16-bit code in the main operating system. This lesson explains why this code exists and what, if any, effect this may have on the rest of the system.

After this lesson you will be able to:

- Explain why 16-bit system code still exists in Windows 95.

Estimated lesson time 10 minutes

Portions of the Windows 95 operating system still use 16-bit code.

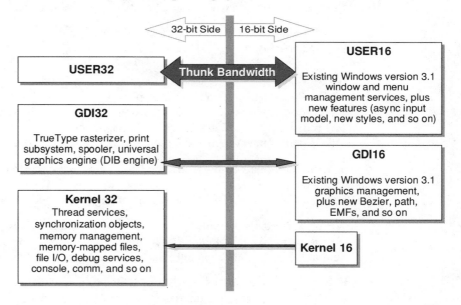

Figure 16.2 Relationship of 32- and 16-bit code in Windows 95 operating system

There are three main reasons that Windows 95 still contains 16-bit code:

- 32-bit code requires more memory for an equivalent amount of 16-bit code. One of the main goals of Windows 95 is to have it work efficiently on a system with limited amounts of RAM. The use of 16-bit code facilitates this requirement.

- In some cases, 16-bit code is faster than the equivalent 32-bit code. In these cases the 16-bit code was used.

- Windows 95 still has 16-bit system code for compatibility reasons with existing programs.

Most 16-bit code is *non-reentrant*. Non-reentrant means that the code module does not have the ability to be used by more than one thread at a time.

To have the capability to run MS-DOS–based, 16-bit and 32-bit Windows-based programs, Windows 95 thunks between 16-bit and 32-bit system code. Thunking is a translation from 16-bit call to 32-bit equivalent call, and from 32-bit to 16-bit.

The User component is almost all 16-bit code. This was done to keep the user component small.

The graphical device interface (GDI) component uses a mix of 16- and 32-bit code. 32-bit code was used where speed was the important issue or when precise floating point measurements are needed, such as when TrueType renders Kanji characters. 16-bit code was used when compatibility was the main concern.

The Kernel uses all 32-bit code. The 16-bit APIs are just entry points that were kept for compatibility reasons.

Win16Mutex

When a process uses a non-reentrant piece of code, a flag is set indicating that no other process can use this piece of code until the process is finished with it. When the process finishes using that code, the flag is reset. If this piece of non-reentrant code is part of the system code, it is called a *critical section*.

In Windows 95, all 16-bit system code is considered part of a critical section, because it was designed for compatibility with 16-bit Windows. When a critical section of code is used by a process, no other process may use that system code.

Win16Mutex is the flag that Windows 95 sets when it calls Windows 16-bit code. Only one thread can hold the Win16Mutex flag at a time. No other program can be running 16-bit system code until the Win16Mutex flag is released.

If the program that set the Win16Mutex flag tries to violate system integrity or stops to responding while the flag is set, the Win16Mutex flag may not get reset. This prevents any program from using 16-bit system code. In this instance, a 16-bit Windows-based program can block a 32-bit Windows-based program from running.

If this situation occurs, the user must close the 16-bit Windows-based program. When the 16-bit Windows-based program closes, the Win16Mutex flag is reset and the critical section of code may be used.

The calls that set the Win16Mutex tend to be very short in duration, for example, a GDI call that paints a single pixel.

Because the Kernel uses all 32-bit code, the Win16Mutex flag does not block kernel code from running.

Lesson Summary

Windows 95 contains 16-bit code to make it smaller and compatible with existing programs. If a process uses a critical section of code, no other program may use that section of system code.

Review

The following questions are intended to reinforce key information presented in this chapter. If you are unable to answer a question, review the appropriate lesson and then try the question again.

1. Why does Windows 95 have both 16-bit and 32-bit system code?

2. A client calls and complains that after closing a 16-bit Windows-based program that had stopped responding, the system resources remain low. Why?

3. A customer complains that after closing various programs, the available resources are still reported lower than they were before the programs were started. No problems are occurring, the complaint is just that the resources are reported lower. Why?

C H A P T E R   1 7

Tuning an MS-DOS–Based Program

Before You Begin

To complete the lessons in this chapter, you must have:

- Completed Chapter 1 and installed Microsoft Windows 95.
- The following file in the C:\LABS folder.
  PIFTEST.EXE

Lesson 1: General Properties

This lesson explains the parameters available on the General tab.

After this lesson you will be able to:

- Create a .PIF file for a Microsoft MS-DOS–based program.

Estimated lesson time 10 minutes

Programs based on all versions of Microsoft Windows contain information in their headers that allow them to easily coexist with other programs. This includes things such as sharing resources, sharing memory, and so on.

MS-DOS–based programs do not contain this information. They were usually designed to use whatever resources were available to the computer.

Microsoft Windows 95 contains default properties for most common MS-DOS–based programs. These properties are stored in the APPS.INF file in the hidden Windows\INF folder. The first time these programs are run, the properties are loaded from this file.

If the program does not perform as desired using the default settings, or if the program is not on the APPS.INF list, you may use the property sheets for an MS-DOS–based program to get a program to perform better in specific circumstances. The property sheets for an MS-DOS–based program can be accessed by clicking the program with the secondary mouse button, and then clicking the Properties option, or by clicking the Properties button on the MS-DOS window toolbar.

▶ **To use the General properties**

1. Explore My Computer and use the Find function to locate COMMAND.COM.
2. Click the secondary mouse button on **command**.
3. Click Properties on the menu.

   The property sheets consists of a series of tabs. Clicking the General tab, which appears at first by default, displays a property sheet that is common to all files.

4. Click the question mark in the upper-right corner. Notice that the mouse pointer has a question mark attached to its side.

5. Click any of the fields on the General tab.

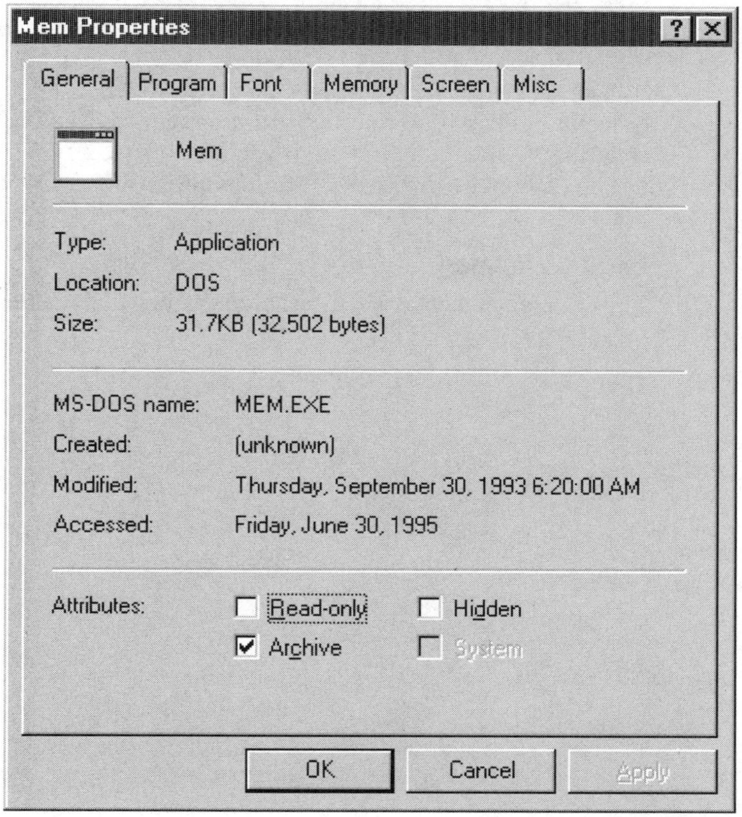

Mem Properties

General | Program | Font | Memory | Screen | Misc

Mem

Type: Application
Location: DOS
Size: 31.7KB (32,502 bytes)

MS-DOS name: MEM.EXE
Created: (unknown)
Modified: Thursday, September 30, 1993 6:20:00 AM
Accessed: Friday, June 30, 1995

Attributes: ☐ Read-only   ☐ Hidden
              ☑ Archive   ☐ System

OK   Cancel   Apply

Figure 17.1 General tab on an MS-DOS–based program property sheet

The remaining tabs are unique to MS-DOS–based programs.

Note If you start the MS-DOS prompt on the Start menu and then click the secondary mouse button on the title bar, the General tab does not appear. The Program tab is the first to appear.

When you modify the property sheets, you are modifying a .PIF (Program Information File) file which is created and stored in the same folder as the program. You may create multiple .PIF files for a single MS-DOS–based program by copying the .PIF file, assigning it a new name, and using the property sheets to assign the new settings.

Note If you have installed an MS-DOS–based program that does not have a .PIF, Windows 95 searches for an APPS.INF file. If you have upgraded from Windows 3.1 or Microsoft Windows for Workgroups 3.11, you will have an APPS.INF file. If there is an entry in APPS.INF, Windows 95 will use it to create a .PIF for the program. If there is no entry for your program, _DEFAULT.PIF will be used to create a .PIF for your program. If you do not have a DEFAULT.PIF, you can create one by copying DOSPRMPT.PIF from the C:\WINDOWS folder.

Lesson Summary

The General tab contains the basic information about a file.

Lesson 2: Program Properties

This lesson explains the parameters available on the Program property sheet.

After this lesson you will be able to:

- Modify the program properties of an MS-DOS–based program.

Estimated lesson time 20 minutes

The Program tab contains some of the general purpose information about the program.

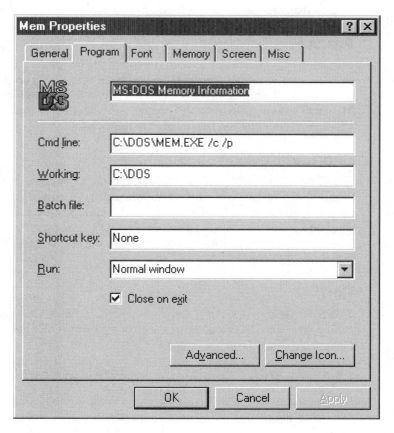

Figure 17.2 Program tab on an MS-DOS–based program property sheet

The following are some of the more common parameters that are set using this tab.

Cmd Line

The command line allows you to type a path and command to start the MS-DOS–based program. This is a complete command line; you may enter any information that you would normally enter at a command prompt, including startup parameters.

Working

If you want to specify a location to store data that is different from the location where the program is stored, you can use the Working field for this. This may include the universal naming convention (UNC) name for a network location.

Batch File

This allows you to specify a batch file to run before running the program. This is a convenient way to start terminate-and-stay-resident (TSR) programs and set other configuration information that is required before a program runs. If there are MS-DOS environment variables that need to be set before running the MS-DOS–based program, they can be specified in this batch file.

Shortcut Key

The Shortcut key field is where you can specify a keyboard shortcut to start this program. However, if you specify a keyboard shortcut, any program that uses the same keystrokes to perform a specialized function loses that capability. The shortcut keys are reserved to start the MS-DOS–based program. Whenever those keys are pressed, even when inside another program, the MS-DOS–based program is activated.

Run

This list box allows you to specify how to run the MS-DOS–based program. The choices are to run the program in a normal window, minimized as an icon, or maximized using the entire screen.

Close on Exit

If a program automatically exits when it is completed, you may not see the results of running the program. If a program that displays information on the screen and then exits has this option set, for example, MEM, DIR, and others, you may never be able to see the information presented on the screen before the window is closed.

If this check box is not selected, Windows 95 will close the window of a full screen program and leave open the window of a program that prints to the screen and then exits.

▶ **To modify program properties**

1. Explore My Computer and use the Find function to locate MEM.EXE.

2. Click the secondary mouse button on **mem**.

3. Click Properties on the menu.

4. Click the Program tab.

5. Click Close on Exit.

6. Click OK.

7. Start **mem** by double-clicking it or opening it.

8. According to the display, what is the total amount of Extended memory? Were you able to read it? Why or why not?

   _____

   _____

   _____

9. Without changing the settings in the .PIF, start a command prompt and run **mem** in it.

10. Were you able to read the total amount of extended memory? Why or why not?

    _____

    _____

    _____

Advanced Program Settings

When you click the Advanced... button on the Program property sheet, the advanced program settings appear. The full path to the .PIF you are modifying appears.

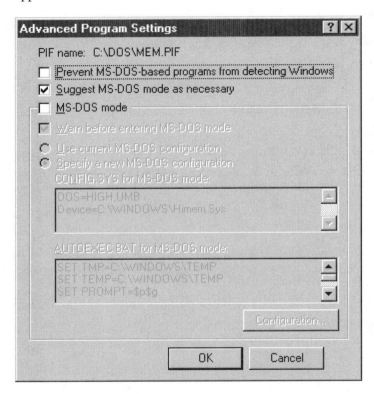

Figure 17.3 Advanced Program Settings for an MS-DOS–based program

Prevent MS-DOS–Based Programs from Detecting Windows

This setting specifies whether this MS-DOS–based program will be able to detect the presence of Windows. Some programs determine whether they are running in a MS-DOS virtual machine or under native MS-DOS, and behave differently for each environment.

If you want to prevent Windows from being detected by this MS-DOS–based program, make sure this box is checked. If you are not sure, or you want to run Windows-based programs from this MS-DOS–based program, clear this check box.

Suggest MS-DOS Mode As Necessary

This setting specifies that when you run this program, Windows detects whether the program requires or runs best in MS-DOS mode. If the program requires MS-DOS mode for best performance, Windows runs a wizard to set up a custom icon to run the program. If the program works best in or requires MS-DOS mode, and you do not select this option, it may run poorly or not run at all.

MS-DOS Mode

Although Windows 95 is designed to run MS-DOS–based programs, it is possible that you may find one that cannot be run from the desktop, such as a game that requires complete control of the computer. For this type of program, you can use the MS-DOS mode. If you select MS-DOS mode, Windows 95 unloads and the MS-DOS–based program is given control of the entire machine. When the MS-DOS–based program completes, Windows 95 restarts. Because you have full control of the machine for this program, you may create specific settings for the CONFIG.SYS and AUTOEXEC.BAT files.

The Select MS-DOS Mode Configuration Options dialog box walks you through the process of creating the program-specific CONFIG.SYS and AUTOEXEC.BAT files.

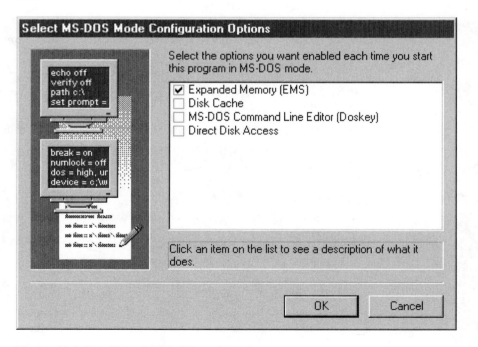

Figure 17.4 Specifying MS-DOS mode settings

▶ **To modify AUTOEXEC.BAT and CONFIG.SYS**

1. Explore My Computer and use the Find function to locate \WINDOWS\COMMAND\MEM.EXE.

2. Click the secondary mouse button on **mem**.

3. Click Properties on the menu.

4. Click the Program tab, and then click the Advanced button.

   You may want to make a backup copy of the CONFIG.SYS and AUTOEXEC.BAT files before you continue to the next step. This can be done by starting a command prompt or in Windows Explorer.

5. Do not select the options available by clicking the check box, but click each of the available options and look at the bottom of the window to see an explanation each option.

6. Click Disk Cache and MS-DOS Command Line Editor (Doskey).

7. Click OK on three different dialog boxes to finish.

8. On the Start menu, click Run.

9. Type **mem** and then press ENTER.

   You will receive the following prompt:

   ```
   This program is set to run in MS-DOS mode and cannot run while other
   programs are running.  All other programs will close if you choose to
   continue.
   Do you want to continue?
   ```

10. If you click Yes to continue, all programs shut down and your computer restarts. Click Yes.

11. Once you exit **mem**, your computer restarts to resume running Windows 95.

12. Before continuing with this chapter, reset the .PIF for **mem,** and cancel the selection of MS-DOS mode.

Lesson Summary

The Program tab allows you to set some general purpose information about the programs.

Lesson 3: Font Properties

This lesson explains the parameters available on the Font property sheet.

After this lesson you will be able to:

- Modify the font properties of an MS-DOS–based program.

Estimated lesson time 10 minutes

The Font tab allows you to specify the font type and size used in the MS-DOS window. Windows 95 adds TrueType font support, in addition to bitmap fonts.

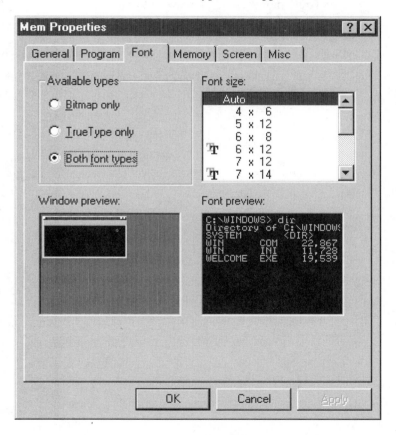

Figure 17.5 Font tab on an MS-DOS–based program property sheet

If you select Auto as the font size, the computer automatically determines the appropriate font as the window is increased or decreased in size.

▶   **To modify the font properties**

1. Start **mem**, located in \WINDOWS\COMMAND, and leave it open.

2. Through Windows Explorer, locate **mem** and display the property sheet.

3. Click the Fonts tab.

4. Notice that Font size is set to Auto by default.

5. Set the fonts to 4 x 6, or the smallest setting.

6. Start a second copy of **mem**.

   Notice the size difference between the two windows running **mem**. Especially on larger monitors, you may want to run programs in smaller windows.

Lesson Summary

MS-DOS–based programs may use various fonts and sizes, including TrueType fonts.

Lesson 4: Memory Properties

This lesson explains the parameters available on the Memory property sheet.

After this lesson you will be able to:

- Modify the memory properties of an MS-DOS–based program.

Estimated lesson time 30 minutes

The Memory tab allows you to specify the amount of the Conventional, Expanded, Extended, and DPMI memory allocated for the MS-DOS–based program. You may also select the Protected check box the Conventional memory area.

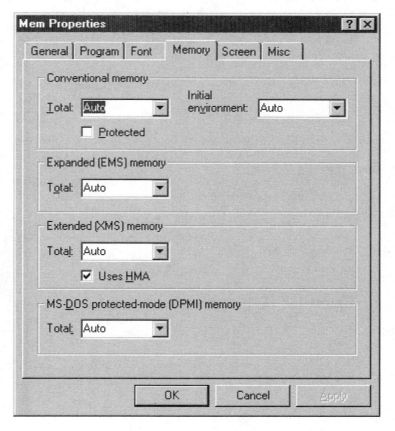

Figure 17.6 Memory tab on an MS-DOS–based program property sheet

Conventional Memory

The conventional memory list box indicates how much conventional memory is required for this program. In most cases, the Auto setting is best.

The Initial environment indicates the amount of memory set aside for the MS-DOS Command Interpreter, COMMAND.COM. This setting is also used for batch files (*.BAT) and for SET variables, such as the path and TEMP directory location. If you increase this amount, you have more space for these variables, but a smaller amount of space for the program. One common use is to make sure there is enough space for a long path. If you have a program that is cutting off the end of the path, you may consider increasing the local environment size. If you have the Initial environment size set to Auto, the size of the environment will be determined by the SHELL= line in your CONFIG.SYS file.

The Protected switch can be used to increase the protection of the memory used by the program by protecting system memory from inappropriate modifications by this program. When this check box is checked, the program might run slightly slower, but your computer is protected from errors or failures in the program.

Expanded Memory

Specifies the maximum amount of expanded memory, in kilobytes, to allocate to this program. If you set this value to Auto, no limit is imposed.

Some programs may have difficulty dealing with an unlimited amount of expanded memory. If this becomes a problem, set this value 8192.

Windows 95 automatically provides expanded memory for MS-DOS–based programs that require it to run. However, if you include a statement in CONFIG.SYS that loads EMM386.EXE with the **noems** parameter, then no expanded memory will be available.

Extended Memory

Specifies the maximum amount of extended memory, in kilobytes, to allocate to the program. If you set this value to Auto, then no limit is imposed.

Some programs may have difficulty dealing with an unlimited amount of extended memory. If this become a problem, set this value 8192.

DPMI Memory

Specifies the maximum amount of MS-DOS protected-mode (DPMI) memory, in kilobytes, to allocate to this program. If you set this value to Auto, then Windows chooses a limit based on your current configuration.

Lesson Summary

The Mem property sheet allows you to configure the various memory settings for an MS-DOS–based program.

Lesson 5: Screen Properties

This lesson explains the how you can modify the screen properties of an MS-DOS–based program.

After this lesson you will be able to:

- Modify the screen properties of an MS-DOS–based program.

Estimated lesson time 10 minutes

The Screen tab is used to define how the program uses the screen functions.

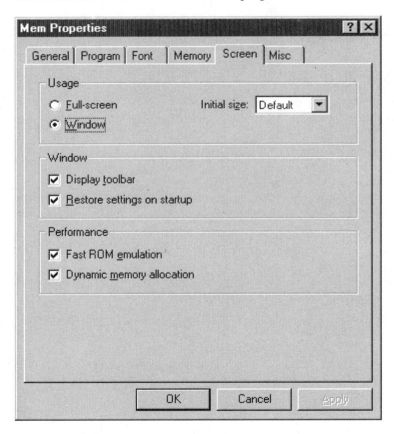

Figure 17.7 Screen tab on an MS-DOS–based program property sheet

Usage

This group determines how the monitor screen is used. The settings in this group are:

- Full-screen—Specifies that the program run in a full screen. This uses the least memory and is mostly used to run graphics.

- Window—Specifies that the program run in a window. This mode makes it easier to share information with other Windows-based programs, and is mostly used for text-based MS-DOS–based programs.

- Initial size—Specifies the initial number of lines on the screen for this program. A program that resets the display to its default number of lines on the screen will override this setting.

Window

These options determine the default appearance of the window where the program runs.

When the Display toolbar option is checked, a toolbar is added to the program window.

The Restore settings on start up option restores window settings when you exit the MS-DOS–based program. This includes the window size, position, and font. It returns the screen to the configuration it had prior to running the MS-DOS–based program.

Performance

There are two settings which affect the performance of the video drivers.

- Fast ROM emulation—Clicking this option allows the computer to emulate the video ROM drivers in protected mode, allowing the computer to write to the screen faster.

  Clear this check box if your program is using nonstandard functions in ROM, or if you experience problems with the program writing text to the screen.

- Dynamic memory allocation—If this switch is set, memory used by the program for video display is held by the program. This is useful when a program frequently switches between text and graphics modes, such as with the print preview function of a word processor. If this is not checked, the memory needs to be reallocated whenever graphics are selected.

Make sure this box is checked if this program uses text and graphics modes and you want to maximize the amount of memory available to other programs when this program is running. When you switch to the mode requiring less memory, Windows makes more memory available to other programs. When you switch back to the mode requiring more memory, Windows attempts to provide the memory.

To ensure that there is always enough memory for Windows to correctly display this program in any mode, make sure this box is not checked.

Lesson Summary

The Screen tab contains the parameters to configure for adjusting video output display.

Lesson 6: Miscellaneous Properties

This lesson explains how you can use the parameters available on the Misc tab to modify an MS-DOS–based program.

After this lesson you will be able to:

- Modify the miscellaneous properties of an MS-DOS–based program.

Estimated lesson time 15 minutes

The Misc tab determines how the computer shares the CPU and other resources.

Figure 17.8 Misc tab on an MS-DOS–based program property sheet

Foreground

If Allow screen saver is not checked, the computer screen saver will be prevented from running when this program is in the foreground. You may find this setting useful if the screen saver triggers time-outs or screen painting problems with the MS-DOS–based program.

Background

When the Always suspend box is checked, the program is suspended when it is not in the foreground. This is not the default setting.

Idle Sensitivity

This setting is used to determine when the computer suspends a program after a certain amount of time of inactivity, such as when waiting for input.

If you are using a program that uses a coprocessor, such as a 3270 communications system, it may appear to the computer that the program is inactive and the program may be suspended while using the coprocessor. If this situation exists, lower the sensitivity to its lowest level.

Mouse

When QuickEdit is selected, the mouse may be used to select text in the MS-DOS window without having to go into a special edit mode. This should not be used when the program uses the mouse itself.

Exclusive mode locks the mouse inside the MS-DOS window. This may be necessary on some programs that lose synchronization with the mouse when it leaves their window.

Termination

Warn if still active should be enabled most of the time. If a program uses open files, such as a database, and is terminated without the files being properly closed, data can be corrupted. By having this option set, the user is warned that the program is about to close and is given the chance to save files and then close the program.

Other

Most programs allow pasting into their window from the Windows 95 Clipboard. If this does not work, deselecting Fast pasting should correct the problem.

Windows Shortcut Keys

These settings determine which of the standard Windows shortcut keys to enable for the MS-DOS–based program. Any key combination selected here is sent to Windows 95 and not to the MS-DOS–based program. If you want the MS-DOS–based program to get the keystroke rather than Windows 95, make sure appropriate check box is not checked.

▶ **To change command window miscellaneous attributes**

1. Shut down all programs.

2. Start two command prompts and put each in a window on your desktop.

3. Arrange the MS-DOS windows so that both are viewable at the same time and one is positioned above the other.

4. In each MS-DOS window, type the following commands:

   **cd ** and then press ENTER

   cls and then press ENTER

   This brings you to the root directory and clears the screen.

5. In each of the command windows, type in the following command:

   c:\labs\piftest

   This starts a counter on the upper-left corner of the windows screen. You may have to scroll up to see the counter running.

6. In the top MS-DOS window, click the MS-DOS icon in the upper-left corner, and then click Properties.

7. Click the Misc tab, and then click the Background Always suspend check box.

8. Click the Apply button, and then click the OK button. Look at both counters—what happened?

   _____

9. Click the bottom MS-DOS window to bring it to the foreground. What happened?

   _____

10. Return to the top MS-DOS window. What happened to the counter in the bottom MS-DOS window?_____

11. Stop the **piftest** counters by pressing the SPACEBAR while in the active window.

12. Deselect all of the changes you made in this exercise before shutting down the two command windows.

Lesson Summary

The Misc tab can be used to configure and tune an MS-DOS–based program.

Review

The following questions are intended to reinforce key information presented in this chapter. If you are unable to answer a question, review the appropriate lesson and then try the question again.

1. A user calls and says, "When I try to switch between my MS-DOS–based program and Windows by using ALT+TAB, nothing happens. I have to quit the program to get back to Windows." How do you help this user?

   _____

   _____

2. A user wants a special batch file to run before she runs her favorite MS-DOS–based program. How can this be set up?

   _____

   _____

3. A user complains that he can no longer get an MS-DOS session to work properly. Each time he tries to start an MS-DOS session on the Programs menu, the system shuts down Windows and goes into MS-DOS mode. A quick glance at the Properties list for the C:\WINDOWS\COMMAND.COM file shows that the MS-DOS mode option is cleared. How do you fix this problem?

   _____

   _____

C H A P T E R   1 8

Display

Before You Begin

To complete the lessons in this chapter, you must have:

- Completed Chapter 1 and installed Microsoft Windows 95.

Lesson 1: Display Architecture

This lesson provides you with an overview of the display subsystem architecture. This information can be very useful when trying to isolate problems.

After this lesson you will be able to:

- Describe the new display driver model in Microsoft Windows 95.
- Describe the benefit of the Device Independent Bitmap (DIB) engine in Windows 95.

Estimated lesson time 20 minutes

Display Driver Model

A Windows *display driver* is a dynamic-link library (DLL) that translates device-independent commands from the graphic-device interface (GDI) into commands and actions that the display adapter uses to draw graphics on the screen. The display driver also gives information to Windows regarding the display hardware, such as color resolution, graphics capabilities, screen size and resolution, and other display features.

Windows 95 Display Drivers

Writing display drivers for previous versions of Windows required independent hardware vendors (IHVs) to compose a great deal of assembly language code covering a variety of display tasks. In the Windows 95 display driver architecture, Microsoft has taken the common software code needed by display drivers and placed it in the Device Independent Bitmap (DIB) engine. The IHV now only needs to write the hardware-specific code for the display and call on the DIB engine for software calls. Should the IHV decide not to take advantage of the DIB engine, they need to write a full display driver that functions similar to the older Windows 3.x model, with added functionality for Windows 95.

The Windows 95 DIB engine (DIBENG.DLL) provided by Microsoft contains most of the functions needed to translate GDI commands. A display driver that uses the DIB engine is called a *display mini-driver*. The mini-driver only contains hardware-specific code for the display adapter and redirects the software calls from the GDI to the DIB engine. Mini-drivers call the functions in this library to perform bitmap operations, manage graphics objects, manage color palettes, and draw lines, curves, filled shapes, and text.

Supported Drivers

Windows 95 supports a variety of display drivers. However, most of the drivers are based on a limited number of chip sets. The chip sets supported by Windows 95 use the following display drivers.

- FRAMEBUF.DRV   Generic frame buffer cards (no acceleration)
- ATIM32.DRV   ATI Mach 32 chip set based cards
- ATIM8.DRV   ATI Mach 8 chip set based cards
- ATIM64.DRV   ATI Mach 64 chip set based cards
- CHIPS.DRV   Chips and Technologies chip set based cards
- CIRRUS.DRV   Cirrus Logic chip set based cards
- CIRRUSMM.DRV   Cirrus Logic memory-mapped chip set series based cards
- COMPAQ.DRV   Compaq chip set based cards
- MGA.DRV   Matrox® MGA chip set based cards
- S3.DRV   S3 chip set based cards
- TSENG.DRV   Tseng Labs chip set based cards
- WD.DRV   Western Digital™ chip set based cards
- XGA.DRV   IBM XGA®–compatible cards

Other drivers may be listed, however these are actually friendly names that point back to one of these listed drivers. This means that the user does not have to know the actual chip set on their hardware, they can use the friendly name to select the appropriate display driver.

Display Subsystem Architecture

The display architecture is similar to the architecture used for printing or networking. It is layered and consists of various drivers that allow for device independence.

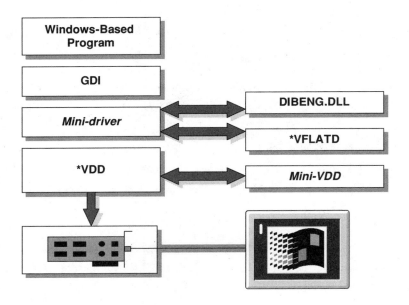

Figure 18.1 Display subsystem architecture

The Windows 95 display subsystem consists of the following major components:

Display Mini-Driver

A hardware-specific DLL to draw output on a video display; written by the IHV. It is a display driver that uses the DIB engine. The mini-driver contains only hardware-specific code for the display adapter and redirects the software calls from the GDI to the DIB engine.

DIB Engine

A generic DLL (DIBENG.DLL) supplied by Microsoft that used by the display mini-driver to draw output. This DLL contains most of the functions needed to translate GDI commands to help developers create more efficient display drivers.

VFLATD.VXD

VFLATD.VXD is a VxD supplied by Microsoft to virtualize frame buffers larger than 64K. There are two ways a display driver can handle video memory: the flat memory model and the flat-frame buffer model. Previous versions of Windows provided only a 64K frame buffer for those display drivers needing one. While the early display drivers worked efficiently within this 64K limit, as resolution and color capabilities increased the 64K limit presented difficulties for the video display driver. The display driver had to devise a method of mapping bytes from the larger buffer needed by the driver into the smaller buffer allocated by the computer.

With Windows 95, the virtual flat-frame buffer device driver (VFLATD.VXD) gives display drivers access to a large logical flat-frame buffer. The exact size of the buffer allocated by VFLATD.VXD is specified by the display driver, up to a maximum allowable size of 1 MB. All memory management issues within this buffer are handled by VFLATD.VXD, thus freeing the display driver to only need to accomplish drawing the display.

This VxD allows the IHVs to write only small device-specific mini-VDD display drivers without worrying about general video memory management. Only display drivers written for Windows 95 can take advantage of VFLATD.VXD.

VDD

VDD is a generic VxD supplied by Microsoft that is used by the mini-VDD to virtualize the video hardware. The VDD is called by the grabber (VGAFULL.3GR) whenever a Microsoft MS-DOS virtual machine needs to display output. The VDD enables the smooth transition from Windows high-resolution mode to full-screen VGA mode and back again. The VDD also receives information from the display mini-driver, which it can pass along to the mini-VDD.

Mini-VDD

A mini-VDD is a hardware-specific VxD supplied by an IHV to virtualize the video hardware so that more than one virtual machine (VM) can share the same display. Virtual display mini-drivers (mini-VDD) support virtualization of the display adapter by helping to manage the display hardware for the virtual display device (VDD). The VDD virtualizes display memory, ports, display modes, and text and graphics output. The mini-VDD handles any interactions with the video hardware that the VDD cannot.

Using the Mini-VDD

The mini-VDD is a virtual device (VxDs) that is called by the Windows 95 VDD. Because the mini-VDD does not have an API address, it can be called only by the VDD. The display driver cannot call the mini-VDD directly and must communicate with the mini-VDD through the VDD. This prevents programs and display drivers from getting direct access to the video hardware and corrupting the display while it is in a virtualized mode.

The VDD and mini-VDD are used to virtualize the display and thus are used in displaying MS-DOS–based programs in a window or full-screen. In Windows 3.x, there were many difficulties in displaying MS-DOS–based programs in windows. Windows 95 allows most MS-DOS–based programs to be used in windows.

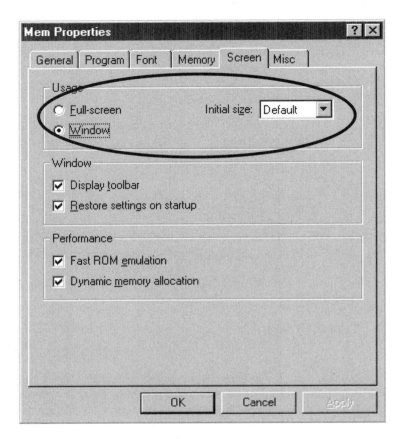

Figure 18.2 MS-DOS-based programs run in a window by default

By default, these programs attempt to run in a window unless they detect a mode that must run full-screen, at which point Windows 95 switches to full-screen mode.

Accelerator cards may also use the new component structure and thus can take advantage of the DIB engine.

Windows 95 Full Display Drivers

This new architecture does not prevent an IHV from writing a Windows 3.1-style Full Display Driver consisting of an IHV written display driver and virtual display driver. They will not get the benefits of using the DIB engine, VFLATD, or the VDD components written by Microsoft.

Interaction of Components

Windows-based programs, MS-DOS–based programs displayed full-screen, and MS-DOS–based programs displayed in a window use the components in the display model differently.

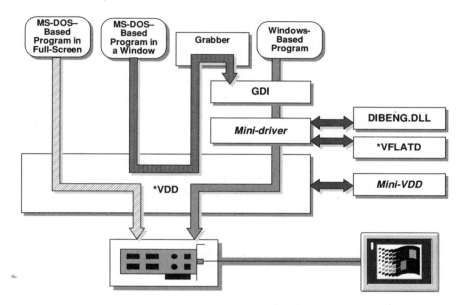

Figure 18.3 How programs interact with display architecture components

The three possible paths through the VDD shown in Figure 18.3 are explained next.

Windows-Based Program

1. Windows-based programs make GDI calls.

2. GDI sends commands to the appropriate device—the display mini-driver.

3. The display mini-driver may require use of the DIB engine or the virtual flat-frame buffer device to generate the image.

4. The completed image is sent to the display adapter by means of the VDD.

Full-Screen MS-DOS–Based Program

1. Program output is trapped by the VDD.

2. The VDD may use the mini-VDD to implement device-specific features.

3. The commands are passed to the display adapter.

Windowed MS-DOS–Based Program

1. MS-DOS–based program output is trapped by the VDD.

2. The VDD may use the mini-VDD to implement device specific features.

3. Output from the VDD is sent to the video grabber.

4. The grabber formats it for GDI.

5. The GDI routes it through the Windows display system as it would a Windows-based program.

Events that occur on the portion of the screen, such as mouse clicks and so forth, occupied by the MS-DOS–based program are passed back through the VDD to the program.

Lesson Summary

The Windows 95 display architecture follows a model similar to printing and other components. Manufacturers that write drivers only need to include a mini-driver, the code included in the DIB engine does the rest.

Lesson 2: Configuring Video

This lesson explains how you can change the video settings to meet the requirements of users and programs.

After this lesson you will be able to:

- Modify the display type, resolution, and colors in Windows 95.
- Explain the importance of setting the monitor type in Windows 95.

Estimated lesson time 20 minutes

The Display property sheet is where the user can change the type of display driver being used by the computer. Each display driver supports all the color and resolution combinations for a given card. Once the driver is loaded, the color and resolution can be changed independently.

The screen resolution can be changed dynamically with a Windows 95 driver as long as the same driver can be used for the new resolution. Changes in resolution which require a new driver or changes in color depth—regardless of the driver—require restarting Windows 95.

The color drop-down list will detail all the choices available for the card at any resolution. Display adapters have 16,256, High color, and True color as options. High color corresponds to a 15- or 16-bit color depth or 32,768 and 65,536 colors respectively. True color is 24-bit color, supporting 16.7 million colors. If a color option is selected that is unavailable in the selected resolution mode, it drops to the highest supported number of colors at that resolution.

The process for changing the display driver and viewing the drivers in use currently is the same.

▶ **To configure your video display**

1. On the Settings menu, or in My Computer, click Control Panel.
2. Click the Display icon.

3. Click the Settings tab on the property sheet.

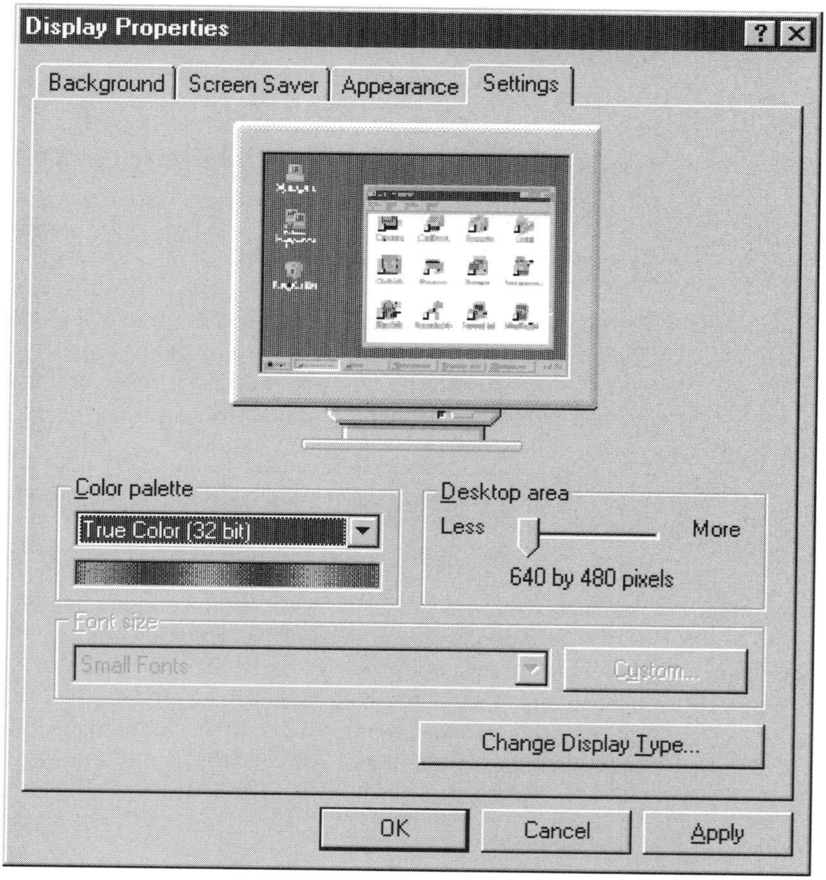

Figure 18.4 Setting tab on the Display property sheet

4. Click the Change Display Type button.

Note   Clicking the desktop with the secondary mouse button and selecting Properties will quickly bring up the Display property sheet.

At this point the following dialog box appears.

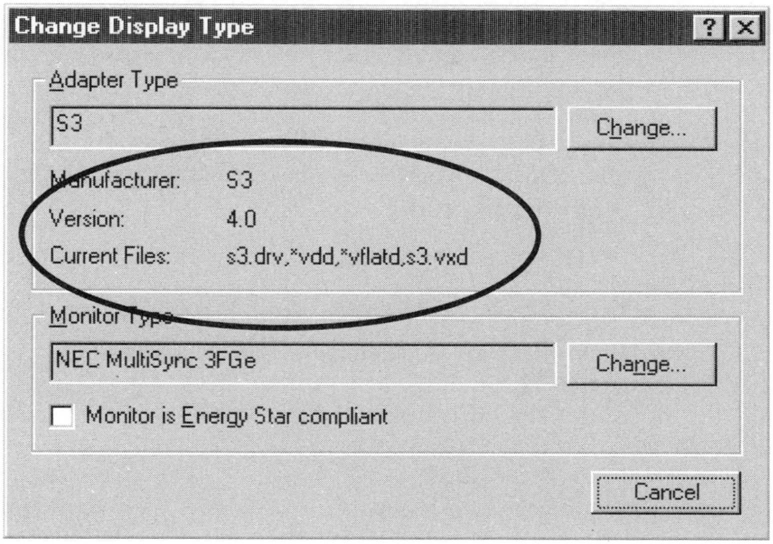

Figure 18.5 Change Display Type dialog box

In the last field under Adapter Type, the drivers currently in use are listed. In the Current Files category of Figure 18.5 , the drivers are listed in the following order.

Device	Driver
Display driver	S3.DRV
VDD	*VDD
Frame buffer memory manager (not always present)	*VFLATD
mini-VDD	S3.VXD

Note that the version of the display driver is also shown.

How to Tell if a Windows 95 Driver Is Being Used

If the Change Display Type dialog box contains the entries *VDD and *VFLATD, then a Windows 95 driver is installed. In some cases, *VFLATD may not be listed. The Windows 95 driver will have an IHV named display driver component, such as S3.DRV in the previous table, and an IHV named mini-VDD, such as S3.VXD in the previous table. Remember, if a Windows 95 mini-driver is being used, it will be using the DIB engine.

If a Windows 3.*x* driver was installed, the dialog box would list the full display driver (<display>.DRV) and virtual display driver supplied by the IHV (<vdisplay>.386). If a Windows 95 full display driver was installed, the dialog box would list the full display driver (<display>.DRV) and virtual display driver supplied by the IHV (<vdisplay>.VXD).

When a Windows 95 display driver is being used, the SYSTEM.INI contains a dummy DISPLAY.DRV entry instead of the actual driver name:

```
[boot]
display.drv=pnpdrvr.drv
```

The registry stores display driver information in the following branch:

```
HKEY_LOCAL_MACHINE
    +SYSTEM
        +CurrentControlSet
            +Services
                +Class
                    +Display
                        +0000
```

Monitor Type

The Monitor Type setting allows the best possible image to be displayed on the monitor. Most monitors and cards support higher refresh rates than standard VGA mode, and at higher resolutions they may have to switch to an interlaced mode.

▶ **To change the monitor type**

1. On the Settings menu, or in My Computer, click Control Panel.

2. Click the Display icon.

3. Click the Settings tab on the property sheet.

4. Click the Change Display Type button.

5. Click the Change button under Monitor Type.

Warning It is possible to damage a monitor if it is driven beyond its capacity for any length of time. Do not choose a monitor option randomly. The user's guide for the monitor should list the maximum resolution and maximum vertical refresh at that resolution. When in doubt, underestimate.

6. By default, Windows 95 has the Show compatible devices button selected. To see the dialog box in Figure 18.6, click the Show all devices button.

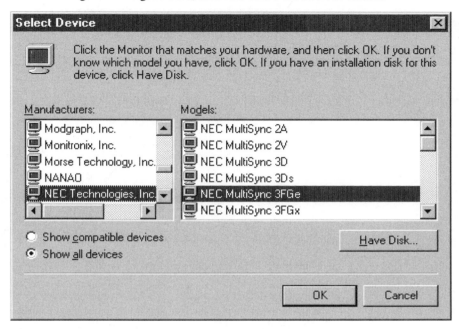

Figure 18.6 Select Device dialog box

The MONITORS.INF file contains maximum resolutions and refresh rates for all of the monitors supported. There is also a Generic monitor option for monitors that do not appear on the list.

7. Click Cancel to return to the Change Display Type dialog box.

Many newer monitors are also Energy Star-compliant. This means they support special energy-saver modes when certain video signals are present.

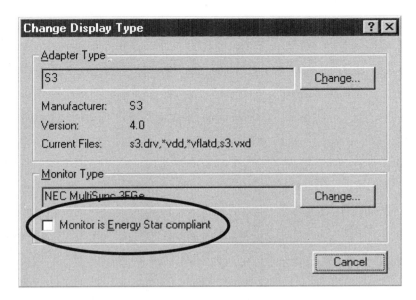

Figure 18.7 Energy Star-compliant setting

Because the monitor is usually the single largest consumer of electricity in a computer system, these monitors are becoming quite common. The switch in the Change Display Type dialog box tells Windows 95 that these energy-saving modes are available on the monitor.

Plug and Play-compliant monitors conform to the Video Electronic Standards Association (VESA) Display Data Channel (DDC) specification. If both the display adapter and the monitor are DDC compliant, display drivers will use timing data from the monitor to optimize refresh rates, centering, and so forth. Also, Image Color Matching will be able to generate a characterization file based on color information from the monitor.

8. Click Cancel to exit the Change Display Type dialog box.

Lesson Summary

The Display property sheet is used to configure the display settings. Windows 95 supports the energy saving features of Energy Star-compliant monitors.

Lesson 3: Troubleshooting Video

There are several common areas where you may have display problems. This lesson explains these areas and what you can do to solve any problems which may occur.

After this lesson you will be able to:

- Diagnose and solve video display problems.

Estimated lesson time 10 minutes

Chip Sets

Most video vendors use standard chip sets in their designs. This allows them to use relatively generic drivers from the chip set vendors and write code only to take advantage of some special feature of their card. If a driver from a particular vendor is not listed, it is quite possible a generic version of that driver will work and provide almost identical functionality as one from the IHV.

The SVGA driver uses the standard VESA mode to access the card. It provides only a few resolution and color options. It also treats all cards as frame buffer devices; if the card has an accelerated chip set, it is not using that functionality. This can obviously have serious performance effects. The feature that this driver offers, however, is that it works on any card with VESA mode BIOS support and provides more than VGA resolution to most cards.

VGA Fallback Mode

Windows 95 also provides VGA fallback mode if it cannot locate the driver for a given card, or if it detects an error when loading the driver. This provides the user with a usable VGA (640x480) display without having to worry about how to upgrade or replace video systems. If a video system is in VGA mode when another mode is explicitly chosen, Windows 95 detects an error initializing the display adapter and switches to VGA. This indicates some problem with the video card or the driver.

When an error occurs, the user is prompted with an error message and then allowed to start Windows 95 in VGA mode. Once in Windows 95, the user must then change the display driver for the correct display adapter or chip set.

Because VGA fallback is not a feature of Windows 3.1, VGA fallback does not work in Windows 95 if Windows 3.1 drivers are being used.

Graphics Performance Tab

In the Control Panel, double-click the System icon. On the Performance tab, click the Graphics button in the Advanced settings group. This button takes you to the Advanced Graphics Settings dialog box.

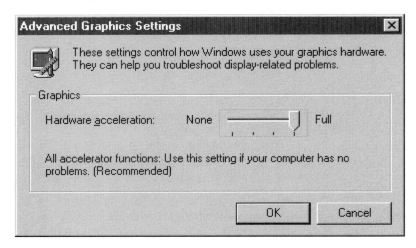

Figure 18.8 Tuning graphics performance

This dialog box contains a slide bar with settings on how Windows 95 uses the graphics hardware. There are four settings:

- Full—This is the default setting. This uses all the accelerator functions. If there are no problems with your display system, this is the setting to use.

- Most—This setting applies to S3 or Western Digital (WD)–compatible drivers. If you have problems with the way your mouse driver appears on the screen, try moving the slide control one notch to the left.

   This setting adds the following line to [display] section the SYSTEM.INI file:

   ```
   SwCursor=1
   ```

   A SWCursor=1 setting disables the hardware cursor. This setting is similar to the /Y switch that can be used with some versions of the MS-DOS–based Microsoft Mouse driver.

- Basic—If the computer uses a mini-driver, and basically all of the display drivers in Windows 95 do except VGA, and it is faulting, the user should try to move the slide control to the left two notches.

  This setting disables all but the essential hardware acceleration in the driver. For most things there probably won't be a noticeable difference.

  This setting adds the following lines to the WIN.INI and SYSTEM.INI files:

  ```
  SafeMode=1 to the [windows] section of the WIN.INI file
  SWCursor=1 to the [Display] section of the WIN.INI file
  MMio=0 to the [display] section of the SYSTEM.INI
  ```

  A SafeMode=1 setting allows for "basic acceleration" only, for example, pattern blt and screen-to-screen blt.

  A SWCursor=1 setting disables the hardware cursor.

  A MMIO=0 setting disables memory-mapped I/O for S3 compatible drivers.

- None—If the fault continues, try moving the slide control all the way to the left. This disables all hardware acceleration.

  This setting adds the following lines to the files indicated:

  ```
  SafeMode=2 to the [Windows] section of the WIN.INI file
  MMIO=0 to the [Display] section of the SYSTEM.INI file.
  SWCursor=1 to the [Display] section of the WIN.INI file
  ```

  A SafeMode=2 setting disables all video card acceleration; the graphical device interface (GDI) calls the device-independent bitmap (DIB) engine directly for screen drawing, rather than going through the display driver.

  A MMIO=0 setting disables memory-mapped I/O for S3 compatible drivers.

  A SWCursor=1 setting disables the hardware cursor.

Lesson Summary

Windows 95 has built-in several features to help isolate display problems. This includes supporting standard chip sets, a VGA fallback mode, and the ability to selectively disable various graphic acceleration settings.

Review

The following questions are intended to reinforce key information presented in this chapter. If you are unable to answer a question, review the appropriate lesson and then try the question again.

1. What is the DIB engine?

2. What is a display mini-driver?

3. Match the component with the appropriate definition.

Component	Definition
A. mini-VDD	1. Generic VxD used by the mini-VDD to virtualize the video hardware; supplied by Microsoft.
B. virtual display device (VDD.VXD)	2. Hardware-specific DRV to draw output on a video display; written by IHV. IHVs need to write only if they cannot write a display mini-driver.
C. VFLATD.VXD	3. Generic VxD to virtualize frame buffers larger than 64K; supplied by Microsoft.
D. full display driver	4. Hardware-specific VxD to virtualize the video hardware so that more than one virtual machine (VM) can share the same display; written by the IHV.

4. Which components of the Windows 95 display system handle virtualizing video graphic services for MS-DOS–based programs running in a Virtual Machine?

5. Why is it important for the correct monitor type to be selected in Windows 95?

6. You receive the following support call from a user. The user states: "I was adjusting my display settings when I was distracted. I accidentally installed the wrong card and monitor and then clicked OK. The system asked me if I wanted to restart the computer and I hit the ENTER key so it would restart. As it was restarting, I realized that I had installed the wrong display and video card and so I shut off the computer." What is the next step to take to help this user?

C H A P T E R   1 9

System Policies and Templates

Before You Begin

To complete the lessons in this chapter, you must have:

- Completed Chapter 1 and installed Microsoft Windows 95.
- An additional computer with Windows 95 installed.
- Access to a Microsoft Windows NT Server with \PUBLIC, \PRIVATE, and other shared folders.
- Domain Username, Domain Password, and Domain name for the Windows NT Server.
- The following files from the course CD-ROM. They should be placed in the \LABS directory of your Windows 95-based computer.

  ADMIN.ADM

  WALPAPER.ADM

  MINIMAL.ADM
- The following files located on the Windows 95 installation CD-ROM and should be placed in the \LABS directory of your Windows 95-based computer.

  POLEDIT.EXE

  POLEDIT.CNT

  POLEDIT.HLP

  POLEDIT.INF

Lesson 1: System Policies

System policies and policy templates can be used to control how a computer is set up and, to some extent, used. This lesson explains and demonstrates the use of polices.

After this lesson you will be able to:

- For a specified set of requirements, use the System Policy Editor to implement appropriate security.
- Use the System Policy Editor to modify a user's computer to meet the requirements for a specific environment.
- Use the System Policy Editor to create default users, groups, and computers.

Estimated lesson time 45 minutes

System Policies

System policies are registry settings that are automatically set when the user logs on to a computer. Policies may be applied to machines, users, or groups of users.

Registry entries can be set, changed, and maintained by administrators on a per-user, per-machine, or per-group basis by establishing system policies. Virtually all configuration settings on the system are available by writing a custom template. The most common administrative options are provided in the sample template.

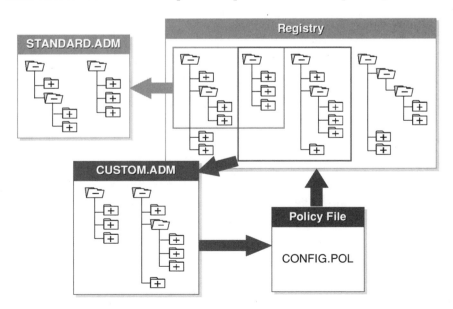

Figure 19.1 Relationship of registry, templates, and policies

Policy files are created by an administrator by using the System Policy Editor. When complete, the policy file is placed in an accessible location on the network and is automatically loaded when the user logs on. By combining policies assigned for that user, the machine they are logging on to, and any groups they are members of, very precise control of the computer and network can be established.

Policy Files

Two groups of Windows 95 files are involved in configuring Windows 95 policies:

- .ADM files. These are template files that establish the scope of administrative policies.

- .POL files. These files enforce the policies.

Administrators responsible for transitioning large numbers of users from an existing environment to Windows 95 will be primarily interested in the .ADM files.

*.ADM Files (Policy Templates)

The .ADM files are templates that determine what parameters will be available to administrators when they want to create a default user or computer. They can be built before, during, or after Setup.

The .ADM templates determine the limits for the policies that are put in place by the .POL files. The .ADM templates do not create the policy, they merely allow for policy creation.

POLEDIT is the engine behind the System Policy Editor. The first time an administrator runs the System Policy Editor, it reads an .ADM file.

A sample of this template comes with Windows 95 on the Installation CD-ROM. However, because this template is such a powerful administration tool, it must be manually copied from the CD-ROM.

*.POL Files

Configuration and limit information from a system policy is stored in the policy (.POL) file. The .POL file is read during startup and its information is merged into the registry.

The .POL files implement system policies based on the options made available through the .ADM templates. System policies are system configurations and limitations determined by the system administrator. Using system policies, administrators have a great deal of control over users' desktop, network, and security settings.

For example, a company may have information kiosks connected to the corporate network in a public area to provide visitors with the latest news, stock price, and so on. The company wants to tightly restrict all the kiosks in the corporation to prevent visitors from using the kiosks to access the corporate network. This can be done by setting a system policy that only allows access to specific programs.

Location of a .POL File

For a .POL file to work, the system must know that it exists. By default, Windows 95 looks for a .POL file in one of three locations.

- On a share-level security computer, or on a computer not on a network, Windows 95 looks in the \WINDOWS folder.

- On a user-level security computer getting its security information from a Windows NT system, the default location for the policy file is the user's home directory.

- On a NetWare network, the default policy file location is in the user's electronic mail directory.

If the policy file is not present, no policies are loaded. However, if the file is in the default location, the policies are loaded into the registry and are enforced when the computer starts.

The location of the .POL file can be changed, but first you must have a policy file in the default location that contains an entry to the new location, or you must manually change the registry to point to the location. This entry is added to the registry. When the computer restarts, the registry has the new location and uses the .POL file found there.

By specifying a network location, the administrator can update policies as needed from a central location and not be required to change the .POL file on every machine.

Setting Policies

If an administrator decides that a certain user or computer requires an environment with a customized configuration, the administrator must change the defaults.

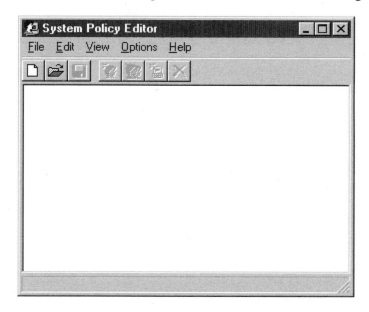

Figure 19.2 System Policy Editor

Changing defaults involves the following steps:

- In the System Policy Editor, click the target user, group, or computer. That user, group, or computer's property sheet appears.
- Proceed through the property sheet's categories selecting parameters as appropriate.

The policy controls may be set in one of the following three states.

- Enabled—When the control is checked, this function is turned on.
- Disabled—When the control is not checked, this function is turned off.
- Neutral—When the control is grayed, the availability of the function is not determined by this policy. This setting exists so different policies may be merged.

The System Policy Editor is not loaded during installation. The System Policy Editor is on the Windows 95 Setup CD-ROM under \ADMIN\APPTOOLS\POLEDIT. To install it, in the Control Panel, click the Add/Remove Programs icon. On the Windows Setup tab, click Have disk. Enter the full path to the \ADMIN\APPTOOLS\POLEDIT folder on the CD-ROM, either with a drive letter or with the universal naming convention (UNC) name, and then press ENTER. Click both Group Policies and System Policy Editor check boxes. Click Install and the files will be installed on your computer. The System Policy Editor is added to the Start menu under Programs/Accessories/System Tools.

▶ **To start the System Policy Editor**

1. On the Start menu, click Run.

2. Type **poledit.exe** and then press ENTER.

The System Policy Editor may be used to directly access the registry or to create and edit .POL files.

▶ **To access the registry**

1. On the File menu, click Open Registry.

   The Local User and Local Computer icons appear in the System Policy Editor.

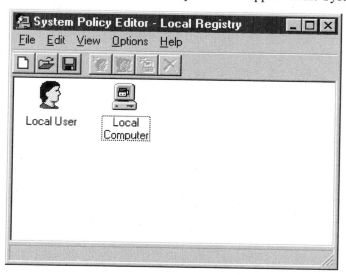

Figure 19.3 Using the System Policy Editor to access the local registry

Local mode is a user interface for direct access to the registry. Using local mode changes registry entries on that machine. No .POL file is created when you use local mode. If a .POL file exists, local changes may be overwritten during the next logon. This is useful for stand-alone computers, computers with no .POL files, troubleshooting, and so on. This interface can also be considered a menu-driven interface for editing the registry.

2. To open the local registry, double-click the Local Computer or Local User icon.

The valid policies appear.

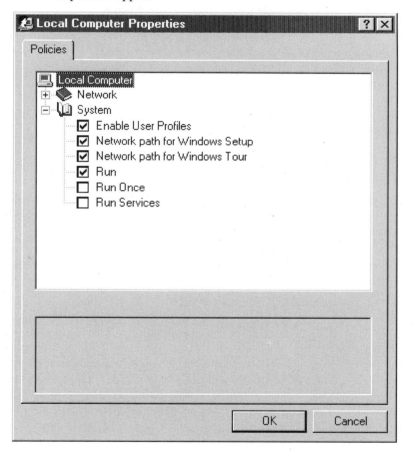

Figure 19.4 Policy editor for local computer

In this screen, you can access and configure the various policies.

3. To accept the changes, you would normally click OK. However, for purposes of this lesson, click Cancel.

Enabling Policies

Before a policy can be enforced on a Windows 95-based computer, the computer must have policy enforcement enabled. Policy enforcement is enabled by using the System Policy Editor.

▶ **To enable system policies**

1. Start the System Policy Editor.
2. On the File menu, click Open Registry.

   The Local User and Local Computer icons appear in the System Policy Editor.
3. Double-click the Local Computer icon.
4. Expand Network by clicking the + sign.
5. Under Network, expand Update.
6. Click the Remote Update check box, and make sure a check mark appears.
7. In the Update Mode box, click Manual.
8. Specify the path for manual update.

   The path should point to the location of the .POL file.
9. Click the Display error messages check box.
10. Click OK on the Local Computer property sheet.
11. Close System Policy Editor.

System policies are enforced the next time you start the computer.

Creating a .POL File

If you want a policy to be implemented every time a computer starts, or to be implemented across several computers, you should create a .POL file.

You may create policies for default or specific users, computers, or groups of users. Use the System Policy Editor to create the file.

▶ **To create a policy file**

1. On the File menu, click New File.

   The Default User and Default Computer icons appear in the System Policy Editor.

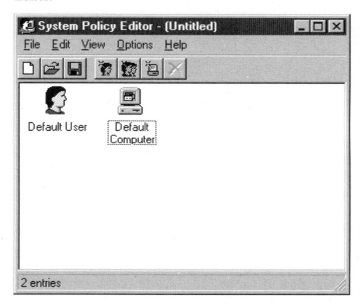

Figure 19.5 Creating a policy with the System Policy Editor

Changing these policies is done the same way as accessing the registry with the local configurations. For example, to restrict default users from access to the computer Control Panel, click the Default User, expand the Control Panel key, expand the system key, and then click the Restrict System Control Panel check box.

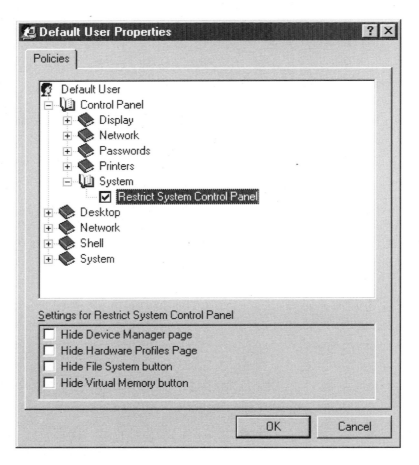

Figure 19.6 Selecting policies

You can then configure the settings on the restriction.

In addition to setting default profiles, you can determine profiles for specific users and computers.

2. To accept the changes, you would normally click OK. However, for purposes of this lesson, click Cancel.

▶ **To add specific users**

1. On the Edit menu, click Add User.

Note The steps for adding and configuring policies for a specific computer are the same as the steps for a specific user.

2. Type the name of the new user and then click OK.

   The new user is added to the System Policy Editor. You may then configure the policies for this specific user.

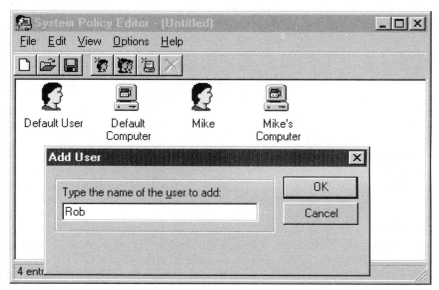

Figure 19.7 Adding a user policy

When you have completed setting the policies, save the file in the desired location. The policies take effect the next time the computer restarts.

Group Policies

Group policies are supported for both Windows NT and NetWare networks.
Creating policies for groups is similar to creating policies for users and computers.

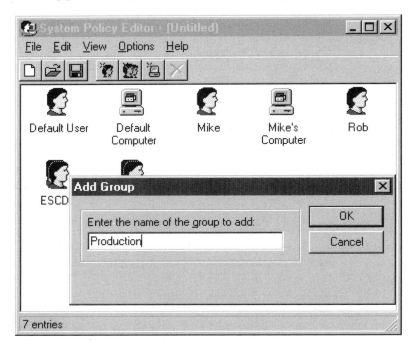

Figure 19.8 Adding a group policy

The group policies must be used with a central security server. Groups allow you to
add specific restrictions to your domain groups.

You cannot create new groups using System Policy Editor; you can only use
existing groups on the NetWare or Windows NT network. To create a new group,
use the tools provided with your network administrative software.

To set group policies, you must first ensure that GROUPPOL.DLL, which supports
group policies, has been successfully installed on each client.

▶ **To install GROUPPOL.DLL**

1. In the Control Panel, double-click the Add/Remove Programs icon.

2. Click the Windows Setup tab.

3. Click the Have Disk button.

4. Enter the full path to the \ADMIN\APPTOOLS\POLEDIT folder on the CD-ROM, either with a drive letter or with the UNC name, and then press ENTER.

5. Click the Group Policies check box. If you have not installed the System Policy Editor, click its check box as well.

6. Click Install and the GROUPPOL.DLL file is installed in your WINDOWS\SYSTEM folder.

▶ **To create system policies for groups**

1. On the Edit menu in System Policy Editor, click Add Group.

   You can either type in the name of the group or browse to find the group and then click the OK button.

2. Double-click the group to bring up the group's properties.

3. Check or clear policies by clicking the policy name.

Important If a policy exists for a specific named user, then group policies are not applied for that user.

Group Processing

Group policies are downloaded in order from the lowest priority group to the highest priority group. All groups are processed. The group with the highest priority is processed last, so that any of its settings are applied that differ from those defined in the other group policies.

▶ **To set priority levels for groups**

1. Open the policy file. Add groups as appropriate, and specify the policy settings you want.

2. Click Options, and then click Group Priority.

3. Use the Move Up and Move Down buttons to place each group in its relative priority.

4. To accept the changes, you would normally click OK. However, for purposes of this lesson, click Cancel.

You can use one policy file for each group, even if some of the client computers in the group do not have support installed for group policies. Client computers that are not configured for using group policies ignore group policy files.

Policy Implementation

Policies are implemented depending on what type of policies exist.

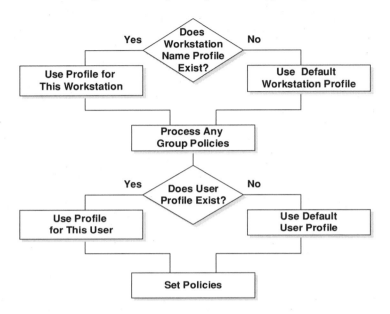

Figure 19.9 Policy implementation process

When someone logs on, the logon process follows the UNC path to the user's configuration and then follows the policy to implement the user's environment according to the following steps:

1. Logon checks the computer's name.

   If a profile for the computer exists, the computer's profile is the same as the one under the computer's name.

   If the computer's name does not exist, logon implements the default computer profile.

2. The policy system checks the user's name against the group listings.

   If the user is a member of a group, that group's policies are processed. This is repeated from lowest to highest groups until all the groups in the policy file are processed.

3. Logon checks the user's name.

   If a profile for the Username exists, the user profile is the same as the one for the Username.

   If a profile for the Username does not exist, logon implements the default user profile.

Lesson Summary

System Policies help the administrator control users computers. System policies (*.POL files) may be set to determine anything that is controlled by the registry. Policies may be applied to machines, users, or groups of users.

Lesson 2: Policy Templates

System policies and policy templates can be used to control how a computer is set up and, to some extent, used. This lesson explains and demonstrates the use of templates to determine what policies can be enforced.

After this lesson you will be able to:
• Create a template that allows a specified set of policies.

Estimated lesson time 30 minutes

Policy templates (.ADM files) determine what policies can be enforced, down to the actual choices presented on the policy editor.

The template may be written to affect anything in the registry. For example, if you have a program that can read the registry, you can have a template that can affect changes in that program. A corporate word processor may be able to store its default layout format in the registry. You can create a template that can change the default layout or point to a new layout format.

Creating a Policy Template

Creating a template involves using the appropriate keywords in the appropriate format. If you want to create the templates, it helps if you have some programming background.

A template is broken into sections. Each section in the template follows a similar hierarchy.

CLASS

    CATEGORY

      POLICY

        PART

        END PART

      END POLICY

    END CATEGORY

CLASS specifies either MACHINE or USER.

CATEGORY is the major heading such as SYSTEM or NETWORK.

POLICY represents an entry under the CATEGORY such as Logon Banner. The POLICY entry often contains multiple PARTs.

PART represents a single setting such as the text of the Logon Banner.

The end of each CATEGORY, POLICY, and PART section is indicated with END CATEGORY, END POLICY, and END PART respectively. The template is not required to be indented in the structured format shown. You can actually write the template as a single line of code as long as you follow the hierarchy. However, by indenting the code you can more easily locate sections to change and modify.

The entries in each section determine what policies are available. A full list of keywords are located in Appendix D, ".ADM Template Keywords."

For example, the following .ADM file

```
CLASS MACHINE
    CATEGORY Category
    KEYNAME Network\Logon
        POLICY Policy
            PART Part EDITTEXT
                VALUENAME UserProfiles
            END PART
        END POLICY
    END CATEGORY
```

produces the following policy:

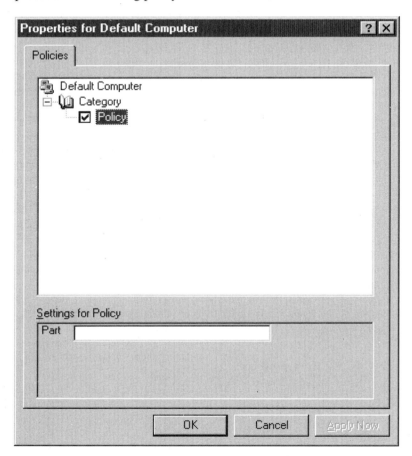

Figure 19.10 Example of policy created using the sample template

Note A complete list of keywords that can be used when creating .ADM templates is included in Appendix D, ".ADM Template Keywords."

Using a Template

In this exercise you will use existing sample templates to understand how restrictions are set up in the .ADM files.

1. Using Notepad, open the \LABS\ADMIN.ADM file.

2. Start the POLEDIT.EXE program and on the File menu, click New File.

    You should tile this window with the Notepad window to make some comparisons.

3. During this exercise, you will build a cross-reference table by scrolling through the ADMIN.ADM file and simultaneously open different parts of the System Policy Editor. Study the template and the tree built by the System Policy Editor side-by-side, and then compare them with the table below.

Template	System Policy Editor
CLASS MACHINE	Default Computer
CATEGORY !!System	System
POLICY !!NetworkSetupPath	Network Path for Microsoft Windows Setup
PART !!NetworkSetupPath_Path EDITTEXT REQUIRED	Path
POLICY !!EnableUserProfiles	Enable User Profiles

4. Complete the right side of this table by examining the template and the System Policy Editor.

Template	System Policy Editor
CLASS USER	Default User
CATEGORY !!ControlPanel	
CATEGORY !!CPL_Display	
POLICY !!CPL_Display_Restrict	
PART !!CPL_Display_Disable CHECKBOX	
PART !!CPL_Display_HideBkgnd CHECKBOX	
!!CPL_Display_HideScrsav CHECKBOX	

Modifying the Templates

You are not required to use the entire ADMIN.ADM template to create a policy for your site. In this exercise, you will examine three templates:

- ADMIN.ADM—The standard template that comes with the product.
- WALPAPER.ADM—A modification of the standard template. It has been modified to install a particular wallpaper.
- MINIMAL.ADM—A minimal template that only contains the modified portion of WALPAPER.ADM.

Note the differences in each of these files; this information will help you in the next exercise.

1. Start the System Policy Editor, POLEDIT.EXE.
2. On the Options menu, click the Template option and make sure the standard template is loaded. The path and filename is C:\LABS\ADMIN.ADM.
3. On the File menu, click New File to create a new System Policy File.
4. Open the Properties box for the default user, click Desktop, and then put a check mark next to Wallpaper.

   Is there a default wallpaper name listed, or is the entry blank?

   _____

   What is the name of the default wallpaper, if there is one?

   _____

5. Close the Properties box for the default user and then click Close on the File menu. Do *not* save your changes.
6. On the Options menu, click Template, and then load the modified template. The path and filename is C:\LABS\WALPAPER.ADM.
7. On the File menu, click New to create a new System Policy File.
8. Open the Properties box for the default user, click Desktop, and then put a check mark next to Wallpaper.

   Is there a default wallpaper name listed, or is the entry blank?

   _____

   What is the name of the default wallpaper, if there is one?

   _____

9. Close the Properties box for the default user and then click Close on the File menu. Do *not* save your changes.

10. On the Options menu, click Template, and then load the modified template. The path and filename is C:\LABS\MINIMAL.ADM.

11. On the File menu, click New to create a new System Policy File.

12. Open the Properties box for the default user, click Desktop, and then put a check mark next to Wallpaper.

    Is there a default wallpaper name listed, or is the entry blank?

    _____

    What is the name of the default wallpaper, if there is one?

    _____

13. What other differences do you notice about the MINIMAL.ADM file?

    _____

14. Use Notepad to open the MINIMAL.ADM file. Try to determine why all the property restrictions—except for the wallpaper settings—for the default user and default computer have disappeared.

15. Close the Properties box for the default user and then click Close on the File menu. Do *not* save your changes. Exit Notepad without saving changes.

Creating a Template (Optional)

In this exercise you will make a copy of the existing sample template, with the path and filename of C:\LABS\ADMIN.ADM, and edit it to allow only restrictions that meet the criteria described below.

- Some users should have specific wallpaper installed. This is usually tiled.

- Some users should not be able to share files or printers.

- Some computers require a logon banner that warns against unauthorized logon. Your legal department prefers that this have a caption of "Important Notice" and that the message states that unauthorized logon is prohibited.

- Some computers which require Dial-Up Networking to dial out should not be allowed to let anyone dial in.

1. You should create an .ADM file that reflects these policies and allows an administrator to make the appropriate settings by loading this .ADM file into the System Policy Editor and creating the appropriate .POL policy file.

2. When you are done, open the System Policy Editor.

3. On the Options menu, click Template, and then click the Open Template button.

   Load the template you just created.

4. Click New on the File menu.

   Examine the choices available to the administrator using this template. They should match the criteria specified in steps 1–4.

Lesson Summary

System policies and policy templates are used together to help the administrator control users' computers. Policy templates (*.ADM files) are used to determine what policies can be enforced, down to the actual choices present on the policy editor.

Review

The following questions are intended to reinforce key information presented in this chapter. If you are unable to answer a question, review the appropriate lesson and then try the question again.

1. Is it possible to restrict a user from starting a single-mode MS-DOS session? If so, how?

   _____

   _____

2. What would be the best way to restrict all users from starting single-mode MS-DOS sessions?

   _____

   _____

3. You are the network manager of a 1000-node, twelve hundred user network—some users share machines—with 950 of these nodes running Windows 95 and the rest running Windows NT. There are 24 different departments sharing resources on the network, and you would like to restrict access to various programs to different groups of users using the following guidelines:

Group A: No Restrictions

Group B: Disable Registry Editing tools

Group C: Group B restrictions + Restrict Network Control Panel

Group D: Group C restrictions + Restrict Passwords Control Panel

Group E: Group D restrictions + Restrict Printer Settings

Group F: Group E restrictions + Restrict System Control Panel

Because these groups are set up on the Windows NT server, there will be users in more than one group. Make sure that if a user is listed in both Group F and in Group C that Group F's restrictions will take effect. How can this be accomplished?

CHAPTER 20

Disk Utilities

Before You Begin

To complete the lessons in this chapter, you must have:

- Completed Chapter 1 and installed Microsoft Windows 95.
- A blank floppy disk.

Lesson 1: ScanDisk

ScanDisk is a program included with Windows 95 that allows you to check a disk for errors. If errors are located, ScanDisk can try and make the necessary repairs. This lesson explains how to use ScanDisk.

After this lesson you will be able to:
- Use ScanDisk to check a disk for damage.

Estimated lesson time 10 minutes

Cross-Linked Files

Files in the FAT file system, including the VFAT implementation, are stored in blocks called clusters. The location of the first cluster is stored in the directory. Each cluster contains the location of the next cluster, along with its data, and this format continues until the end of the file.

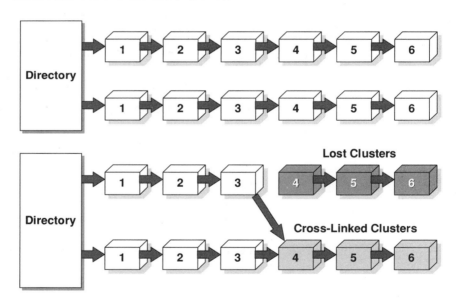

Figure 20.1 Example of cross-linked files

If the pointer in one of these clusters is corrupted so that it points to a cluster in another file, this is called cross linking. The clusters that were "orphaned" by the corrupted pointer are called lost clusters.

To repair cross-linked clusters and files, you can use ScanDisk.

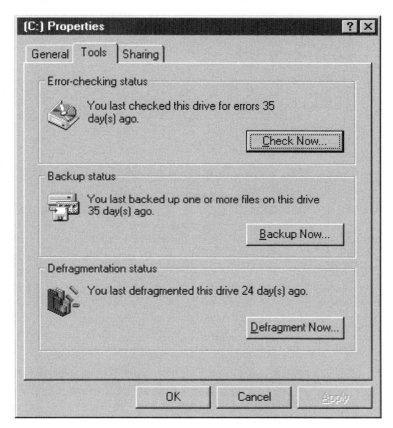

Figure 20.2 Tools tab on the selected drive's property sheet

ScanDisk, Backup, and Disk Defragmenter can be accessed from Tools tab on the Disk property sheet for a specified disk drive, or from the System Tools menu.

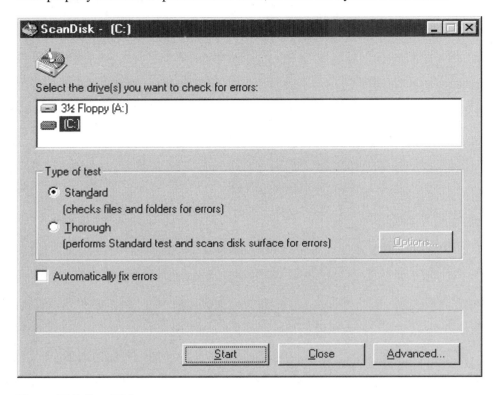

Figure 20.3 ScanDisk

You may start the disk check process by clicking the Start button. The type of tests performed depends on how the test is configured.

- Standard—Checks files and folders for errors.
- Thorough—Performs the Standard test and scans the disk surface for any errors. The options for this test allow you to configure which areas of the disk are scanned and how ScanDisk performs certain checks.

Configuring the Tests

The Advanced button allows you to configure the types of tests performed. When you click this button, you receive the following dialog box.

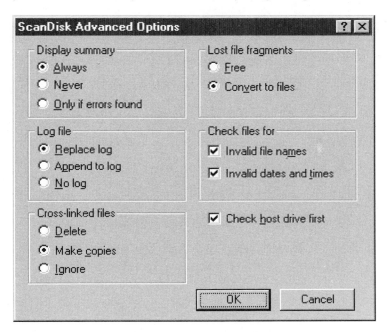

Figure 20.4 Advanced Options for ScanDisk

The Lost file fragments Free option unmarks the lost clusters and returns them to use. The Convert to files option creates files in the root directory of the drive that can be examined for possible data salvaging.

Cross-linked files occur when two files end up using the same clusters. The problem with cross-linked files is that it is impossible to determine which of the files is corrupt and which is good. The default option, Make copies, will copy the shared data clusters so that each file has a copy. This increases the likelihood of saving at least one of the files.

By selecting the various options, you can configure a set of tests that work the best for specific situations.

When ScanDisk locates a potential error you may receive a dialog box with options, such as the following.

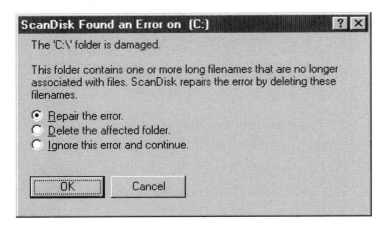

Figure 20.5 Example of error displayed when ScanDisk discovers an error

This allows you to determine if an error requires fixing or if it is the result of some other tests you have been performing on the computer.

Lesson Summary

ScanDisk can detect and repair errors on hard drives. ScanDisk can be configured to perform tests ranging from basic to advanced.

Lesson 2: Microsoft Backup

Windows 95 includes Microsoft Backup, a backup program to simplify backing up and restoring files. This lesson demonstrates the backup process.

After this lesson you will be able to:
- Use Backup to back up and restore data.

Estimated lesson time 40 minutes

This program gives you a graphical interface to select various files, folders, or drives to back up.

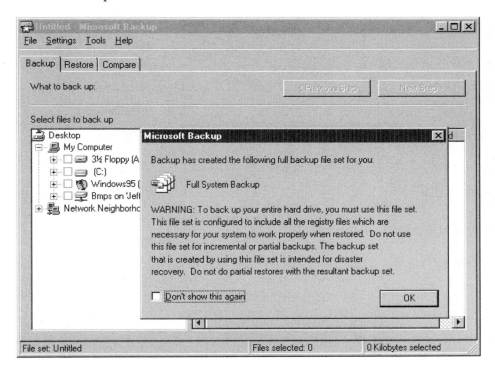

Figure 20.6 Backup dialog box

To use Backup, select the files, folders, or drives you want to back up and indicate where the backup copies should be placed. The program takes care of the rest.

▶ **To back up a folder**

1. On the Start menu, point to Programs, Accessories, System Tools, and then click Backup.

2. Click the drive you want to back up to display the folders on that drive.

Tip Do not click the check box for the drive. Clicking the check box selects all the folders and files on that drive.

---

3. Click the empty check box beside the objects you want to back up.

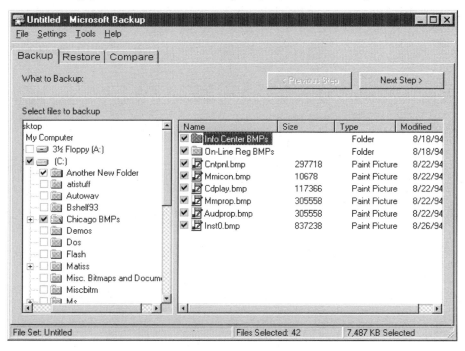

Figure 20.7 Selecting files and folders to back up

4. Click the Next Step button.

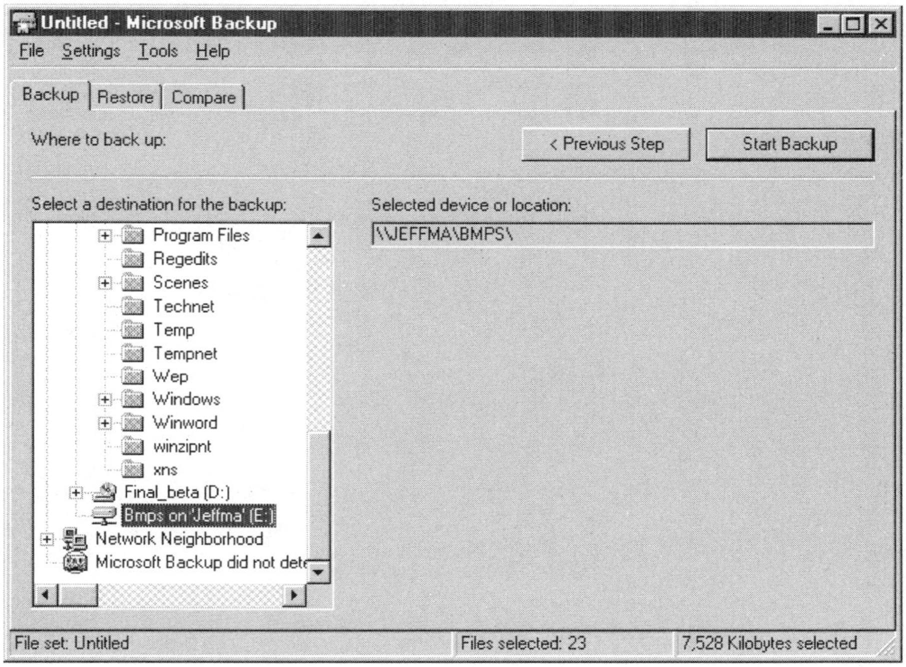

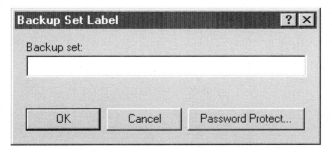

Figure 20.8 Specifying location for backup files

5. Click the location where the backed-up objects will be stored. This can be another drive, a network location, or a tape device.

   The location selected appears in the Selected device or location text box.

6. Click the Start Backup button.

Figure 20.9 Specifying label for backup set

7. In the Backup set text box, type a name for the backup set. You may specify a password. Click OK.

Backup begins backing up the objects you selected.

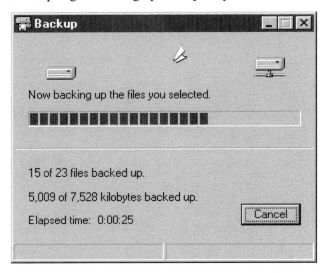

Figure 20.10 Backup in progress

The progress indicator tells you how the backup is going. When the backup is complete, a message appears and indicates if any errors in copying occurred. The Restore and Compare utilities work in the same manner.

Restore

The Restore tab is used restore files from the backup set. It functions similarly to the Backup function. When restoring files, you can selectively restore single files, folders, or entire systems.

Compare

Compare allows you to compare the files on the backup set with another version of the files.

Settings

You can configure the backup by using the three settings under the Settings menu.

File Filtering

These settings allow you to decide which files are backed up.

- Last modified date—Excludes only files that were last modified within this range of dates.

- File types—Specifies types of files, such as .TMP that you want to exclude from the backup, restore, or compare operation.

- Exclude file types—This setting allows you to list new types of files or modify existing file types that will be excluded from the backup, restore, or compare operation.

Drag and Drop

- Run Backup minimized—Specifies that the Backup window should be minimized while a file set you have dragged onto the Backup icon is being backed up.

- Confirm operation before beginning—Displays a message confirming which files are backed up after you have dragged a file set onto the Backup icon.

- Quit Backup after operation is finished—Closes Backup when the file set you dragged onto the Backup icon has been backed up.

Options

The General tab options toggle audible prompts and allow you to overwrite old status log files.

There are specific options for Backup, Restore, and Compare.

- Backup options include specifying the type of backup, full or partial; auto-verification, compares backed up data to original data after the backup completes; toggling data compression; and setting the various options used with tape backups.

- Restore options include locations, verifications, and the capability to overwrite files.

- Compare options include the ability to quit when finished and to specify the location for the comparisons.

Back Up Local Drives

In this exercise, you will use the Full Backup file set to back up local drives. In the interest of time, the backup will be halted after backing up the first floppy disk.

▶ **To back up local drives**

1. Insert a floppy disk in the floppy disk drive.

2. On the Start menu, point to Programs, Accessories, System Tools, and then click Backup.

   The Welcome to Microsoft Backup dialog box appears.

3. After noting the instructions, click the OK button.

   If you receive the error message No Drive detected, click OK.

4. The first time you run Backup, a dialog box appears stating "Backup has created the following full backup file set for you: Full System Backup." The statement is followed by a warning that the file set must be used to back up your entire hard drive. Click the OK button.

   The Microsoft Backup dialog box appears.

5. On the File menu, click Open File Set.

   The Open dialog box appears.

6. In the File name text box, click Full System Backup Set.

7. Click Open.

   The File Selection dialog box appears.

   Backup begins populating the File Select dialog box based on FULLBKUP.SET.

8. In the left pane, double-click My Computer, the C drive, and then the Windows folder to explore which directories are included in the Full Backup file set.

   Each folder and drive in the dialog box is preceded with a box. An empty box means no files and folders within the folder will be backed up. A checked box indicates that *all* files and folders within the folder will be backed up. A grayed checked box indicates that *some* files and folders within the folder will be backed up.

   What is *not* included in the Full Backup set?

   _____

9. Click the Next Step button.

   The Backup dialog box appears.

10. Click the floppy disk drive icon and then click the Start Backup button.

    The Backup Set Label dialog box appears.

11. In the Backup set prompt, enter your first name and then click Password Protect.

12. In the Password Protect Backup Set dialog box, type **password** in both password prompts, and then click OK.

    You will be returned to the Backup Set Label dialog box.

13. Click the OK button.

    Backup will begin backing up files. Allow backup to finish creating the first floppy disk.

14. After Backup has finished with the first disk, you would normally insert another disk to continue the process. For the purposes of this exercise, click Cancel when prompted to insert the next disk.

    You will be notified that the operation has been halted.

15. Click OK twice to return to the Microsoft Backup dialog box.

16. Click the Restore tab, and then click the floppy disk drive icon. The backup you just created will appear in the Backup Set window.

17. Click the backup set you just created and then click the Next Step button.

    Did Backup prompt you for a password?_____

18. Normally, to complete the backup you would continue this process. For the purposes of this exercise, click Cancel.

19. In the Microsoft Backup dialog box, click Close on the File menu to close the fileset.

Backup Individual Files (Optional)

In this exercise, you will create three files, Overwrite, Delete, and Remove Directory, using WordPad, and back them up to a floppy disk drive. You will see the effect of restoring over an existing file, over a newer file, and from a file with a folder that has been deleted.

▶ **To create test files**

1. On the Start menu, point to Programs, Accessories, and then click WordPad.

2. Type **Overwrite** in the text area.

3. On the File menu, click Save. The Save As dialog box appears.

4. Double-click My Computer to show its drives.

5. Double-click the C drive to show its folders.

6. Click the Create New Folder button on the toolbar to create a new folder.

7. Name the folder Test Directory.

8. Double-click the Test Directory folder.

9. Type **Overwrite** in the File name prompt, and then click Save.

   The WordPad dialog box appears.

10. In WordPad, backspace over the word Overwrite, and then type **Delete** in the text area.

11. On the File menu, click Save As.

12. Type **Delete** in the File name prompt, and then click Save to save the file in Test Directory.

    The WordPad dialog box appears.

13. In WordPad, backspace over the word Delete, and then type **Remove Directory** in the text area.

14. On the File menu, click Save As.

15. Click the Up One Level button on the toolbar to display the file folders on the C drive.

16. Click the Create New Folder button and name the new directory **Test Delete**.

17. Double-click the Test Delete folder.

18. Type **Remove Directory** in the File Name prompt, and then click Save.

19. On the File menu, click Exit to exit WordPad.

▶   **To back up files**

1. On the Start menu, point to Programs, Accessories, System Tools, and then click Backup to start Backup.

2. In the Welcome to Microsoft Backup dialog box, click OK.

3. Click the Backup tab.

4. In the left pane, the box next to My Computer has either a + or a - symbol. If the box contains a +, click the + to see the drives within My Computer.

   Drives appear underneath the My Computer icon.

5. If the box in front of the C: drive icon contains a + symbol, click the + to display its folders.

6. Open the Test Directory folder.

   The files within the folder appear in the right pane in Backup.

7. Click the empty box in front of the Overwrite.doc file you just created.

   A check mark appears in the box.

   The box next to the Test Directory folder is now grayed and checked indicating that at least one file, but not all the files in the folder, is checked.

8. Click the empty box next to the Delete.doc file. The box next to Test Directory is no longer grayed, indicating that all the files within the directory are selected.

9. Click the box next to the Test Delete folder to select the files within the folder.

10. Click the Next Step button.

11. Click the A: drive icon under My Computer to backup the files to the floppy drive.

12. Place a new disk in the A drive.

13. Click the Start Backup button.

    The Backup Set Label dialog box appears.

14. Type **Test Backup** in the Backup set prompt, and then click OK.

15. Click OK when the backup is finished.

▶ **To create a custom file set**

1. Perform steps 3–11 of the To back up files procedure.

2. On the File menu, click Save As.

3. The Save in prompt should be changed to Desktop.

4. In the File Name prompt, type **My File Set**, and then click Save.

   A My File Set icon appears on the desktop.

5. On the File menu, click Exit to exit Microsoft Backup.

▶ **To back up using a file set**

1. Double-click the My File Set icon on the desktop.

   A prompt appears asking: Are you sure you want to continue with this operation?

2. Place the disk used to backup the files in the floppy disk drive and then click Yes.

3. Backup creates a backup of the files you selected on the floppy disk.

▶ **To restore backed up files**

1. To determine how Backup handles various circumstances, explore the C drive.

2. Delete the Test Delete folder.

3. Delete the Delete.doc file in the Test Directory folder.

4. Make a change to the Overwrite.doc file in the Test Directory folder.

5. Start Backup. Click the Restore tab.

6. In the left pane, click the floppy disk drive.

   The Backup dialog box appears.

7. Click My File Set_00.

8. Click Next Step.

9. Click the empty boxes next to the Test Delete and Test Directory folders to restore the files within the directories.

10. Click Start Restore to begin restoring the file.

11. Click OK when done.

12. Did Backup recreate the Test Delete directory?

_____

13. Did Backup restore the deleted Delete.doc and Remove Directory.doc files?

_____

14. Did Backup overwrite the Overwrite.doc file in the Test Directory folder with the original, older file?

_____

15. On the Settings menu in Backup, click Options.

Which setting prevents Restore from overwriting newer files?

_____

How does enabling incremental backup affect making backups?

_____

_____

16. Exit the Backup program.

Lesson Summary

The Backup program allows you to back up and restore any combination of drives, folders, and files.

Lesson 3: Disk Defragmenter

During the day-to-day use of a computer, files on the drives may become fragmented. This can cause performance problems. This lesson explains how to defragment the a disk to correct these problems.

After this lesson you will be able to:

• Use Disk Defragmenter to improve the performance of a disk drive.

Estimated lesson time 10 minutes

On a fragmented disk, the heads must skip from fragment to fragment to access some files. This can affect disk performance. To correct this problem, you can defragment the disk.

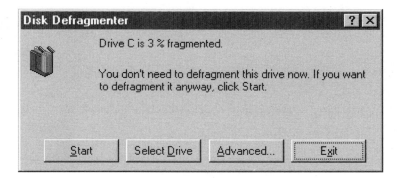

Figure 20.11 Disk Defragmenter status dialog box

When you click the Defragment Now button, the disk is checked for fragmented files. The report returned indicates whether or not the drive requires defragmenting at this time. By keeping track of the state of a disk drive, the drives can be managed to provide optimum performance.

You can determine the type of defragmentation performed by clicking the Advanced button.

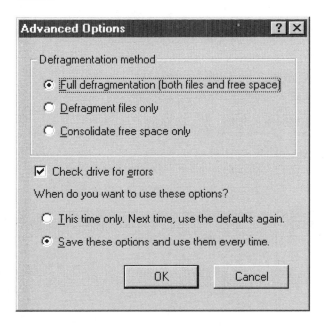

Figure 20.12 Advanced defragmentation options

The options include determining the type of defragmenting, defragmenting of special files, and if you want to save these options as a default.

During the defragmentation process, you can obtain complete details by clicking the Show Details button. Clicking the Legend button displays an explanation of the symbols that appear on the details screen during the defragmentation process.

Figure 20.13 Defragmentation legend

Lesson Summary

Defragmenting a disk can improve performance by enhancing file access time. Disk Defragmenter may be run in the background, you can pause the defragment process, or you can even halt the defragmenting process at any time without risking any data.

Lesson 4: DriveSpace

Windows 95 includes support for disk compression including Microsoft DriveSpace, Microsoft DoubleSpace® disc compression utility, and STAC Electronics Stacker®. This lesson explains how to use the various compression methods to increase disk space.

After this lesson you will be able to:

- Use Microsoft DriveSpace to compress a disk drive.
- Use the Compression Agent from Microsoft Plus! for Windows 95 to manage types of disk compression.

Estimated lesson time 30 minutes

A compressed drive is not a real disk drive, although it appears that way to Windows 95 and your programs. The contents of a compressed drive are stored in a single file, called a compressed volume file, .CVF. The CVF is located on an uncompressed drive, called a host drive.

For example, suppose you want to compress your hard disk, drive C. The first thing DriveSpace does is assign a different drive letter to your disk, such as H. DriveSpace then compresses the contents of your hard disk into a compressed volume file stored on drive H. Drive H will be the host for drive C. To Windows 95 and your programs, the compressed volume file on drive H appears to be your original drive C, but drive C has more free space than it originally had.

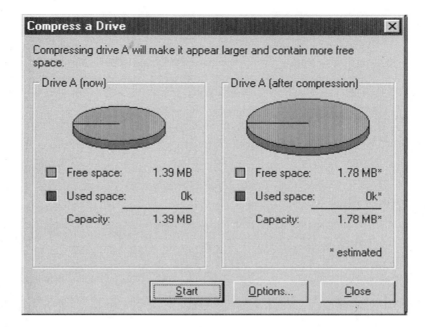

Figure 20.14 Possible results of using DriveSpace

When you view the contents of your computer by using My Computer or Windows Explorer, the host drive is hidden unless it contains more than 2 MB of free space. This is done to reduce confusion and free up a drive letter. If the host drive is less than 2 MB in size, it is assumed that the entire drive is used as a compressed drive and the host drive will not be used on a regular basis. If the host drive contains more than 2 MB of free space, it is visible and you can work with it as you would any other drive.

In addition to compressing the contents of an entire drive, DriveSpace can use the free space on an uncompressed drive to create a new, empty, compressed drive. For example, instead of compressing drive C, you could use 10 MB of the free space on drive C to create a new drive, drive G. Drive G will contain approximately 20 MB of free space.

If you are only compressing removable media such as floppy disks, the DriveSpace driver is only loaded when the disk is in the drive and mounted. By default, Windows 95 will automatically mount the drive when it detects compressed media. When there are no compressed drives in use, Windows 95 will unload the driver to free up memory.

Compressing a Drive

DriveSpace is started from the System Tools menu by clicking the Start menu, pointing to Programs, Accessories, System Tools, and then clicking DriveSpace. DriveSpace can compress any locally attached drive that has at least 512 kilobytes (K) of free space. The maximum size of the compressed drive with the version of DriveSpace included with Windows 95 is 512 MB.

▶ **To compress a floppy disk**

The following example compresses a floppy disk in the A drive.

1. On the Start menu, point to Programs, Accessories, System Tools, and then click DriveSpace.

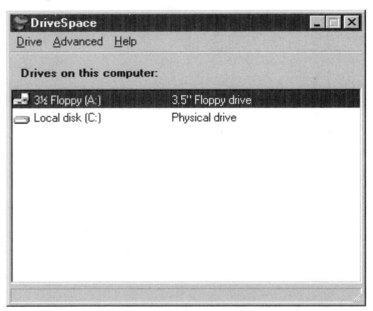

Figure 20.15 DriveSpace status dialog box

2. Highlight a floppy disk drive, and from the Drive menu, click Compress.

   DriveSpace shows the space on the selected drive and the estimated space after compression.

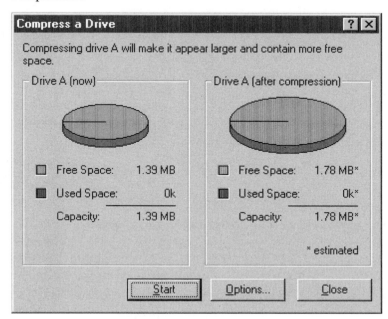

Figure 20.16 Estimated results of using DriveSpace

The Options button allows you to select what drive letter is used for the host drive, how much free space to leave on the host drive after creating the CVF, and whether to hide the host drive.

Remember If there is less than 2 MB free space on the host drive, it is hidden by default.

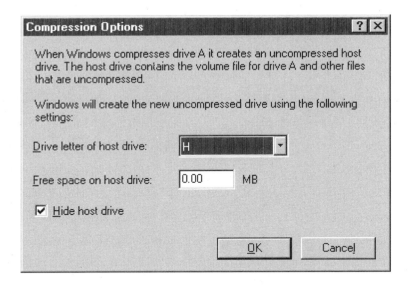

Figure 20.17 DriveSpace compression options

3. Click the Start button to begin the compression process.

   When you start compressing the drive, several actions are taken.

   a. The drive is checked using the ScanDisk Thorough tests.

   b. The CVF is created and prepared.

   c. The CVF is resized.

Figure 20.18 DriveSpace compression in progress

Note If you have more than one operating system installed on your computer, you receive the following caution:

Windows NT, OS/2, or another operating system may be installed on your computer. If you compress drive A, you may not be able to access its contents while using another operating system.

When the compression is complete, DriveSpace displays the size of the drive before and after compression.

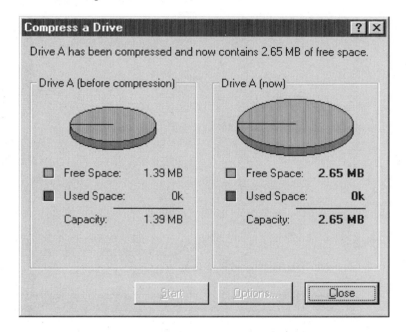

Figure 20.19 Results of DriveSpace compression

The amount of compressed free space is still an estimate. For example, if you are storing compressed files such as GIF graphics or ZIP archives, these are not compressed further. However, they increase the number of bytes used by the size of the file, and will reduce the amount of free bytes available by approximately twice their size. The following example shows why the free space is only an estimate.

The compressed floppy disk in drive A has 868,530 bytes used and 1,359,872 bytes free. A compressed file, 388,233 bytes in size, is copied to the floppy. The floppy now shows 1,259,872 bytes used, but only 565,248 bytes free. The used value went up by the size of the compressed file, while the free bytes went down by more than twice the size of the file.

Although the host drive is hidden, DriveSpace shows both the compressed and the host drives.

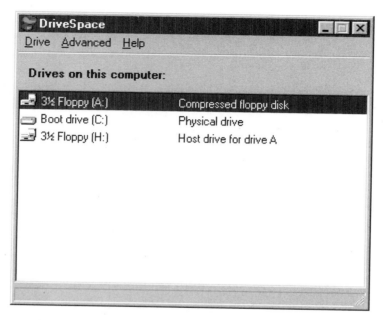

Figure 20.20 Host drive

If you look at the host of a compressed drive, you will notice that it contains two files: Dblspace.000 and Readthis.

Name	Size	Type	Modified
Dblspace.000	1,423KB	000 File	3/22/95 2:05 PM
Readthis	1KB	Text Document	3/22/95 2:05 PM

Figure 20.21 Files contained on a compressed host drive

Readthis is a text document that will be visible even if the floppy is read on a computer that has no disk compression such as an MS-DOS 5.*x* or earlier system. This file is placed there as a reminder that the floppy is not blank, but is compressed. The Readthis file contains the following text:

```
This disk was compressed using Windows 95 DriveSpace.
To use this disk, you must first mount it. To mount it:

1. Run DriveSpace in Windows.
2. In the Drives list, click the drive that contains the disk,
   and then click Mount on the Advanced menu.
To automatically mount all compressed devices, use the Settings
command on the Advanced menu.
(If this file is located on a drive other than the drive that
contains the compressed disk, then the disk is already mounted).
```

The CVF file is stored as Dblspace.000 and is hidden.

Uncompressing the Drive

A drive can be uncompressed in place. This is done by selecting the compressed disk (drive A in Figure 20.20) and selecting Uncompress from the Drive menu. If there are no compressed drives in the computer after the compression is removed, DriveSpace removes the DriveSpace driver from memory.

Paging with Compressed Drives

Unlike earlier versions of Windows, the DriveSpace driver is fully integrated in the Windows 95 32-bit disk components. This means that if necessary, the computer's paging file can be stored on a DriveSpace virtual drive.

Lesson Summary

The DriveSpace utility can be used to increase apparent disk size.

Lesson 5: DriveSpace 3 and Compression Agent

In addition to the normal DriveSpace compression offered by Windows 95, the Microsoft Plus! for Windows 95 package offers a more advanced compression suite. This lesson explains how to use the enhanced compression tools.

After this lesson you will be able to:
- Compress a drive using DriveSpace 3.
- Use the Compression Agent from Microsoft Plus! for Windows 95 automate disk maintenance tasks.

Estimated lesson time 20 minutes

DriveSpace 3

Included with Microsoft Plus! for Windows 95 is a more powerful version of DriveSpace, DriveSpace 3, which can handle compressed drives up to 2 gigabytes in size. In addition, the advanced compression utilities can create compressed drives with different levels of compression on a per file basis on the same compressed drive.

▶ **To compress a drive with DriveSpace 3**

In this exercise, you will compress a floppy disk using DriveSpace 3.

1. If you have the Microsoft Plus! installed, you will notice the 3 added to the Start DriveSpace icon in System Tools. Start Drive Space 3.
2. Place a floppy disk in the floppy disk drive.
3. On the Advanced menu, click Settings...

   There are four compression methods listed. A drive compressed with the DriveSpace 3 can contain any or all of four different compression methods.

Compression method	Characteristics	Notes
No Compression	Files are not compressed when you save them to a compressed drive.	This provides the best performance when writing and reading files to and from a compressed drive.
No Compression unless drive is at least XX% full.	Uses standard compression to save files to a compressed drive only if the drive is as full as you specify. If the drive is not that full, then files are saved uncompressed.	This setting is useful for maintaining performance when you have ample disk space, and for conserving space when the free space on a compressed drive is low. The default percentage is 90 percent full.

(*continued*)

Compression method	Characteristics	Notes
Standard Compression	The same compression used in normal DriveSpace.	This setting provides good compression without sacrificing performance when writing and reading files to and from a compressed drive.
HiPack	Files are compressed using a drive-wide compression table.	This method maintains the most disk space, but writing files to a compressed drive may be slower.

Note HiPack compression only applies to saving files to a DriveSpace 3 compressed drive. If you are using a compressed drive that was created using MS-DOS or Windows 95 DriveSpace or MS-DOS DoubleSpace, and you have not yet upgraded the drive, your files will be saved using standard compression, even if you select the HiPack option.

4. Click the HiPack Compression option, and then click OK.

5. On the Drive menu, click Compress..., and then write down the numbers.

   For example, using a blank 1.44 MB floppy disk, the computer indicated 1.39 MB of free space and after compression, 1.78 MB would be available.

6. Click Start to begin compressing the drive.

   After compressing with HiPack, the computer reported 2.56 MB of free space and an increase of 1.17 MB of space. You may want to compare this with the standard compression run on a floppy in an earlier exercise.

Note If DriveSpace 3 should fail while compressing, after the computer restarts DriveSpace 3 attempts to restart the compression process. If the compression cannot be restarted, you can manually complete the compression by copying certain files into root directory and then continuing the compression. The files you need are located on \FAILSAFE.DRV, a hidden folder. From this folder copy CONFIG.PSS to C:\CONFIG.SYS, and AUTOEXEC.PSS to C:\AUTOEXEC.BAT.

Compression Agent

To manage these additional compression features, there are some additions to the compression user interface.

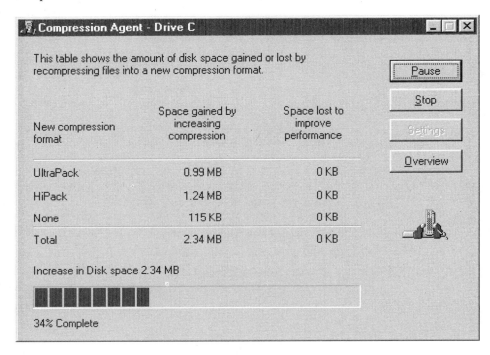

Figure 20.22 Compression Agent in progress

An extra tab is added to the drive properties showing the amount of the drive compressed with each type of compression and the space recovered.

The Compression Agent utility allows the user to manage the varying levels and types of compression.

Types of Compression

A drive compressed with the Microsoft Plus! for Windows 95 Compression Agent can contain any or all of four different compression methods.

Compression type	Characteristics	Notes
None	Files are not compressed when you save them to a compressed drive.	While this may seem useless, because even uncompressed files in a CVF are stored without regard to block size, there is no disk space lost to the large block size needed on large hard drives.
Standard Compression		This setting provides good compression without sacrificing performance when writing and reading files to and from a compressed drive.
HiPack	Files are compressed using a drive-wide compression table. HiPack compression compresses files to just under half their original size.	Maintains excellent performance during reads, but writing files to a compressed drive may be slower.
UltraPack	A Pentium-optimized highly compressed format. UltraPack compresses files to about one third of their original size.	This format may be slower on 80486-based machines.

Due to the nature of UltraPack compression, the Compression Agent utility can be set up to only use UltraPack on files that have not been accessed in more than a specific number of days. This allows for unused files to be archived with only a minimal loss of performance.

▶ **To use Compression Agent**

1. Make sure the compressed floppy is still in drive A. On the Start menu, point to Programs, Accessories, System Tools, and then click Compression Agent.

2. Click the Settings button to display the Compression Agent Settings screen.

3. Under the Which files do you want to UltraPack, click UltraPack all files. Click OK.

4. When prompted "Do you want Compression Agent to use these updated settings when started by System Agent?" click No.

5. Click Start. When Compression Agent is finished, click Exit.

Lesson Summary

Microsoft Plus! for Windows 95 includes advanced compression tools. These tools can be used to increase available disk space.

Lesson 6: System Agent

To make disk maintenance simpler, Microsoft Plus! for Windows 95 includes the System Agent utility. This lesson explains how to use the System Agent.

After this lesson you will be able to:

- Use System Agent to schedule programs.

Estimated lesson time 15 minutes

System Agent is a system task scheduler that can run programs at predetermined times.

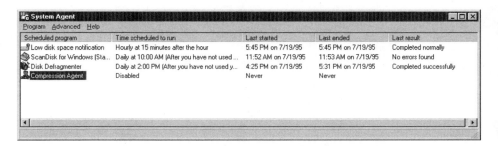

Figure 20.23 Default System Agent tasks

By default, System Agent runs the following tasks:

- Every Hour—Checks for low disk space and warns the user if disk space falls below a preset level.
- Daily—Runs a standard pass with ScanDisk to check the integrity of the hard drives on the computer.
- Daily—Defragments the drives on the computer.
- Monthly—Runs a thorough pass with ScanDisk on the hard drives including a full surface scan to detect flaws in the drive medium.

In addition, if any of the fixed drives on the computer are compressed with DriveSpace, System Agent will run the Compression Agent daily to compress new files and use UltraPack on any files that have aged into UltraPack archive status.

All of the disk maintenance tasks except the low space notification are also dependent on the computer not being in use and, in the case of portable computers, not being run on batteries.

Adding Tasks to System Agent

Any program can be scheduled to run by System Agent.

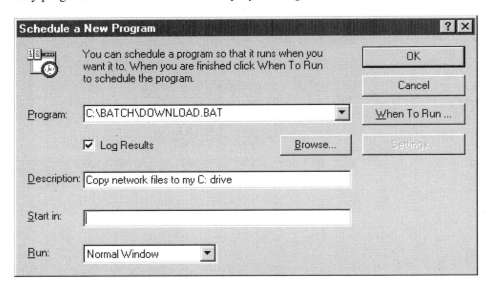

Figure 20.24 Adding tasks to System Agent

Schedule a New Program

When the System Agent starts, it shows a list of all the scheduled programs, when they are scheduled to run, when they last started and ended, and any result information they provided on their last run.

You can add a program to System Agent at any time.

▶ **To add Compression Agent to the schedule**

1. On the Start menu, point to Programs, Accessories, System Tools, and then click System Agent.

2. On the Program menu, click Schedule a new program...

   You can list a program to run, add a friendly description, and specify what type of window to run it in.

3. Click the down arrow to display a selection of programs to schedule, and then click Compression Agent. Click OK.

4. Click OK and Compression Agent is added to the schedule.

5. When prompted "Do you want to postpone running this program until its next scheduled time?" click Yes.

6. Close System Agent.

Change Schedule of a Program

By selecting When To Run... when adding a program or selecting the program you want to modify and selecting Change Schedule from the Program menu, you can specify when the program should be run.

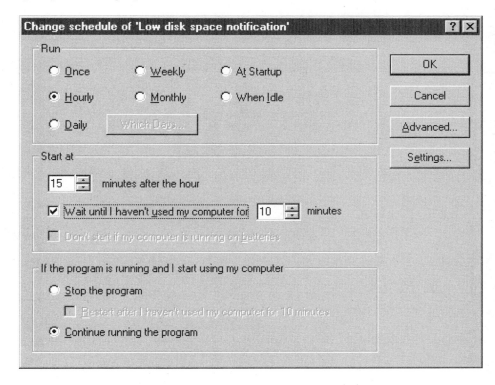

Figure 20.25 System Agent scheduling options

The default is to run a program once a day. You can change the default to run a program any of the following sequences:

- Once
- Hourly
- Daily
- Weekly
- Monthly
- At Startup
- When Idle

The Change schedule dialog box also allows you to specify whether the computer must be idle to run the program, whether to run on a portable computer running on batteries, and what to do if the user starts using the computer while the program is running.

Advanced Options

The Advanced... button allows you to specify deadline information.

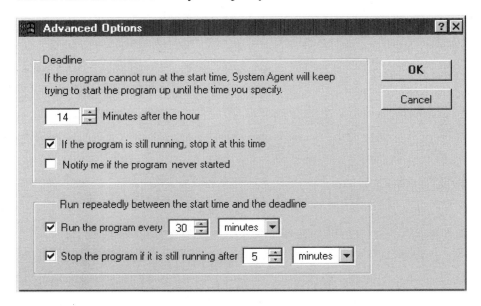

Figure 20.26 Advanced scheduling options

If the program has not been run by a specified time, you can specify whether to stop trying and whether to put up a notification window. In addition, the advanced options allow you to set the program to run repeatedly during a specified time interval.

▶ **To change the schedule of Compression Agent**

In the following exercise, you will configure the schedule for Compression Agent to run every Friday at 3:00 PM.

1. Start System Agent.
2. Under Scheduled programs, double-click Compression Agent.
3. Click Change Schedule...

4. Click the Weekly button.

   When you set the program to run weekly, an additional field in the Start at options appears. This field allows you to indicate which day of the week you want to run the program.

5. In the Start at group, specify that this program should start at 3:00 PM on Friday.

6. Click the Advanced button.

   The Advanced options include the ability to set a deadline and options to run the program repeatedly. You can use these options to tell the program what to do if it cannot run at the normally scheduled time.

7. Click OK to exit the Advanced options dialog box, and then click OK to exit the Change schedule dialog box.

8. Exit System Agent.

Lesson Summary

Microsoft Plus! for Windows 95 includes a System Agent that allows you to automatically run programs at predetermined times. This greatly simplifies some of the more basic computer maintenance tasks.

Review

The following questions are intended to reinforce key information presented in this chapter. If you are unable to answer a question, review the appropriate lesson and then try the question again.

1. When is it most important to run ScanDisk?

_____

_____

2. When is it important to run Disk Defragmenter?

_____

_____

3. List the different media types that Windows 95 Backup can use.

_____

_____

C H A P T E R   2 1

The Boot Sequence

Before You Begin

To complete the lessons in this chapter, you must have:

- Completed Chapter 1 and installed Microsoft Windows 95.
- A CONFIG.SYS file and AUTOEXEC.BAT file on the root directory.

Lesson 1: Bootstrapping Phase

In addition to performing traditional self tests, computers with Plug and Play BIOS perform some additional steps. This lesson describes the initial steps when a computer is first turned on.

After this lesson you will be able to:

- Explain the bootstrapping phase of the boot sequence.

Estimated lesson time 10 minutes

When a computer is first turned on, it performs a Power On Self Test (POST). This is a set of tests to determine that the main hardware is functioning properly. The tests run from the computer's BIOS. This means that the actual tests performed may differ between manufacturers. The OEM for each computer determines the specific POST.

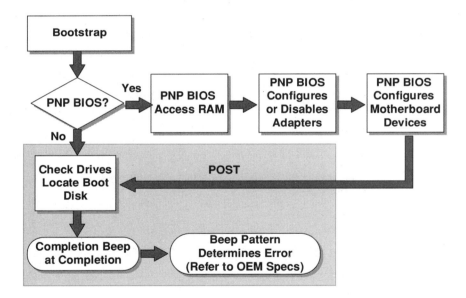

Figure 21.1 Generic POST process

In general, a POST:

- Checks the computer's RAM; this is usually indicated by a count of memory being displayed.
- Performs various computer checks such as displays and other devices.
- Locates the boot drive.

When the POST completes, the computer emits a beep or several beeps. If there is a problem detected during POST, the pattern of beeps—long or short, and the number and sequence of each—may be an indicator to the problem. Check with your original equipment manufacturer (OEM) for more information.

Plug and Play BIOS

If the BIOS is Plug and Play-compatible, there are a few additional ROM routines that occur before the operating system loads. These steps are not strictly part of the POST because they are not a test. However, the specific ROM routines performed are dependent on the hardware vendor.

If the BIOS is not Plug and Play-compatible, the Plug and Play-compliant devices are enumerated in protected mode.

The following steps outline a typical flow of an ISA (Industry Standard Architecture) Plug and Play-compatible computer BIOS POST. All of the standard ISA functionality has been eliminated for clarity in understanding the Plug and Play ROM routine enhancements. Other devices follow a similar pattern.

1. Disable all configurable devices.
2. Assign identifiers to Plug and Play-compliant ISA devices, but keep devices disabled.

   The Plug and Play BIOS constructs a map of resources that are statically allocated to devices in the computer.

   Some computers have Extended System Configuration Data (ESCD) nonvolatile storage, typically battery-backed CMOS or EPROM that the BIOS uses for storing local configuration data. The system software explicitly assigns computer resources for certain devices, such as the monitor, keyboard, and mouse, in the computer through the Write ESCD function of the run-time services. This information is used to construct the resource map and to configure the remaining devices in the computer.

3. Enable input and output devices.

   Devices in the computer that are not configurable always have precedence over devices that can be configured. For example, a standard VGA adapter would become the primary output device. If configurable input and output devices exist, then these devices are enabled at this time. If Plug and Play-compliant input and output devices are selected, then any existing option ROM, such as an ISA option ROM, for these devices is initialized using the Plug and Play option ROM initialization procedure.

4. Perform ISA ROM scan.

   The ISA ROM scan is performed from C0000H to EFFFFH on every 2K boundary searching for a 55AAh header. A checksum is performed to determine and if valid, the option ROM is initialized. Plug and Play-compliant Option ROMs are disabled at this time, except for input and output boot devices, and are not included in the ISA ROM scan.

5. Configure the initial program load (IPL) device.

   If a Plug and Play-compliant device has been selected as the IPL device, then the computer uses the Plug and Play-compliant option ROM procedure to initialize the device. If the IPL device is known to the system BIOS, then the computer must ensure that interrupt 19H is still controlled by the system BIOS.

6. Enable Plug and Play-compliant ISA devices and other configurable devices.

   At this time, the Plug and Play-compliant ISA cards with conflict-free resource assignments are enabled. The computer initializes the option ROMs similar to an ISA ROM scan but, in addition, pass along the defined parameters. All other configurable devices are enabled, if possible, at this time.

7. Initiate the Interrupt 19H IPL sequence.

   The bootstrap loader starts. If the operating system fails to load and a previous ISA option ROM exists, the interrupt 19H vector is restored to the ISA option ROM and the Interrupt 19H bootstrap loader is re-run.

8. Operating system takes over resource management.

   If the loaded operating system is Plug and Play-compliant, it takes over management of the computer's resources. The operating system uses the run-time services of the system BIOS to determine the current allocation of these resources.

Lesson Summary

The steps a computer performs during POST is determined by the OEM. After POST, a Plug and Play BIOS identifies and initializes various devices needed to complete the boot process.

For more information on	See
Plug and Play BIOS	The Plug and Play BIOS Specification as issued by Compaq Computer Corporation, Phoenix Technologies, Ltd. and Intel Corporation. A copy of this document (PNPBIOS.DOC) is included on the CD-ROM for this course in the \RESOURCE folder.

Lesson 2: Real-Mode Compatibility Phase

Once the boot strap phase is complete, the components needed for real-mode loads. This lesson explains this process.

After this lesson you will be able to:
- Explain the real-mode compatibility phase of the boot sequence.

Estimated lesson time 30 minutes

Once the computer has completed the bootstrapping phase, the real-mode phase begins.

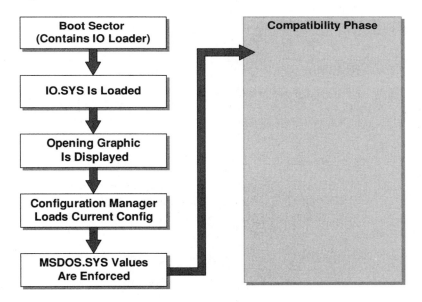

Figure 21.2 Real-mode compatibility phase

Boot Sector
Once the devices are initialized, the computer locates and reads the boot track. The boot sector contains an IO.SYS loader which locates the IO.SYS file on the boot drive, loads it into memory, and then turns control of the system over to it.

IO.SYS

IO.SYS contains the following functions:

- The real-mode Configuration Manager
- Opening graphic screen
- Real-mode Windows 95

IO.SYS loads a minimal file system. This system contains only enough functionality to read the CONFIG.SYS file, if it exists, and the startup graphic file. Other files cannot be read at this point.

Opening Graphic Appears

The opening graphic screen appears on the video monitor during the loading of the real-mode and protected-mode operating system.

Real-Mode PNP Configuration Manager

The real-mode Configuration Manager determines the hardware profile before processing the CONFIG.SYS file. If there is not a hardware profile available, the Configuration Manager creates one. The Configuration Manager can then initialize the hardware devices for the real-mode portion of the operating system.

MSDOS.SYS

Setup creates a hidden, system, read-only file in the root of your boot drive named MSDOS.SYS. This file contains important paths used to locate other Windows 95 files, including the registry. In addition, it contains bootup options for Windows 95.

The values in the MSDOS.SYS are read after the real-mode Plug and Play Configuration Manager has chosen a hardware profile for the computer.

Note Although the MSDOS.SYS file can be edited, the size of it must be greater than 1024 bytes for compatibility with some Microsoft MS-DOS–based programs.

Sample MSDOS.SYS File

```
[Paths]
WinDir=C:\WINDOWS
WinBootDir=C:\WINDOWS
HostWinBootDrv=C

[Options]
BootGUI=1
Network=1
;
;The following lines are required for compatibility with other programs.
;Do not remove them (MSDOS.SYS needs to be >1024 bytes).
;xxxxxxxxxxxxxxxxxxxxxxxxxxxxxxxxxxxxxxxxxxxxxxxxxxxxxxxxxxxxxxxxxxxxxxa
;xxxxxxxxxxxxxxxxxxxxxxxxxxxxxxxxxxxxxxxxxxxxxxxxxxxxxxxxxxxxxxxxxxxxxxb
;xxxxxxxxxxxxxxxxxxxxxxxxxxxxxxxxxxxxxxxxxxxxxxxxxxxxxxxxxxxxxxxxxxxxxxc
;xxxxxxxxxxxxxxxxxxxxxxxxxxxxxxxxxxxxxxxxxxxxxxxxxxxxxxxxxxxxxxxxxxxxxxd
;xxxxxxxxxxxxxxxxxxxxxxxxxxxxxxxxxxxxxxxxxxxxxxxxxxxxxxxxxxxxxxxxxxxxxxe
;xxxxxxxxxxxxxxxxxxxxxxxxxxxxxxxxxxxxxxxxxxxxxxxxxxxxxxxxxxxxxxxxxxxxxxf
;xxxxxxxxxxxxxxxxxxxxxxxxxxxxxxxxxxxxxxxxxxxxxxxxxxxxxxxxxxxxxxxxxxxxxxg
;xxxxxxxxxxxxxxxxxxxxxxxxxxxxxxxxxxxxxxxxxxxxxxxxxxxxxxxxxxxxxxxxxxxxxxh
;xxxxxxxxxxxxxxxxxxxxxxxxxxxxxxxxxxxxxxxxxxxxxxxxxxxxxxxxxxxxxxxxxxxxxxi
;xxxxxxxxxxxxxxxxxxxxxxxxxxxxxxxxxxxxxxxxxxxxxxxxxxxxxxxxxxxxxxxxxxxxxxj
;xxxxxxxxxxxxxxxxxxxxxxxxxxxxxxxxxxxxxxxxxxxxxxxxxxxxxxxxxxxxxxxxxxxxxxk
;xxxxxxxxxxxxxxxxxxxxxxxxxxxxxxxxxxxxxxxxxxxxxxxxxxxxxxxxxxxxxxxxxxxxxxl
;xxxxxxxxxxxxxxxxxxxxxxxxxxxxxxxxxxxxxxxxxxxxxxxxxxxxxxxxxxxxxxxxxxxxxxm
;xxxxxxxxxxxxxxxxxxxxxxxxxxxxxxxxxxxxxxxxxxxxxxxxxxxxxxxxxxxxxxxxxxxxxxn
;xxxxxxxxxxxxxxxxxxxxxxxxxxxxxxxxxxxxxxxxxxxxxxxxxxxxxxxxxxxxxxxxxxxxxxo
;xxxxxxxxxxxxxxxxxxxxxxxxxxxxxxxxxxxxxxxxxxxxxxxxxxxxxxxxxxxxxxxxxxxxxxp
;xxxxxxxxxxxxxxxxxxxxxxxxxxxxxxxxxxxxxxxxxxxxxxxxxxxxxxxxxxxxxxxxxxxxxxq
;xxxxxxxxxxxxxxxxxxxxxxxxxxxxxxxxxxxxxxxxxxxxxxxxxxxxxxxxxxxxxxxxxxxxxxr
;xxxxxxxxxxxxxxxxxxxxxxxxxxxxxxxxxxxxxxxxxxxxxxxxxxxxxxxxxxxxxxxxxxxxxxs
DoubleBuffer=1
```

MSDOS.SYS Path Values

Entry	Description
[Paths] section	
HostWinBootDrv=	Defines the location of the boot drive root directory.
WinBootDir=	Defines the location of the necessary startup files. The default is the directory specified during Setup; for example, C:\WINDOWS.
WinDir=	Defines the location of the Windows 95 directory as specified during Setup.

Note The values shown above are defaults.

MSDOS.SYS also supports an **[Options]** section, which you can tailor the boot process to your specific needs. The following are the entries that may be included in this section.

MSDOS.SYS Option Values

Entry	Description
[Options] section	
BootDelay=n	Sets the initial startup delay to n seconds. The default is 2. **BootKeys=0** disables the delay. The only purpose of the delay is to give the user sufficient time to press the F8 function key after the Starting Windows message appears.
BootFailSafe=	Enables safe mode for computer startup. The default is 0. This setting is enabled typically by equipment manufacturers for installation.
BootGUI=	Enables automatic graphical startup into Windows 95. The default is 1.
BootKeys=	Enables the startup option keys (F5, F6, and F8). The default is 1. Setting this value to 0 overrides the value of **BootDelay=**n and prevents any startup keys from functioning. This setting allows system administrators to configure more secure systems.
BootMenu=	Enables automatic display of the Windows 95 Startup menu, so that the user must press F8 to see the menu. The default is 0. Setting this value to 1 eliminates the need to press F8 to see the menu.
BootMenuDefault=#	Sets the default menu item on the Windows Startup menu; the default is 3 for a computer with no networking components, and 4 for a networked computer.
BootMenuDelay=#	Sets the number of seconds to display the Windows Startup menu before running the default menu item. The default is 30.
BootMulti=	Enables dual-boot capabilities. The default is 0. Setting this value to 1 enables the ability to start the previously installed copy of MS-DOS by pressing F4, or by pressing F8 to use the Windows Startup menu.
BootWarn=	Enables the safe mode startup warning. The default is 1.
BootWin=	Enables Windows 95 as the default operating system. Setting this value to 0 disables Windows 95 as the default; this is useful only with MS-DOS version 5 or 6.x on the computer. The default is 1.
DblSpace=	Enables automatic loading of DBLSPACE.BIN. The default is 1.

(*continued*)

Entry	Description
DoubleBuffer=	Enables loading of a double-buffering driver for a SCSI controller. The default is 0. Setting this value to 1 enables double-buffering, if required by the SCSI controller.
DrvSpace=	Enables automatic loading of DRVSPACE.BIN. The default is 1.
LoadTop=	Enables loading of COMMAND.COM or DRVSPACE.BIN at the top of 640K memory. The default is 1. Set this value to 0 with Novell NetWare or any software that makes assumptions about what is used in specific memory areas.
Logo=	Enables display of the animated logo. The default is 1. Setting this value to 0 also avoids hooking a variety of interrupts that can create incompatibilities with certain memory managers from other vendors.
Network=	Enables Safe Mode With Networking as a menu option. The default is 1 for computers with networking installed. This value should be 0 if network software components are not installed.

After the MSDOS.SYS Values Have Been Read

Windows 95 loads any Setup entries from the default system files for the operating system.

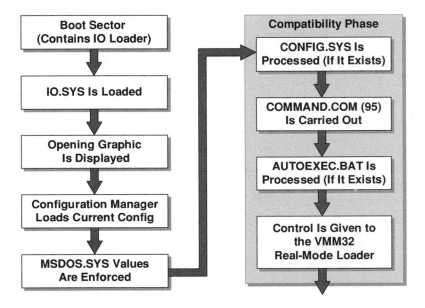

Figure 21.3 Compatibility phase

Most of the common functionality provided by the various CONFIG.SYS file entries are now provided by default by Windows 95. The following are some of the more common (optional) lines in the CONFIG.SYS file that are now incorporated into Windows 95.

Default entries	Description
DOS=High,Auto	Tells the computer to load MS-DOS into the high memory area (HMA).
HIMEM.SYS	Enables access to the HMA. This line loads and runs the Real Mode Memory Manager.
IFSHLP.SYS	The Installable File System Helper (IFSHLP) loads device drivers. This allows the computer to make real file system calls.
SETVER.EXE	Some MS-DOS–based programs require a specific version of MS-DOS to be running. This file responds to queries from those programs with the version number that the program wants to receive. This file is a TSR file that is included for compatibility reasons.
FILES=60	Specifies the number of file handle buffers to create. This is specifically for files opened using IO.SYS calls and is not required by Windows 95. It is included for compatibility with older programs.
LASTDRIVE=Z	Specifies the last drive letter available for assignment. This is not required for Windows 95 but is included for compatibility with older programs. This setting is overridden by the property in the Microsoft Client for NetWare Networks property sheet, if set.
BUFFERS=30	Specifies the number of file buffers to create. This is specifically for programs using IO.SYS calls and is not required by Windows 95.
STACKS=9,256	Specifies the number, 9 is the default for Windows 95, and size (256 is the default) of stack frames. This is not required for Windows 95 but is included for compatibility with older programs.
SHELL=COMMAND.COM /p	Indicates the command process to use. The **/p** switch indicates that the command process is permanent and should not be unloaded. If **/p** is not used, the command process can be unloaded on exit.

Windows 95 will load default entries of the operating environment for the command prompt or MS-DOS–based programs.

The default Windows 95 environment includes:

- TMP=C:\WINDOWS
- TEMP=C:\WINDOWS
- PROMPT=pg
- PATH=C:\WINDOWS;C:\WINDOWS\COMMAND added to the existing path
- COMSPEC=C:\WINDOWS\COMMAND.COM

The following commands are the equivalent default settings for Windows 95.

Default entries	Description
net start	Binds the real-mode network components and validates the binding. Any errors received at this point would be placed in the NDISLOG.TXT file.
set path =*path*	Sets the path as specified.
setcfg	Populates the Plug and Play table with the device information received during the boot initialization and identification process. Arbitrates resource allocation.
set variables, **temp=** **tmp=**	Indicates locations for temporary directories. Both are specified for compatibility reasons.

Processing the CONFIG.SYS and AUTOEXEC.BAT Files

The CONFIG.SYS file is not required for Windows 95. It is retained for compatibility reasons with other programs and to allow the loading of any other-vendor real-mode device drivers. However, computers that require certain real-mode drivers or terminate-and-stay-resident (TSR) programs continue to need those files. CONFIG.SYS and AUTOEXEC.BAT may still be required to enable certain software options. However, some options, such as long command lines, can also be enabled by using the COMMAND.COM Program property sheet command line, for example, place **/P /L:xxx** to include the **/L:xxx** after **SHELL=**.

Similarly, startup batch files, as specified on the Environment property sheet, can be used to do all the environment initialization previously performed by the AUTOEXEC.BAT file.

In Windows 95, CONFIG.SYS and AUTOEXEC.BAT are processed similarly to the way they are processed under MS-DOS version 6.*x*. MS-DOS drivers and TSRs are loaded in real mode.

CONFIG.SYS

If a CONFIG.SYS file exists, it is read at this point. Each line in the CONFIG.SYS file is processed in sequence.

Most of the common functionality provided by the various CONFIG.SYS file entries are now provided by default by Windows 95. The following are some of the more common (optional) lines in the CONFIG.SYS file that are now incorporated into Windows 95.

At this point the base CONFIG.SYS file has been read, and devices are loaded.

COMMAND.COM (Windows 95 Real-Mode Command Processor) Runs

At this point in the process, COMMAND.COM runs. This provides a nongraphical user interface and allows Windows 95 to load an AUTOEXEC.BAT file for compatibility with MS-DOS–based programs that require specific settings.

It also is useful for a command level environment for troubleshooting. For example, suppose Windows 95 stops responding once the graphical interface is loaded, even though you are running in safe mode. You could restart, press F8, and then choose the command prompt and have access to the computer.

AUTOEXEC.BAT

The AUTOEXEC.BAT file is not required for Windows 95, it is included for compatibility purposes. If a computer has an AUTOEXEC.BAT file, it is read at this point and each line is processed in sequence.

The AUTOEXEC.BAT file may contain additional program-specific entries. These are run in the sequence they are listed.

Control Is Given to VMM32

At this point the base AUTOEXEC.BAT file has been read and, if there is no WIN.COM in the AUTOEXEC.BAT, Windows-based components start to load. This is an automatic process with Windows 95. It is at this point that control is given to VMM32.

If There Is a WIN.COM File in the AUTOEXEC.BAT File

WIN.COM is an optional method of starting Windows 95 that allows you to include various switches, usually for troubleshooting. For example, if you needed to perform a safe mode system start due to a problem, you would have the option to add a switch to WIN.COM. The following is the syntax for using switches with WIN.COM.

win [/d:[f][m][n][s][v][x]]

/d: This switch is used for troubleshooting when Windows 95 does not start correctly. The following are the options for the **/d:** switch:

f   Turns off 32-bit disk access. Try this if the computer appears to have disk problems, or if Windows 95 stops responding. This is equivalent to the SYSTEM.INI file setting: **32BitDiskAccess=FALSE**.

m   Enables safe mode. This is automatically enabled during safe mode startup by pressing F5.

n   Enables safe mode with networking. This is automatically enabled during safe mode startup by pressing F6.

s   Specifies that Windows 95 should not use ROM address space between F000:0000 and 1 MB for a break point. Equivalent to the SYSTEM.INI file setting **SystemROMBreakPoint=FALSE**.

v   Specifies that the ROM routine will handle interrupts from the hard disk controller. Equivalent to the SYSTEM.INI file setting **VirtualHDIRQ=FALSE**.

x   Excludes all of the adapter area from the range of memory that Windows 95 scans to find unused space. Equivalent to the SYSTEM.INI file setting **EMMExclude=A000-FFFF**.

If WIN.COM is used to start Windows 95, the real-mode operating system gives control of the computer to WIN.COM. The purpose of this is for troubleshooting.

The WIN.COM switches are passed to VMM32.VXD; at this point control is given to VMM32.VXD.

▶ **To use WIN.COM to start in safe mode**

1. Edit your AUTOEXEC.BAT file to add the following line to the end of the file:

   If you are on a network, add:

   win /d:n

   If you are on a stand-alone computer (not on a network), add:

   win /d:m

2. Notice the message you receive indicating the Windows 95 is running in safe mode.

3. After trying any of the other WIN.COM switches you want to try, be sure to remove the WIN.COM line from your AUTOEXEC.BAT file.

Lesson Summary

Before the system can move into protected mode, the real-mode components need to be initialized.

Lesson 3: Static VxDs and Protected-Mode Load

Once the real-mode components have been loaded, the drivers needed for protected mode are loaded. This lesson explains this process.

After this lesson you will be able to:

- Explain the loading of static virtual device drivers (VxDs) and protected-mode load of the boot sequence.

Estimated lesson time 10 minutes

Static Virtual Drivers Loaded

For compatibility reasons, the VMM32 loader first loads devices specified in SYSTEM.INI. Next, for every device node that exists in the tree, the loader attempts to find the appropriate .VXD driver for the device. If the driver is found then it is automatically loaded.

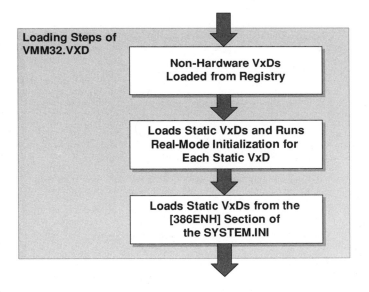

Figure 21.4 Static virtual driver loading sequence

When the enumerator's real-mode initialization routine returns to the loader, VMM32.VXD attempts to load a static VxD for each of the newly identified devices. Devices such as VPICD and VDMAD are passed a handle to the device node that caused them to load.

If WIN.COM was not used to start Windows 95, after all the necessary drivers are loaded, VMM32.VXD switches the processor to operate in protected mode.

At setup, all known required drivers are combined into single file, VMM32.VXD. If additional hardware is added later, the drivers are stored in \\WINDOWS\SYSTEM\VMM32. If a subsequent setup is performed, additional drivers are merged into VMM32.VXD. Because VMM32.VXD is dynamically built for each computer during setup, this file may vary in size for different computer configurations.

Loading and Initializing of the Protected-Mode VxDs

When the real-mode phase is complete, the protected-mode load begins.

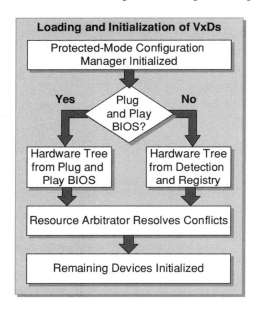

Figure 21.5 Protected-mode virtual driver load and initialize sequence

The protected-mode configuration is an iterative process.

1. The protected-mode Configuration Manager initializes. This includes initializing existing VxDs, and identifying and loading additional VxDs.

   At the Init_Complete phase of VxD initialization, the Configuration Manager begins to enumerate devices and loads the dynamically loadable device drivers.

2. Obtaining the information for the hardware tree depends on whether or not there is a Plug and Play BIOS. If there is a Plug and Play BIOS on the system, the hardware tree is obtained directly from the BIOS which has gathered information from the various bus enumerators.

If there is not a Plug and Play BIOS present, the hardware tree is built from information provided by the bus enumerators themselves and from the static information provided by the Setup hardware detection routines stored in the registry. Drivers update any device information in the device node before resources are allocated.

3. Resolve resource conflicts.

   The next phase resolves device resource conflicts for every device in the tree.

4. Initialize devices.

   The final step informs the devices of their selected configuration.

Lesson Summary

The protected-mode components are loaded and the processor switches to protected mode after all the appropriate drivers are loaded.

Lesson 4: Windows 95 Operating System Load and Desktop Initialization

When the processor is in protected mode and all the necessary devices drivers are loaded, the operating system components are loaded and the desktop is initialized. This lesson explains the steps that occur during this process.

After this lesson you will be able to:

- Explain the process of loading the Windows 95 operating system and initializing the desktop.

Estimated lesson time 10 minutes

This phase of the boot process is loading the Windows 95 operating system.

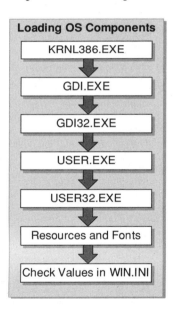

Figure 21.6 Windows 95 operating system loading sequence

When Windows 95 loads, the remaining components are loaded in the following sequence:

- Registry—Contains the base system information.
- SYSTEM.INI—Contains system configuration. This file is being phased out in favor of the registry.
- KERNEL32.DLL—Main operating system code.

- GDI.EXE and GDI32.DLL (graphical device interface)—Windows 95 graphics engine. This contains the base code that performs the drawing to all graphic devices.

- USER.EXE and USER32.DLL—Contains the code for managing the user interface including the window manager.

- Associated resources and fonts.

- WIN.INI—Contains program and user configuration. This file is being phased out in favor of the registry.

Note   The WIN.INI file is not required by Windows 95, but it is included for compatibility reasons.

Desktop Initialization

The last phase of the boot process is loading the Windows 95 system.

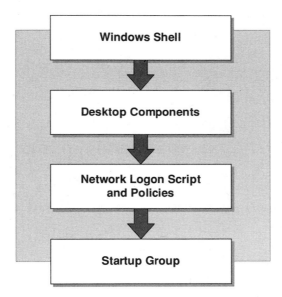

Figure 21.7   Desktop initialization sequence

Windows 95 now loads the shell and the user can log on to the system:

- Windows shell loads, normally this is the EXPLORER.EXE shell. Also, the machine policies are enforced at this point.

- Desktop components—The initial programs that are loaded when Windows 95 starts.

- If you are connected to a network, you will be prompted to log on to the network. After you log on, the login scripts are carried out and policies are enforced for the user. You are prompted to log on to Windows 95 at this point. The log on process involves entering a user name and a password.

  If the user name and password used to log on to the network are the same as the user name and password used to log on to Windows 95, you will not receive the second prompt. You will be automatically logged on.

  Once the user logs on, the system can process user-specific configuration information and load any user-specific policy files. If the user does not log on, default settings are used to determine user preferences and such. If network logon is set, the user may be logged on to the network during this process.

Lesson Summary

The last phases of the boot sequence are loading the Windows 95 operating system components and initializing the desktop.

Lesson 5: Troubleshooting Startup

This lesson explains some of the steps you can take if you have problems starting Windows 95.

After this lesson you will be able to:

- Diagnose and solve problems that may occur during the boot sequence.
- Determine which startup option to use when diagnosing problems.
- Use the switches for WIN.COM to troubleshoot startup problems.

Estimated lesson time 30 minutes

Startup Options

In normal circumstances, when you start the system the Windows 95 logo appears and the load process starts. If you are having startup problems, you may want to use one of the startup options. To use one of these options, press the F8 function key when the following message appears.

```
Starting Windows...
```

The following menu of options appears.

```
Microsoft Windows 95 Startup Menu
================================

1. Normal
2. Logged (\BOOTLOG.TXT)
3. Safe Mode
4. Safe Mode with network support
5. Step-by-step confirmation
6. Command prompt only
7. Safe mode command prompt
8. Previous version of MS-DOS

Enter a choice:  __

F5=Safe mode  Shift+F5=Command prompt  Shift+F8=Step-by-step
confirmation[n]
```

Any of these options may be used to start Windows 95.

- Normal—Windows 95 starts without any troubleshooting options.
- Logged—Starts Windows 95 and creates a log that lists components loaded either successfully or not.

- Safe mode—This boot sequence loads COMMAND.COM but bypasses the AUTOEXEC.BAT and CONFIG.SYS files if they are present on the system. This also loads only the minimal drivers (such as VGA graphics) to allow recovery from an incorrect device configuration.

- Safe mode with network support—Loads COMMAND.COM and network drivers, but bypasses the AUTOEXEC.BAT and CONFIG.SYS files if they are present on the system. This choice allows for safe mode functionality when the driver files needed to restore the system reside on a network share.

- Step-by-step confirmation—Steps through each line in the CONFIG.SYS file. You are prompted (Y/N) whether or not to carry out each line. This option also gives you the option of doing the same single-step process for the AUTOEXEC.BAT file.

In addition to all the line-by-line questions, the interactive start also provides prompts at the following stages:

- Load DoubleSpace driver [Enter=Y,Esc=N]?

- Process the system registry [Enter=Y,Esc=N]?

- Create a startup log file (BOOTLOG.TXT) [Enter=Y,Esc=N]?

- Process your startup command file (AUTOEXEC.BAT) [Enter=Y,Esc=N]?

- WIN [Enter=Y,Esc=N]?

- Load all Windows drivers [Enter=Y,Esc=N]?

If you answer Yes to each prompt, the result of the boot is the same as booting normally, with the exceptions that the logo does not appear and a boot log is created.

- Command prompt only—Brings up a command prompt, does not load the graphical components of Windows 95. This is useful for troubleshooting.

- Safe mode command prompt—Brings up a command prompt, does not process AUTOEXEC.BAT or CONFIG.SYS files, and does not load the graphical components of Windows 95.

- Previous version of MS-DOS—Boots into the operating system that was loaded before Windows 95. If the computer contains an OEM-installed version of Windows 95 (one with no previous version of MS-DOS), the computer boots to a command line.

Note If Windows 95 fails during a boot completely, the last option on this menu may allow you to perform a safe mode boot with networking options intact.

WIN.COM Troubleshooting Switches

WIN.COM has a variety of debug switches which can be used to troubleshoot various problems.

The following are the syntax and switches available for WIN.COM.

win [/b][/d:[f][m][n][s][v][x]]

/b   Creates a file, BOOTLOG.TXT, that records system messages generated during system startup (boot).

/d: Used for troubleshooting when Windows 95 does not start correctly.

    f   Turns off 32-bit disk access. Equivalent to SYSTEM.INI file setting: **32BitDiskAccess=FALSE**.

    m   Enables safe mode. This is automatically enabled during safe mode startup.

    n   Enables safe mode with networking. This is automatically enabled during safe mode startup.

    s   Specifies that Windows 95 should not use ROM address space between F000:0000 and 1 MB for a break point. Equivalent to the SYSTEM.INI file setting **SystemROMBreakPoint=FALSE**.

    v   Specifies that the ROM routine handles interrupts from the hard disk controller. Equivalent to the SYSTEM.INI file setting **VirtualHDIRQ=FALSE**.

    x   Excludes all of the adapter area from the range of memory that Windows 95 scans to find unused space. Equivalent to the SYSTEM.INI file setting **EMMExclude=A000-FFFF**.

Examine the Boot Process

In the following exercise, you will single-step through the boot process, recording what happens during each step.

▶ **To single-step boot (note: read all instructions first)**

1. Restart your computer.

2. After the POST, the Starting Windows... message appears. As soon as this message appears, press F8. Highlight Step-by-Step confirmation, and then press the ENTER key.

3. Windows 95 prompts you to confirm each startup command. The following is a sample of what you may see. In this example, Windows 95 was installed in the default C:\WINDOWS directory. If you installed Windows 95 in another location, your path will vary.

```
Load DoubleSpace driver [Enter=Y,Esc=n]?
Process the system registry [Enter=Y,Esc=N]?
Create a startup log file (BOOTLOG.TXT) [Enter=Y,Esc=N]?
Process your startup device drivers (CONFIG.SYS) [Enter=Y,Esc=N]?
DEVICE=C:\WINDOWS\HIMEM.SYS [Enter=Y,Esc=N]?
LASTDRIVE=Z [Enter=Y,Esc=N]?
DEVICE=C:\WINDOWS\IFSHLP.SYS [Enter=Y,Esc=N]?
DEVICE=C:\WINDOWS\SETVER.EXE [Enter=Y,Esc=N]?
Process your startup command file (AUTOEXEC.BAT) [Enter=Y,Esc=N]?
PATH C:\WINDOWS;C:\DOS [Enter=Y,Esc=N]?
C:\WINDOWS\COMMAND\doskey [Enter=Y,Esc=N]?
WIN [Enter=Y,Esc=N]?
Load all Windows drivers [Enter=Y,Esc=N]?
```

4. Restart your computer as often as necessary to answer the following questions. If any of the following prevents Windows 95 from loading, cold boot your computer by turning it off, waiting five seconds, and then turning it back on.

5. Will Windows 95 start without creating a BOOTLOG.TXT?_____

Does Windows 95 have full functionality?_____

Why or why not?_____

_____

6. Will Windows 95 start without running the CONFIG.SYS file?_____

Does Windows 95 have full functionality?_____

Why or why not?_____

_____

7. Will Windows 95 start without loading HIMEM.SYS?_____

Does Windows 95 have full functionality?_____

Why or why not?_____

_____

8. Will Windows 95 start without running IFSHLP.SYS?_____

Does Windows 95 have full functionality?_____

Why or why not?_____

_____

9. Will Windows 95 start without running the AUTOEXEC.BAT file?_____

    Does Windows 95 have full functionality?_____

    Why or why not?_____

    _____

10. Will Windows 95 start without loading all Windows-based drivers?_____

    Does Windows 95 have full functionality?_____

    Why or why not?_____

    _____

11. Can you break out of the boot process into MS-DOS?_____

    If yes, how?_____

    Why or why not?_____

Shut down the computer and then choose to restart it. When the Starting
Windows 95 message appears during the boot process, press the key combinations
below. If the starting logo appears immediately after pressing a key combination,
press ESC to see the startup files as they are processed.

SHIFT + F5

    What happened?_____

    When would this be useful?_____

F5

    What happened?_____

    When would this be useful?_____

Lesson Summary

Startup problems can be isolated by using a variety of tools. The Startup options
include safe mode (with or without network functions), step-by-step loads, and
using WIN.COM with troubleshooting switches.

Review

The following questions are intended to reinforce key information presented in this chapter. If you are unable to answer a question, review the appropriate lesson and then try the question again.

1. What are three functions of the POST?

2. What additional capabilities does a Plug and Play ROM BIOS provide beyond a legacy ROM BIOS?

3. List the sequence of events during protected-mode Plug and Play initialization.

4. What is the registry? What is its purpose?

CHAPTER 22

Microsoft Exchange

Before You Begin

To complete the lessons in this chapter, you must have:

- Completed Chapter 1 and installed Microsoft Windows 95.
- An additional Windows 95-based computer in the same workgroup is needed to complete all the exercises.

Lesson 1: Microsoft Exchange

This lesson introduces MAPI and how different MAPI-compliant mail systems can communicate with each other.

After this lesson you will be able to:
- Define MAPI and explain how it is used.
- Define Microsoft Exchange.

Estimated lesson time 10 minutes

MAPI Overview

The Messaging Application Programming Interface (MAPI) is a set of common commands that allow programs to communicate with mail systems and other MAPI-compliant programs.

Windows 95 includes Messaging API (MAPI), a set of API functions, and Microsoft OLE Component Object Model (COM) interfaces that enable programs in Windows 95 to interact with many different messaging systems using a single interface. MAPI architecture defines messaging clients, such as Microsoft Exchange, that interact with various message service providers, such as Microsoft Mail, through the MAPI programming interfaces. Windows 95 includes the following messaging service providers to connect with the Microsoft Exchange messaging client:

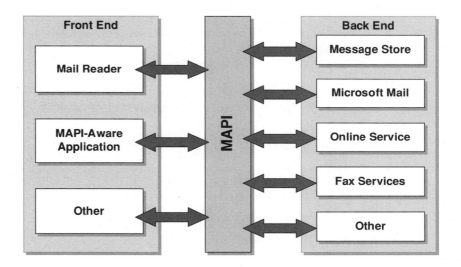

Figure 22.1 Messaging Applications Programming Interface (MAPI)

All the services are considered back-end. They are ways to transmit data, store data, and so on.

The front-ends are the user interfaces. They are independent from the back end.

Any MAPI-compliant front end can communicate to any MAPI-compliant back end by using MAPI.

For example, if you have a Microsoft Visual Basic® programming system program that is MAPI-aware, you can send data from this program to someone else as a mail message, a fax message, a CompuServe message, or whatever format they can receive.

The only commonality needed between the programs is that they use MAPI commands.

Microsoft Exchange

Microsoft Exchange is a central access point for all messages sent and received through the network and other external sources. It acts as a coordinator between MAPI-aware programs such as mail readers, and back ends such as Microsoft Mail or CompuServe MAPI Services.

The Microsoft Exchange client is an advanced messaging and workgroup client that is built directly into Windows 95. Through MAPI, Microsoft Exchange can communicate with any electronic mail system or messaging program that is a *MAPI service provider*. A MAPI service provider is similar to a personal gateway. It specifies all the connection and addressing settings needed to communicate with a network on one end and with the Microsoft Exchange client on another end. MAPI helps Microsoft Exchange define the purpose and content of messages, and manage stored messages.

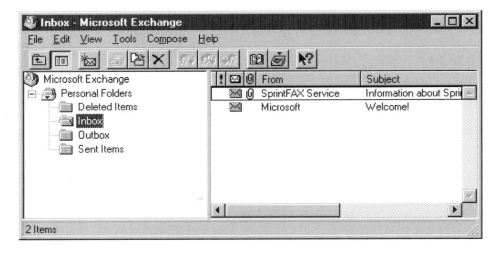

Figure 22.2 Microsoft Exchange client

Microsoft Exchange contains entries for various messaging resources, including:

- Information services
- Address books
- Information stores

Lesson Summary

The Microsoft Exchange client included with Windows 95 is MAPI-compliant. This allows the Microsoft Exchange client to communicate with other MAPI-compliant mail services and vice versa.

Lesson 2: Setting Up a Workgroup Postoffice

Before setting up a Microsoft Exchange client, you would normally assign the client to a postoffice. Windows 95 comes with the capability to set up a workgroup postoffice; that functionality is discussed in this lesson.

After this lesson you will be able to:

- Set up a workgroup postoffice.

Estimated lesson time 20 minutes

Connecting to a Postoffice

Microsoft Exchange can connect to either the workgroup postoffice built into Windows 95 or a full Microsoft Mail Server acquired separately from Windows 95.

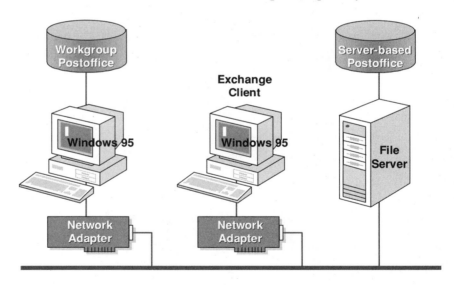

Figure 22.3 Types of postoffices

The Microsoft Mail MAPI service provider connects to Microsoft Mail Server postoffices that you may have on a Microsoft Windows NT or Novell NetWare server, or the built-in Windows 95 Microsoft Mail postoffice.

Setting Up a Workgroup Postoffice

Before you can install and use mail, you must have an account on a postoffice. Windows 95 includes a workgroup postoffice.

▶ **To create a Workgroup Postoffice**

1. In the Control Panel, double-click the Microsoft Mail Postoffice icon.

   The Workgroup Postoffice Admin utility starts.

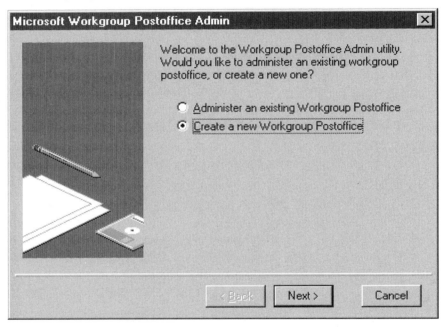

Figure 22.4 Creating a workgroup postoffice

2. Click the Create a new Workgroup Postoffice radio button, and then click Next. You are prompted for the location of the postoffice.

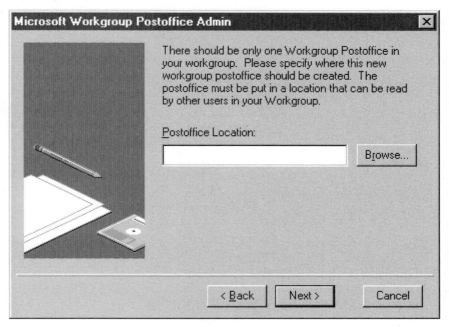

Figure 22.5 Specifying the location of a postoffice

The workgroup postoffice can be set up on a stand-alone computer or on a computer used by a member of the workgroup.

The user who creates the postoffice is automatically made the postoffice administrator. The administrator is the person responsible for managing the workgroup postoffice. His or her job is to add, modify, and remove Mail users and to manage workgroup postoffice disk space. The postoffice itself does not have to be on the administrator's computer. It can be located on any workgroup computer that has the available disk space. Remember that the postoffice administrator must be able to access the computer where the postoffice resides to perform various administrative functions.

Note If users want 24-hour access to the postoffice, the computer with the postoffice must be left on.

It is also useful if the postoffice is on a computer which is not used as often as the other computers in the workgroup.

3. Type the location of the postoffice. If you are creating the postoffice on your on computer, you can simply enter C:\. Click Next.

   If you entered C:\ as the location of the postoffice and there are no other postoffices on C:\, when you clicked Next the computer indicates that the Workgroup Postoffice will be created in the C:\wgpo0000 directory.

4. Click Next.

   The Administrator account details screen appears.

Figure 22.6 Specifying administrator account details

5. Enter the account details for the administrator. The Mailbox defaults to your user logon name, but you may change it to something else. The default password is PASSWORD; it may also be changed. The Administrator account requires a name, mailbox, and password. The other details are optional.

6. After entering the detail information, click the OK button.

Mail

> Workgroup Postoffice created in C:\wgpo\wgpo0000
>
> To allow other users in your workgroup to access the Workgroup Postoffice you just created, you must share the above directory. This can be done from the Explorer. Be sure to allow full access to the shared directory. You can assign a password if you want.
>
> OK

Figure 22.7 Workgroup Postoffice created dialog box

7. Click OK again.

   Make sure that the folder on the postoffice computer is set up as a shared directory with Full access. The WGPO0000 folder contains the shared folders that can be accessed by all members of the workgroup. The postoffice cannot function properly unless this directory is shared.

8. Share your \WGPO0000 folder.

   a. Explore My Computer.

   b. Expand C:\ or the location where you indicated to create the postoffice.

   c. With the secondary mouse button, click wgpo0000.

   d. Click Sharing from the menu.

   e. Click the Shared As option.

   f. Under Access Type, click Full.

   g. Click OK.

   The wpgo0000 folder is shared if a hand appears beneath it.

Administering the Workgroup Postoffice

The Postoffice administrator maintains and administers the Workgroup Postoffice. This job consists of adding and deleting users, maintaining user information, and cleaning up the hard drive.

Adding and Deleting Users

As users are added or dropped from the workgroup, the postoffice administrator can add or delete their mailbox, but not the user's local Personal Folders. This is accomplished from the Postoffice Manager menu by selecting the user and clicking the appropriate button.

Maintaining User Information

If user information such as a phone number, office, or department changes, the postoffice administrator can update this information in Mail. From the Postoffice Manager menu, select the user, and then click the Details button. Included as part of the detail information is a starred section for the user's password. The postoffice administrator can give the user a new password when necessary.

▶ **To add a user to the postoffice**

1. In the Control Panel, double-click the Microsoft Mail Postoffice icon.

2. Make sure the Administer and existing Workgroup Postoffice option is selected, and then click Next.

3. Enter the name of the postoffice to administer, for example, c:\wgpo0000, and then click Next.

4. Enter your mailbox and password to administer the Workgroup Postoffice. The Postoffice Manager dialog box appears.

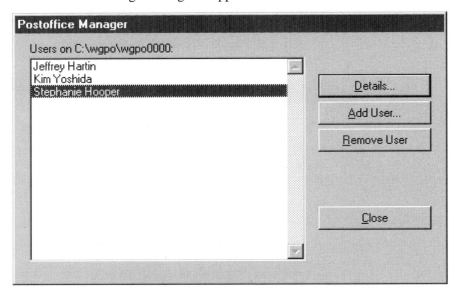

Figure 22.8 Postoffice Manager dialog box

5. Click the Add User button.

   When adding or changing user details, the details sheet appears.

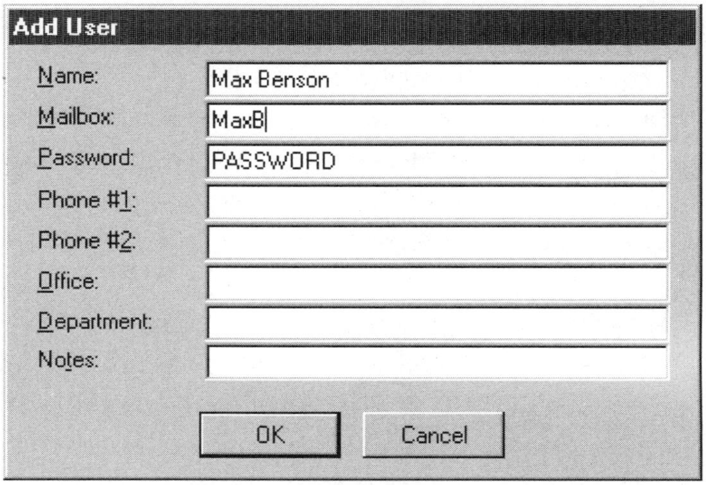

Add User	
Name:	Max Benson
Mailbox:	MaxB
Password:	PASSWORD
Phone #1:	
Phone #2:	
Office:	
Department:	
Notes:	

   [OK]   [Cancel]

   Figure 22.9   Adding a user to postoffice

   Complete the required information and then click OK. The user is added, or the details information is changed.

Lesson Summary

Before setting up Microsoft Exchange clients, you should assign them to a postoffice. The ability to create a workgroup postoffice is included with Windows 95, though you may also assign the client to other postoffices.

Lesson 3: Configuring Microsoft Exchange

The Microsoft Exchange client that is included with Windows 95 can be configured to meet a variety of needs. This lesson explains how to configure the client.

After this lesson you will be able to:

- Implement the various mail options to meet a specific set of user requirements.
- Implement the various messaging/communications functions for Microsoft Windows 95.

Estimated lesson time 30 minutes

Configuring Microsoft Exchange

The first time you access Microsoft Exchange, a wizard will appear that helps you configure the various services. You can also reach this information in the Control Panel by clicking the Mail and Fax icon.

Figure 22.10 The Inbox Setup wizard

As you use the Inbox Setup wizard, you need to provide certain information.

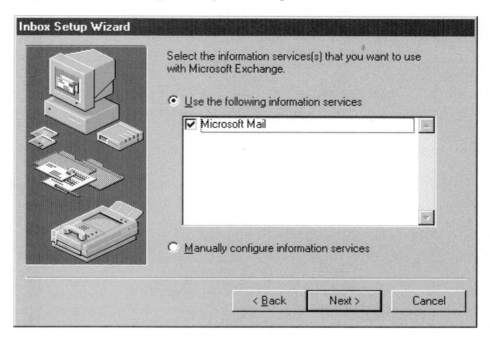

Figure 22.11 Selecting services window in the Inbox Setup wizard

The information services are services that have the ability to send and receive messages. For example; Mail systems, Fax, online services, and so on. Click the services you use.

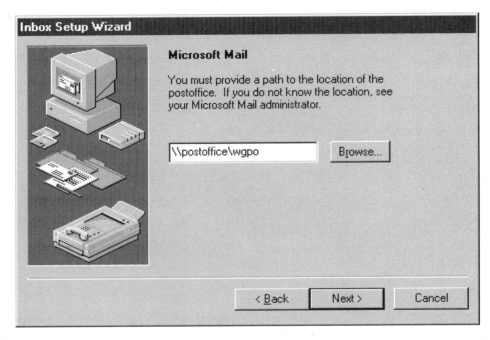

Figure 22.12 Designating a postoffice location in the Inbox Setup wizard

To use mail, you need to specify a postoffice location. This may be on the local machine or a server.

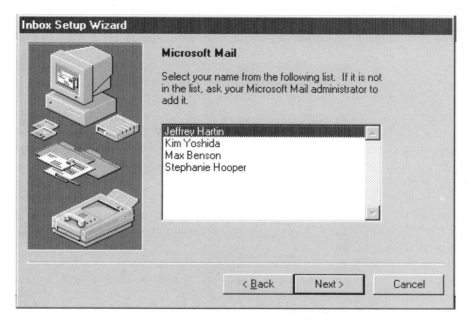

Figure 22.13 Selecting a name in the Inbox Setup wizard

After you select the postoffice, select your name and enter your password to complete the initial configuration of Microsoft Exchange.

Message Profiles

Windows 95 uses message profiles to determine what type of messages to produce and how to produce them. A message profile lists all the services, resources, and configuration information for messages.

Figure 22.14 Microsoft Exchange profiles

The message profile contains service configuration information. It can contain generic settings, locations, delivery order, and other message settings.

You may have more than one message profile, for example, one profile that specifies how to contact people when you are in your office, another profile that has different specifications when you are traveling and away from your network.

A message profile consists of the following components.

- Services—Have the ability to send and receive messages.

- Delivery—Where outgoing messages are sent and where incoming messages are stored.

- Addressing—Where to find an address.

The information you provided to the configuration wizard is used to create a default profile called MS Exchange Settings. This default profile allows you to use the basic Microsoft Exchange features. To use the advanced functions, you need to edit this profile.

To change or to add a profile, double-click the Mail and Fax icon in the Control Panel. Click the Show Profiles, and then click Add or Copy.

Services—Microsoft Mail

The Microsoft Mail service allows you to send electronic mail between other workstations.

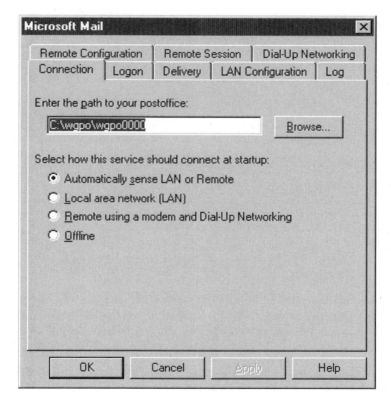

Figure 22.15 Connection tab on the Microsoft Mail property sheet

Microsoft Mail is added by default. You can configure your connection information form the Connection property sheet. You may connect to your postoffice across the local area network (LAN), using remote access, or you can work with your mail messages offline.

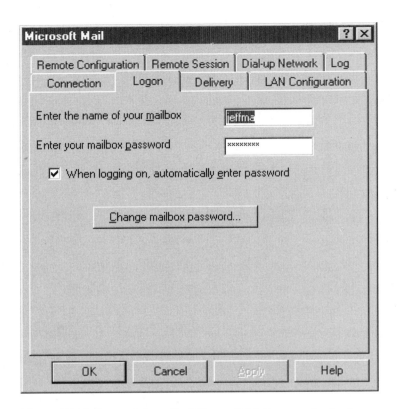

Figure 22.16 Logon tab on the Microsoft Mail property sheet

The Logon property sheet allows you to configure how you are required to access your mailbox.

The Logon and Connection property sheets are the only sheets required to minimally configure Microsoft Mail. If you install Microsoft Exchange using the wizard, these property sheets will already contain default information, allowing you to use the mail service without any additional configuration.

The remaining property sheet tabs allow you to configure the Microsoft Mail service to meet virtually any requirement.

Services—Address Book

An Address Book contains a list of people and where they are located.

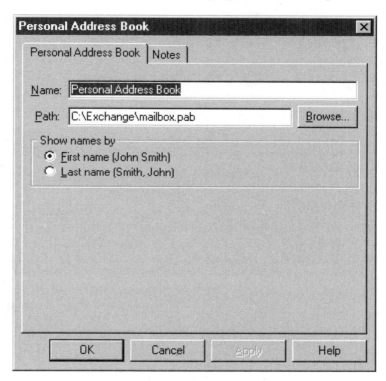

Figure 22.17 Personal Address Book property sheet

An address may be a local mail address, a fax phone number, an internal electronic mail address, or any of a variety of information. The address books indicate how to contact an individual. You may have multiple address books, such as local, remote, one for work, and another for travel. The message profiles allow you to specify the order the address books are searched.

Your address book may reside on your local machine or on a remote server.

Services—Personal Folders

Personal Folders are message containers. These may be on a local drive or on a remote server.

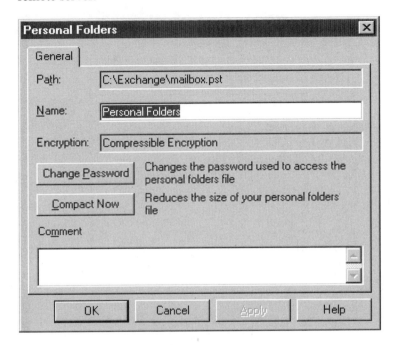

Figure 22.18 Personal Folders property sheet

Windows 95 includes the Microsoft Personal Folder (.PST) file that stores all messages in this one file. However, multiple Personal Folders may be used.

The property sheet for your Personal Folders allows you to specify a location and friendly name for the folder. You can change your password, encrypt, and compress the size of the information store using the buttons on the property sheet.

Adding Services

Additional information services can be added by clicking Tools menu, clicking Services, and then clicking the Add button.

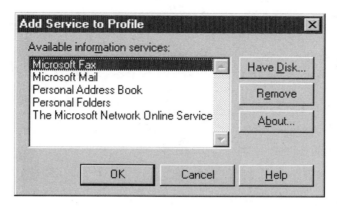

Figure 22.19 Add Service to Profile dialog box

From the list of available information services, select the new service you want to add to your profile and then click OK.

When you add a service, you are prompted for configuration information. For example, one of the services you can add is the Microsoft Fax. This allows you to send and receive faxes through Microsoft Exchange just like any other message.

When you select the fax service, you receive the Microsoft Fax property sheet.

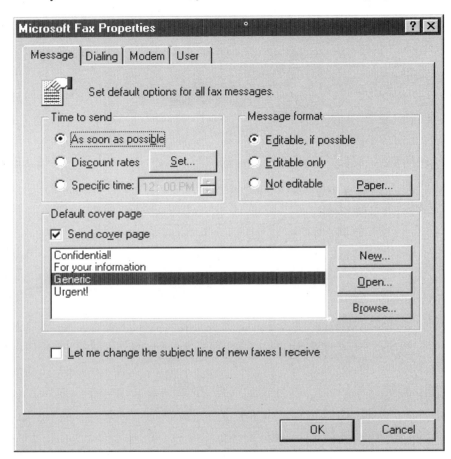

Figure 22.20 Message tab on the Microsoft Fax property sheet

The Message tab properties allows you to configure the message format, specify the cover page, indicate when to send the fax, and other functions.

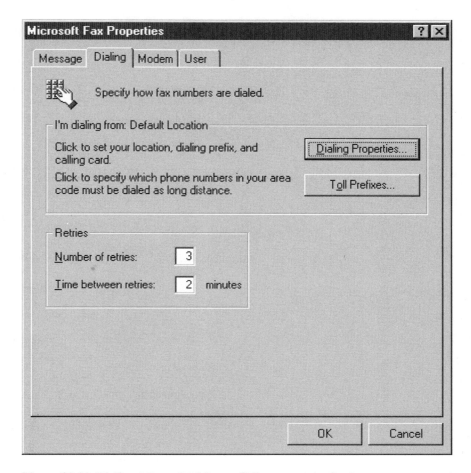

Figure 22.21 Dialing tab on the Microsoft Fax property sheet

The Dialing tab properties allows you to specify how fax numbers are retried when the number cannot be connected. You can access the telephony application programming interface (TAPI) configuration information by clicking the Dialing Properties button.

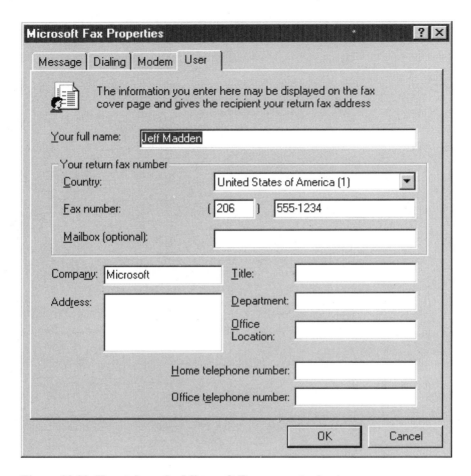

Figure 22.22 User tab on the Microsoft Fax property sheet

The User tab is where you specify the information that appears on the fax cover page and provide a return address. You must enter a name and a fax number; the remaining fields are optional.

When you click OK, you return to the Add Service to Profile property sheet.

Delivery

The method of delivery may be specified for incoming and outgoing messages on the Tools menu Options item.

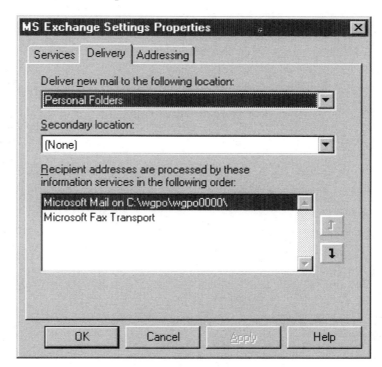

Figure 22.23 Delivery tab on the MS Exchange Settings property sheet

Incoming

All new messages go into one message store (a *.PST file). You can specify which message store to use on this field. Your message store may be on your local machine or on a remote server.

Outgoing

This determines where the mail is sent. The services are listed in order and you may change this order by using the arrow buttons on the side of the list box. This allows messages to be sent to someone with multiple addresses, with Microsoft Exchange selecting which service to use. You can even specify to send a message through all the delivery mechanisms.

Addressing

The addressing properties configure where to look for and store an address. The default address is the first place that the computer looks when you address a piece of electronic mail.

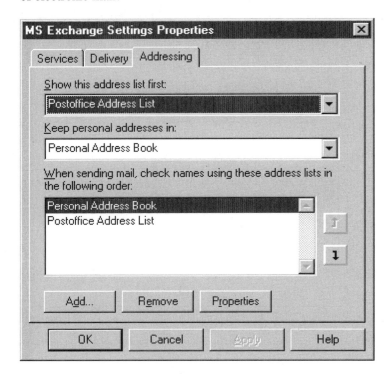

Figure 22.24 Addressing tab on the MS Exchange Settings property sheet

Normally, you would have a personal address book and an address book for each information provider. The Personal Address Book is open for you to make additions and changes, while the information provider's lists are often controlled by their administrator.

The search order indicates the order to search the various address books for a specific address. You can configure the order by using the arrow buttons on the side of the list box.

▶ **To create a postoffice**

1. On the root of the C drive, create a new folder called WGPO.

2. Share the WGPO folder with full access and no password.

3. In the Control Panel, double-click the Microsoft Mail Postoffice icon.

4. Click Create a new Workgroup Postoffice, and then click Next.

5. Click Next to confirm C:\wgpo\wgpo0000 as your postoffice location.

6. Enter your administrator account information.

   Your mailbox name defaults to your logon name. You mailbox name must be unique. Change your password from the default of PASSWORD. Enter your name and complete the other information.

7. Click OK.

   You are prompted that the postoffice has been created.

▶ **To add users to a postoffice**

1. In the Control Panel, open the Microsoft Mail Postoffice icon.

2. Click Administer an existing Workgroup Postoffice, and then click Next.

3. Specify the location of the postoffice as C:\WGPO, and then click Next.

4. Enter your Administrator account information, and then click Next.

5. Click Add User... and add the following users:

Name	Mailbox	Password	Phone 1	Office	Dept.	Notes
Beverly Jones	bevjo	bevjo	555-1234	1403	Sales	VP
Tom Johnston	tomjo	tomjo	555-1236	2206	Mkt.	
Steve Alboucq	stevea	stevea	555-1238	1102	Sales	NW

6. Click Close.

▶ **To configure Microsoft Exchange**

1. In the Control Panel, double-click the Mail and Fax icon.

2. Click the Show Profiles button and then click Add.

3. Click Microsoft Mail, do not click any other information service, and then click Next.

4. For the profile name, type **Mine**

5. For the Postoffice path, type **c:\wgpo\wgpo0000** and then click Next.

6. Click your logon name on the list, and then click Next.

7. Type your password, and then click Next.

8. When prompted, accept the default location for your Personal Address Book—the computer creates one for you—and then click Next.

9. When prompted, accept the default location for your Personal Folder—the computer creates one for you—and then click Next.

10. You will be prompted to determine if you would like to automatically run Microsoft Exchange when you start Windows 95. Click Do not add Inbox to the StartUp group, and then click Next.

11. A Done message appears. Click Finish.

▶ **To copy a profile**

1. From the Microsoft Exchange Profiles window, click the Copy... button.

2. In the New Profile Name, type **bevjo** and then click OK.

3. Click the When starting Microsoft Exchange, use the profile box and then make bevjo the default profile.

▶ **To edit a Profile**

1. In the top part of the Microsoft Exchange Profiles window, select bevjo and click the Properties button.

2. Click Add...

3. Click Microsoft Fax and then click OK.

4. Enter your country, area or city code, and if needed, any number you must dial to reach an outside line. Click OK.

   You are asked if you want to provide your name, fax number, and fax mode.

5. Click Yes.

6. Enter the appropriate information and then click OK.

   You are asked if you want to specify the fax modem to use when sending faxes.

7. Click Yes.

8. Click the Add... button.

9. Click Fax modem and then click OK.

10. An Install New Modem wizard appears.

11. If you actually have a modem attached to the machine, you can let Windows 95 detect the modem by clicking Next.

    If you do not have a modem attached, click the Don't run the Hardware Installation wizard option and then click Next.

12. If you do not have a modem installed, click the Practical Peripherals PM14400FX and then click Next.

13. Click COM1 for your port and then click Next.

14. Click Finish.

15. Make sure your modem is selected as the Active fax device.

    If your modem is not selected as the active fax device, click your modem name and then click Set as Active Fax Device.

16. Click the User tab.

17. Complete the information you would normally want printed on a fax cover sheet.

    You need to enter at least your name and return fax phone number. Click OK.

18. Click OK and then click Close.

Lesson Summary

Microsoft Exchange can be configured to be used in a variety of manners. You may specify multiple mail providers, multiple addresses, and other information.

Lesson 4: Using Mail

The Microsoft Exchange client is included with Windows 95. This lesson explains how you can use this to send and receive messages.

After this lesson you will be able to:

* Create, send, and receive mail messages.

Estimated lesson time 20 minutes

The Microsoft Mail client included with Windows 95 stores messages in RTF format. It is an OLE container, which means that OLE objects, such as a .WAV sound file, may be embedded in the message.

When Microsoft Mail is used with the appropriate profiles, you can have an extremely versatile messaging system. For example, you can send electronic mail to a project group that is specified in the address book. This project group may consist of individuals who receive mail by means of CompuServe, the Internet, internal mail systems, and faxes. As long as every member of the group has their address properly assigned in the address books, you only need to send one message. The messages are automatically routed to through the appropriate mechanisms.

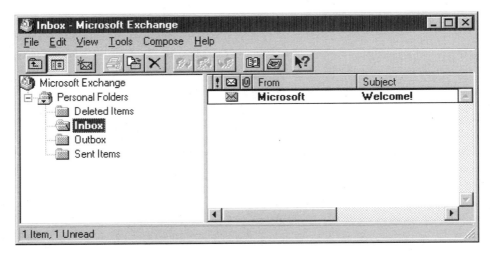

Figure 22.25 Microsoft Exchange Inbox

The use of multiple profiles allows you to use these same address books and aliases even when your capabilities change. When you send mail to someone, it might be sent by means of electronic mail on the network when you are in the office but by means of fax when you are away from the office.

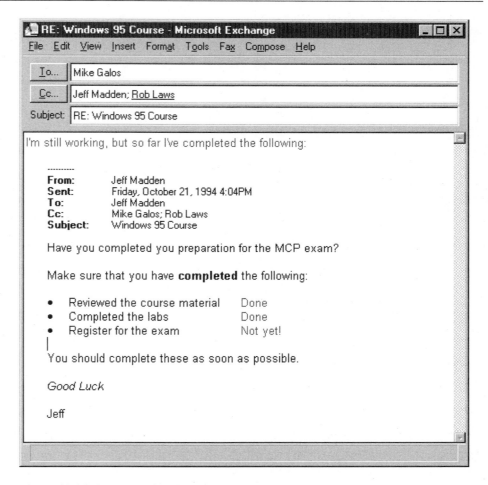

Figure 22.26 Example of mail with RTF

Microsoft Mail now supports the rich text format (RTF). This includes support of different fonts, bullets, and other formatting features. The following sample shows some of the various formats available, including the ability to have responses appear in a different font than the original message used.

In the following exercise, you will create and send an electronic mail message to another user in your postoffice.

▶ **To send a message**

1. On the Start menu, point to Programs, and then click Microsoft Exchange.

   You may be asked to log on to Microsoft Mail, and the fax server will start if you have a fax modem installed.

2. On the Compose menu, click New Message.

3. Click the To... button.

4. On the Tools menu, click Address Book.

5. Click the name of the person to receive the mail, Beverly Johnson, and then click the To button.

   The name is added to the Message recipients list.

6. Click your name and then click the Cc button.

7. Click OK to enter the addresses.

8. Move to the subject line and then enter a topic.

9. Type a message in the main text entry area.

   You may choose to change fonts, use italic or bold text, or change the color of the text. You may also embed OLE objects or files in the message.

10. Send the file by clicking Send on the File menu.

    A letter appears in the status area of the taskbar when the mail has arrived. You may view it by opening Microsoft Exchange, and then opening MS Personal Information Store. Inside you will see four folders, the Inbox entry is bold indicating unread mail. Open the Inbox and you see your messages.

Connecting to Other Services

Through MAPI, you can send and receive messages to and from multiple service providers, such as Microsoft Mail, Microsoft Fax, and CompuServe Mail Services, from Microsoft Exchange. Each of these services have different setup requirements. For example, some service providers may require that you have a modem and an account.

► **To add a service provider**

1. In the Control Panel, double-click the Mail and Fax icon, and then click Add.

   –Or–

   In Microsoft Exchange, on the Tools menu, click Options. Click the Services tab, and then click Add.

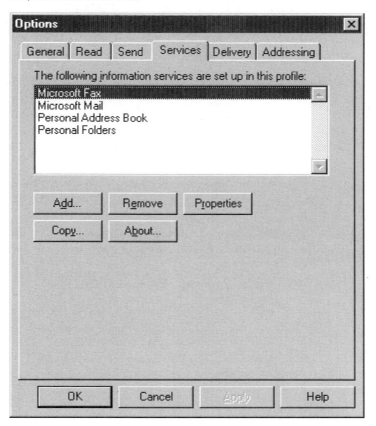

Figure 22.27 Adding services

2. In the Add Services to Profile dialog box, click the service providers you want to add.

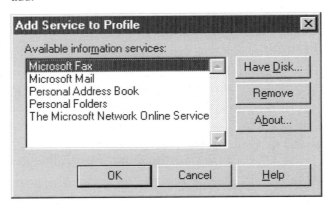

Figure 22.28 Selecting service to add

3. Click OK and specify the information service you want to add.

The service you select determines what specific DLLs are enabled when Microsoft Exchange is started. For example, if the Microsoft Mail service is added, the MSFS32.DLL file in the Windows SYSTEM directory is enabled. To find out which DLLs are loaded for a service, click the name of that service, and then click About.

The information services each provide a Setup wizard which prompts you for any required configuration information.

Tip   When you're troubleshooting Windows 95 mail issues, first remove additional service providers—except Personal Address Book and Personal Folders—and then add each service provider back, one at a time.

Lesson Summary

Windows 95 includes a Microsoft Exchange client. This client can be used to interface with any MAPI-compliant messaging service, including Microsoft Mail. The Microsoft Exchange client supports RTF, which allows you to enhance the look of your mail messages. Support of additional services such as Microsoft Fax can be added as they become available to you.

Review

The following questions are intended to reinforce key information presented in this chapter. If you are unable to answer a question, review the appropriate lesson and then try the question again.

1. What is MAPI?

2. What is the purpose of a message profile?

C H A P T E R   2 3

File Synchronization

Before You Begin

To complete the lessons in this chapter, you must have:

- Completed Chapter 1 and installed Microsoft Windows 95.
- The following files should be installed in the \LABS directory on your computer.

  X.RTF

  Y.RTF

  Z.RTF

  W.RTF

- A floppy disk with at least 50K of free space is also required.

Lesson 1: Briefcase

Briefcase is a utility that updates, synchronizes, and automatically tracks files so that a file from one source is identical to a file from another source. This lesson introduces Briefcase and its functions.

After this lesson you will be able to:

- Explain how Briefcase functions.

Estimated lesson time 5 minutes

Briefcase was designed for the user who needs to work on a file on more than one personal computer and needs to make sure that all versions of the file from all the different sources are the same.

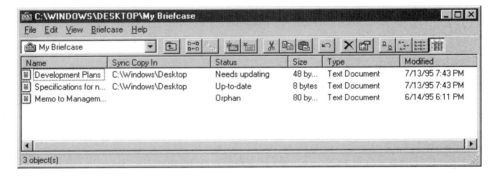

Figure 23.1 Briefcase contents

A salesperson, for example, might need to collect data in certain files during a business trip. Later, it will be important for the files on that salesperson's office computer to match, or synchronize, the files which were changed during the trip. Briefcase synchronizes the files.

With Briefcase, a user can:

- Create a Briefcase folder.
- Check the status of files in Briefcase and their related files.
- Update related files, either individually or all at once.
- Split the connection between related files to maintain them separately.

Note Briefcase is not designed to be shared between multiple users. The design concept was of one user on multiple machines.

How Briefcase Works

At the office desktop, drag copies of the files to be worked on to Briefcase. Briefcase establishes a "sync relationship" between the copy and the original files. Move the entire Briefcase from the desktop computer to a floppy or another hard drive, such as a hard drive on a portable computer. A network directory may also be used, simply choose a network directory that you want to synchronize with, drop it on a Briefcase. Briefcase contains copies of the selected files, not just synchronization information. A directory with 10 MB of files remains 10 MB.

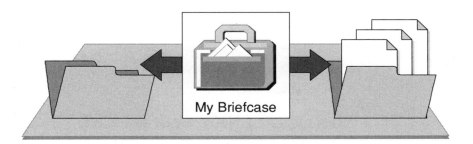

Figure 23.2 Briefcase works by synchronizing complete files

At the new computer, open Briefcase. When you open Briefcase, it goes into Update mode and allows you to synchronize files.

The time/date stamp is the arbitrator that decides which version takes precedence. However, you can select the version to update.

Note While you may have more than one Briefcase on your computer, you can reduce potential confusion if you only create one Briefcase.

Lesson Summary

Briefcase is used to synchronize files that may be worked on in different locations and computers.

Lesson 2: Managing Briefcase

Briefcase is designed to be used easily as a drag and drop application. This lesson explains the steps necessary to fully utilize Briefcase.

After this lesson you will be able to:

- Use Briefcase to synchronize files.

Estimated lesson time 30 minutes

Opening the Briefcase folder presents the administrator with all the menus and programs necessary to:

- Check the status of any file in Briefcase.
- Update the files in Briefcase.
- Split related files.

Briefcase and Network Directories

Briefcase can be used to synchronize with entire network directories. Simply drop the icon for the network directory you want to synchronize with on Briefcase. Briefcase synchronizes the network directory with Briefcase.

Managing Files in Briefcase

Briefcase itself can replace one copy of a file with another, but it can't merge files. The program is responsible for any merging. Briefcase can, however, tell the program when a merge should be done.

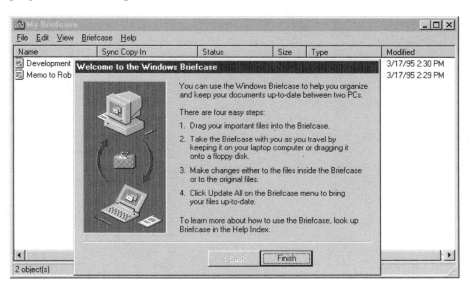

Figure 23.3   Opening Briefcase for the first time

To open Briefcase, double-click the Briefcase icon. If this is the first time you have opened Briefcase, you receive a Welcome screen that contains an explanation on how to use Briefcase.

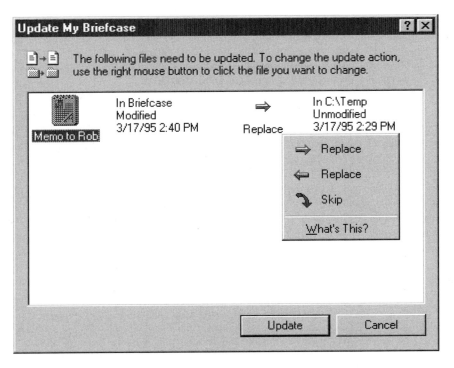

Figure 23.4 Updating a file

To update a file using Briefcase, select the file to update, and from the Briefcase menu, click Update Selection. The Update My Briefcase dialog box appears.

With the secondary mouse button, click the file icon. A dialog box appears with the following choices:

- Replace—Indicates that you want to replace the original file with the updated version in Briefcase.

- Replace—Indicates that you want to replace the version in Briefcase with the original version, which has been updated since the version in Briefcase was copied.

- Skip—Do not do anything about the file being out of synchronization at this time.

You may select multiple files and select the replacement for each, or skip specific files.

Note   A Merge option may be available if the program that created the file supports merging.

Using Briefcase

In this exercise, you will create a Briefcase and populate it with several files from your computer. You will then move the Briefcase to a floppy disk. After you modify some of the existing files, you will synchronize the files on the floppy disk, with the original files still located on your computer.

Briefcase is created on the desktop by default during installation. If Briefcase is missing, you may add one to your desktop.

▶   **To enable Briefcase**

1.   Open Briefcase on the desktop.

2.   Read the directions in the dialog box.

3.   Click the Finish button.

▶   **To populate Briefcase with files**

1.   Locate the Labs folder and open it to reveal four files: W, X, Y, and Z (these are .RTF files).

     Open each file in WordPad to see the data that is currently in the files.

2.   Drag the entire Labs folder to Briefcase and drop it there. This copies all of the files in the folder to Briefcase.

3.   Close the Briefcase window.

▶   **To move Briefcase to another machine**

•   Insert a blank disk in the floppy drive and drag Briefcase to the floppy icon.

     Briefcase should move to the floppy.

Modifying the Contents of Briefcase

The following change relationships will be observed in this part of the exercise.

	Original	Briefcase
File X	Modified	Not Modified
File Y	Not Modified	Modified
File Z	Modified	Modified
File W	Not Modified	Modified

▶ **To modify the contents of file X**

1. Locate the Labs folder on your computer.

2. Open file X in the Labs folder.

3. Select all of the text by pressing CTRL+A.

4. Save the information on the Clipboard by typing CTRL+C.

5. Position the cursor at the end of the file by typing CTRL+END.

6. Paste the information from the Clipboard into this file by typing CTRL+V.

7. Exit the file by typing ALT+F4.

   Be sure to save the changes you have made to the file.

   You have now modified your original file X. You will not be modifying the file X in your Briefcase.

▶ **To modify the contents of file Y**

1. Locate the Labs folder in Briefcase on your floppy disk.

2. Open file Y in the Labs folder.

3. Select all of the text by typing CTRL+A.

4. Save the information onto the Clipboard by typing CTRL+C.

5. Position the cursor at the end of the file by typing CTRL+END.

6. Paste the information by typing CTRL +V.

7. Exit the file by typing ALT+F4.

   Be sure to save the changes you have made to the file.

   You have now modified the copy of file Y in Briefcase. You will not be modifying the original file Y.

▶ **To modify the contents of file Z**

1. Open file Z in the Labs folder and then type in today's date.

2. Save the file in the Labs folder.

3. Open file Z in Briefcase on your floppy disk and then type the name of your company.

4. Save the file in Briefcase.

   You have now modified your original file Z and you have made a different modification to the copy of file Z in your Briefcase.

▶ **To modify the contents of file W**

1. Open file W in Briefcase on your floppy disk.

2. Make a modification to file W by placing the following data at the beginning of the file:

   My name is *[your name]*. I have modified this file.

   Be sure to save the changes you have made to the file.

   You have now modified file W in your Briefcase. You will not modify the original file W.

▶ **To synchronize your files**

1. Drag Briefcase from the floppy back to the desktop.

   Briefcase should move to the desktop.

2. Open Briefcase and click the Update All option on the Briefcase menu.

3. Click the Update button to update the files which can be updated.

4. Click the Update All option again to see what is left.

   File Z is the only file in the dialog box. Because the original and Briefcase copy were both modified, Briefcase cannot decide which direction to copy the file. You can use the secondary mouse button to force a copy in either direction or, if a merge function is defined for the appropriate file type, the merge function can be called. A merge function is not defined for .TXT files.

5. Open each of the files to see the changes.

Lesson Summary

Briefcase allows you to copy, transport, and update multiple version of files while maintaining the version you want.

Lesson 3: Briefcase Internals

In addition to the files you place in Briefcase for synchronizing, there are several other files that Briefcase interacts with. This lesson explains the functions of those files.

After this lesson you will be able to:
- List and describe the function of the files that Briefcase uses.

Estimated lesson time 5 minutes

Briefcase is a folder. Files stored in Briefcase are maintained in their original location. Copies of the files are placed in the Briefcase folder.

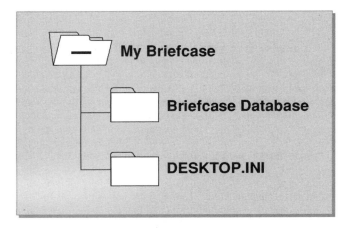

Figure 23.5 Hidden files in Briefcase

Briefcase Files

The Briefcase folder contains the following hidden files.

- Briefcase Database—Contains the date, time, size, status, and the location of the original files in Briefcase at the time they were last synchronized.

- DESKTOP.INI—Contains the OLE registration information for Briefcase and the setting for confirmation.

These files are hidden so that the only files normally seen in Briefcase are the files being synchronized. These files should not be deleted.

To prevent these files from accidentally being deleted, you cannot view these files when in the actual Briefcase, even if you set the view options to show hidden files. You can view these two files using the **attrib** command in a command prompt, or the directory command with show hidden attributes parameters (**dir /a:h**).

The following files are also used by Briefcase and are contained in the System folder.

- SYNCENG.DLL—Checks to determine whether files match.
- LINKINFO.DLL—Keeps track of the path of the files to be updated, adjusts the path to create a universal naming convention (UNC) or volume name depending on the location of Briefcase, for example, in a docked or undocked portable.
- SYNCUI.DLL—Provides the user interface for My Briefcase.

Orphan Files

A copied file that does not have a master file with which to synchronize is called an orphan file. This could be due to the original file being deleted or the file being created inside Briefcase.

Troubleshooting Briefcase

If one of the synchronized files is deleted, the copy in Briefcase is tagged as an orphan. If the original is renamed or moved, the Microsoft Windows 95 link tracking system attempts to keep track of the link. If this is not possible, you must create a new link after you find the file.

Briefcase can and will update files across Remote Access connections. Briefcase automatically makes the remote access connection to the server. However, Briefcase does not hang up the connection. The remote access connection must be disconnected manually.

Lesson Summary

Briefcase is a folder that contains two hidden files. It is important that these files are not deleted. If an original file is moved, Briefcase tries to locate it before tagging the file as an orphan.

Review

The following questions are intended to reinforce key information presented in this chapter. If you are unable to answer a question, review the appropriate lesson and then try the question again.

1. What is the purpose of Briefcase?

    _____

    _____

2. What is an orphan file?

    _____

    _____

CHAPTER 24

Dial-Up Networking Functions

Before You Begin

To complete the lessons in this chapter, you must have:

- Completed Chapter 1 and installed Microsoft Windows 95.
- A null modem or parallel cable in order to complete the Direct Cable Connect exercise. The cable connects the two computers.
- A second computer with Windows 95 installed.
- A modem and phone line if you actually want to dial out, however, the exercises can be completed without them.

Lesson 1: Dial-Up Networking

Dial-Up Networking allows you to connect to your network from a remote location not normally on the network. This lesson explains the features and functions of Dial-Up Networking.

After this lesson you will be able to:

- Describe the features and functions of Dial-Up Networking.

Estimated lesson time 30 minutes

Dial-Up Networking allows you to be a remote node on a network. You may connect to the network using various services and, once connected, you can access all the available network resources. Your computer can be set up to start the connection (Microsoft Dial-Up Networking client) or answer an incoming connection (Dial-Up Networking host).

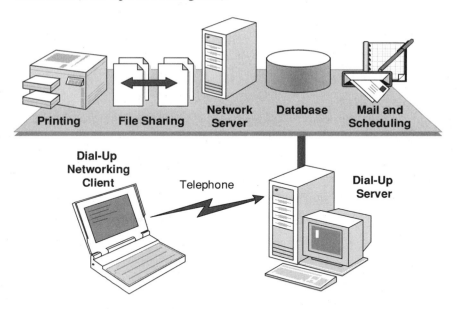

Figure 24.1 Dial-Up Networking allows remote access to network resources

For example, a user may connect to the network from their home through a phone line to the office. When the connection is made, the user can access all network resources as if they were at a computer in the office. Dial-Up Networking can be thought of as turning a modem into a network card.

To be more technically accurate, the Dial-Up Networking server acts as a gateway between the remote client and the network.

Dial-Up Networking Features

Some of the features of Windows 95 Dial-Up Networking service are the following.

- Down-level compatibility—Any Dial-Up Networking client can connect to any Microsoft Windows NT, Microsoft LAN Manager, Microsoft Windows for Workgroups, LAN Manager for UNIX, IBM LAN servers, Shiva® LanRover and other dial-up routers, or other computers supporting either Microsoft RAS, Novell NetWare Connect, Serial Line Internet Protocol (SLIP), or Point-to-Point Protocol (PPP) protocols. SLIP support is included in the CD-ROM release of Windows 95. Dial-Up Networking allows you to use additional protocols on top of these line protocols.

- LAN topology-independent—A Windows 95 Dial-Up Networking server supports all topologies currently supported by Windows 95 including the following:

  - Ethernet
  - Token Ring
  - FDDI
  - ArcNet

- Advanced security—Dial-Up Networking can require that passwords be encrypted to prevent their capture over telephone lines.

- Advanced modem support—Dial-Up Networking supports all modems which work with the Unimodem driver system.

- Compression (hardware or software)—Data sent by means of Dial-Up Networking can be automatically compressed to increase the effective speed of the connection.

- Slow Links—Dial-Up Networking has a "slow link" application programming interface (API) that Windows 95 makes available to programs to indicate to the program if it is running over a slow link.

Caution Dial-Up Networking works best in a situation where the programs are already installed on the remote computer and only the data is downloaded across the communications link. Dial-Up Networking will appear to work slowly if it has to download both the data and the program.

Dial-Up Networking Architecture

The architecture of Dial-Up Networking is a series of layers. When a program needs a remote resource, it sends a request to the interface layer.

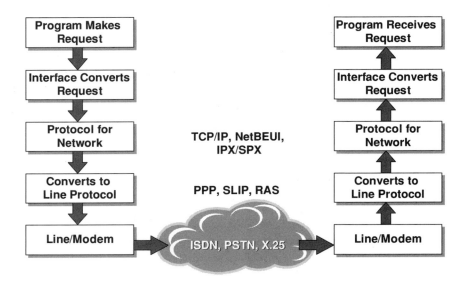

Figure 24.2 Dial-Up Networking architecture

The interface layer converts the request into a request that the network can understand. The request is then passed on to the protocol layer.

The protocol takes the request and packages it in exactly the same way it would on a normal network. It passes the converted request to the line protocol layer.

The line protocol encapsulates the request into a format that can be transmitted across the line and then sends the request to the line.

The line is the actual media that transmits the request. The line may be a modem and phone line combination, a cable connected through serial or parallel ports, or a number of other alternatives.

Supported Network Interfaces

Dial-Up Networking offers full interface support. Any network program that uses any of the following interfaces works over Dial-Up Networking:

- NetBIOS
- Mailslots
- Named pipes
- Remote procedure calls (RPCs)
- LAN Manager APIs
- TCP/IP utilities
- WinSockets

Network Protocols

Dial-Up Networking is protocol independent. The following network protocols are supported by Dial-Up Networking.

- NetBEUI
- IPX/SPX-compatible
- TCP/IP

It is important to note that line protocols support different network protocols.

The Data Link Control (DLC) protocol is supported over Dial-Up Networking as an add-in product.

Note To run Dial-Up Networking, the computer must have a protected-mode client, that is, one that can use the Windows 95 protected-mode transports, or others that use NDIS and provide appropriate PPP drivers. This means that you cannot use a Novell real-mode client over Dial-Up Networking, but you can use Microsoft Client for NetWare Networks.

Troubleshooting Tip: Binding Protocols to a Dial-Up Adapter

To make sure the correct protocols are bound to the Microsoft Dial-Up adapter or other network adapter, in the Network option in the Control Panel, each protocol in the Components list box that is bound to the Microsoft Dial-Up adapter will show an arrow pointing to the adapter.

Line Protocols

Windows 95 Dial-Up Networking supports the following line protocols.

Point-to-Point Protocol (PPP)

Dial-Up Networking is compliant with the industry standard Point-to-Point communications protocol (PPP). PPP is a standard protocol for low-speed access that grew out of the TCP/IP world and is now in common usage. It is a more widely recognized and more flexible standard than the RAS AsyBEUI protocol which it replaces. PPP also has the advantage over SLIP in dynamically assigning IP addresses to clients.

The Dial-Up Networking PPP driver implements a subset of the Link Control Protocol and Network Control Protocols defined by the IETF (Internet Engineering Task Force).

Serial Line Internet Protocol (SLIP)

Serial Line Internet Protocol (SLIP) is an older standard also from the TCP/IP suite. It is currently being phased out in favor of PPP because it is considerably less flexible. Support for SLIP as a client can be found on the Windows 95 CD-ROM in the ADMIN\APPTOOLS\SLIP directory. You can install SLIP by using the Add/Remove Programs option in the Control Panel. Installing SLIP also installs support for CSLIP (SLIP with Compressed IP headers).

Windows NT RAS

The AsyBEUI was used in earlier Microsoft Dial-Up Networking products such as LAN Manager Dial-Up Networking Services (RAS).

NetWare Connect

NetWare Connect is a proprietary connection protocol that allows a Windows 95 client to dial into a NetWare server. The NetWare Connect connection type allows a computer running Windows 95 to directly connect to a NetWare Connect server and, if running a NetWare-compatible network client, connect to NetWare servers. Windows 95 can only act as a client for connecting to a NetWare Connect server. NetWare Connect clients themselves cannot connect to a Windows 95 Dial-Up Networking server directly through Dial-Up Networking. Only the IPX/SPX (with or without NetBIOS enabled over IPX/SPX) network protocol can be used with NetWare Connect.

Multiple Protocols

Because Windows 95 can accommodate multiple protocols, Dial-Up Networking can coexist with other protocols loaded on top of it.

Connection protocols	Network protocols (APIs)
NetWare Connect	IPX/SPX (Windows Sockets/NetBIOS)
PPP	TCP/IP (Windows Sockets/NetBIOS) IPX/SPX (Windows Sockets/NetBIOS) NetBEUI (NetBIOS)
RAS for Windows NT 3.1 or Windows for Workgroups 3.11	NetBEUI (NetBIOS)
SLIP	TCP/IP (Windows Sockets/NetBIOS)

Note You do not need to install any network protocols when you install Dial-Up Networking; NetBEUI and the IPX/SPX-compatible protocol are automatically installed and bound to the Microsoft Dial-Up adapter. You can add protocols by using the Network option in the Control Panel.

Troubleshooting Tip: PPP Log File

You can record how the PPP layers process a call by enabling the PPPLOG file. This file contains some of the basic layers and points of any Dial-Up Networking session, and is especially useful for monitoring PPP sessions. It is recorded and stored in the Windows directory.

For more information on the PPP dial-up sequence, see Appendix E, "PPP Dial-Up Sequence."

▶ **To enable PPP logging**

1. In the Control Panel, double-click the Network icon, and then double-click Dial-Up Adapter on the list of installed network components.

2. In the Dial-Up Adapter property sheet, click the Advanced tab. On the Property list, click the option named Record a log file, and on the Value list, click Yes. Click OK.

3. Shut down and restart the computer for these settings to take effect.

The following is sample content of a PPPLOG.TXT file:

Sample PPPLOG.TXT

09-01-1994 18:14:22 - Remote access driver log opened.

09-01-1994 18:14:22 - Server type is PPP (Point-to-Point Protocol).

09-01-1994 18:14:22 - CCP : Layer initialized.

09-01-1994 18:14:22 - NBFCP : Layer initialized.

09-01-1994 18:14:22 - FSA : Control protocol 2180 will not be negotiated.

09-01-1994 18:14:22 - IPXCP : Layer initialized.

09-01-1994 18:14:22 - FSA : Encrypted password required.

09-01-1994 18:14:22 - LCP : Layer initialized.

09-01-1994 18:14:22 - LCP : Will try to negotiate callback.

09-01-1994 18:14:22 - LCP : Layer started.

09-01-1994 18:14:22 - LCP : Received and accepted ACCM of 0.

WAN Support

Dial-Up Networking runs over the modem mini-driver and telephony application programming interface (TAPI) interfaces and supports the same types of communication lines.

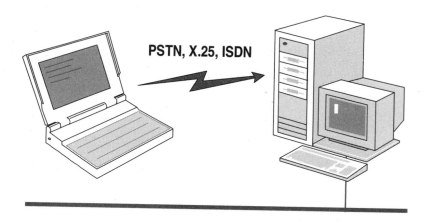

Figure 24.3 Supported WANs

Public Switched Telephone Networks (PSTN)

Windows 95 Dial-Up Networking uses normal modem connections over Public Switched Telephone Networks. This is the normal phone service for most of the world.

X.25

An X.25 network transmits data with a packet-switching protocol. This protocol relies on an elaborate worldwide network of packet-forwarding nodes that participate in delivering an X.25 packet to the correct address. Locally, a device called a Packet Assembler/Disassembler (PAD) is used in place of a modem.

Integrated Services Digital Network (ISDN)

ISDN is a series of standards for digital telephony. ISDN offers much faster communication speed than a standard analog telephone line. ISDN communicates at speeds of 64 to 128 kilobits per second.

Clients

There are various client, server, and protocol configurations that can be used with Dial-Up Networking.

This server type	Connects to
PPP: Windows 95, Windows NT 3.5, Internet	This is the default. Selecting this allows Windows 95 to automatically detect and connect to other remote access servers that are running TCP/IP, NetBEUI, or IPX/SPX over PPP.
NRN: NetWare Connect	Novell NetWare Connect running IPX/SPX over NetWare Connect (Note: You must be running user-level security.)
Windows for Workgroups and Windows NT 3.1	Windows 95 Dial-Up server; Windows NT version 3.1 or 3.5x; Windows for Workgroups version 3.11 running NetBEUI over RAS.
SLIP: UNIX Connection	Any SLIP server over TCP/IP.

Modem Support

Dial-Up Networking supports any modem supported by the new mini-port driver including generic AT command set modems.

Dial-Up Networking provides support for advanced features in modems, such as MNP/5 and V.42bis compression, and error control. In addition, RTS/CTS and XON/XOFF software flow control are supported.

Windows 95 Dial-Up Networking supports a variety of modems. Check the Windows 95 Hardware Compatibility List for the current list.

Flow Control and Compression

A key feature of Dial-Up Networking is its recognition of flow control, which regulates data traffic between communication devices. This feature is essential in implementing modem hardware error-correction and data compression.

Dial-Up Networking supports the following forms of error correction:

- v.42bis and MNP/5 compression
- v.42 error correction

Windows NT clients, Windows NT Server, and Windows for Workgroups version 3.11 currently implement support for flow control. There is no support for flow control (or software compression) in the MS-DOS RAS client software.

Dial-Up Networking supports any modem supported by mini-port drivers.

Lesson Summary

Dial-Up Networking allows your computer to become a remote node on a network using a variety of connection methods.

Lesson 2: Creating a Dial-Up Networking Connection

Once you create a Dial-Up Network connection, you can reestablish the connection by clicking the icon. This lesson explains the process of creating a Dial-Up Networking connection.

After this lesson you will be able to:
- Create a dial-up connection.

Estimated lesson time 15 minutes

Dial-Up Networking is installed automatically as part of a default installation. If it was not initially installed it can be added by using the Add/Remove Programs icon in the Control Panel. On the Add/Remove Programs property sheet, click the Windows Setup tab, and then double-click Communications. Make sure that Dial-Up Networking is selected, and then click OK.

Requirements

The Windows 95 Dial-Up Networking service requires:

- One or more compatible modems.

  See the Windows 95 Hardware Compatibility List for a complete list of compatible modems.

- About 2 MB of free disk space to install the client, server, and administration portions of Dial-Up Networking.

Installation

Installing Dial-Up Networking consists of two parts.

1. Setting up the modem (refer to Chapter 13, "Communications," for information on setting up modems).

2. Creating a connection.

You can complete these parts individually or at the same time. The modem may be installed from the Control Panel or you can install a modem when you first set up Dial-Up Networking.

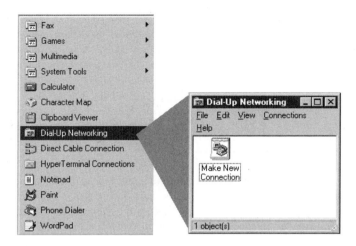

Figure 24.4 Dial-Up Networking on the Accessories menu

You can reach the Dial-Up Networking folder by clicking the Start menu button, pointing to Programs, Accessories, and then clicking Dial-Up Networking.

▶ **To create a connection**

1. From the Dial-Up Networking folder, double-click the New Connection icon.

Note If this is your first time activating Dial-Up Networking, you will not have a New Connection icon. When you double-click the Dial-Up Networking folder, the New Connection wizard starts.

The New Connection wizard starts.

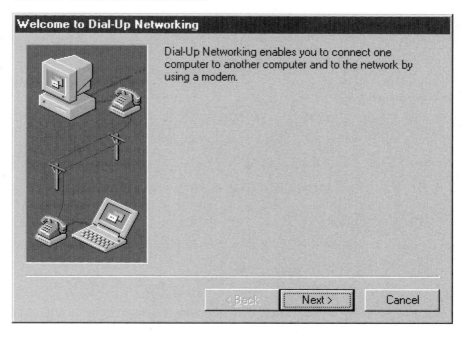

Figure 24.5 Starting Dial-Up Networking

2. Click the Next button.

The Make New Connection dialog box appears.

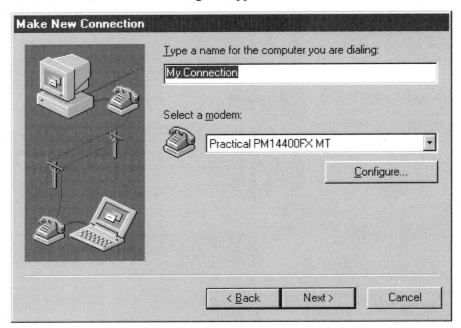

Figure 24.6 Specifying a new connection in the Make New Connection dialog box

3. Enter the name of the computer you are dialing.
4. Select a modem.

5. Click Next.

You are prompted for the phone number of the computer.

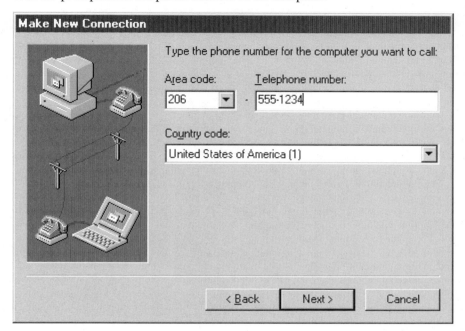

Figure 24.7 Specifying a phone number in the Make New Connection dialog box

6. Enter the area code, phone number, and country code.

7. Click the Next button.

The confirmation information displays.

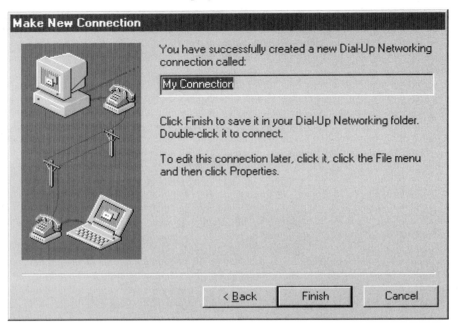

Figure 24.8 New connection complete dialog box

8. Click the Finish button to complete the creation of the new connection.

You may be prompted to provide a driver. When the files are finished copying, an icon for the new connection appears in your Dial-Up Networking folder.

Figure 24.9 Dial-Up Networking folder with new connection added

As part of the Windows 95 Setup process, existing Dial-Up Networking System or other communication programs are updated.

Because Dial-Up Networking treats your modem as an additional network card and needs the PPP protocol, these need to be installed. You do not need to do this manually because the Dial-Up Networking Setup wizard installs it for you.

Lesson Summary

Creating a Dial-Up Network connection is simply a matter of following the prompts in the New Connection wizard.

Lesson 3: Connecting with Dial-Up Networking

You can use Dial-Up Networking to connect as a client or server to remote networks. However, to function as a server requires the installation of the Microsoft Plus! for Windows 95 pack. This lesson explains the procedures on how to make these connections.

After this lesson you will be able to:

- Implement Dial-Up Networking as both a client and server on a Microsoft Windows 95-based computer.

Estimated lesson time 15 minutes

Once a connection is created, you can implement the connection by double-clicking the icon.

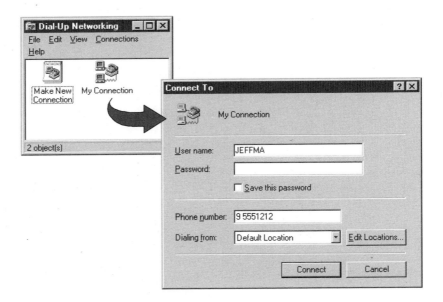

Figure 24.10 Connecting with Dial-Up Networking

▶ **To connect to a remote computer using Dial-Up Networking**

   1. Double-click the icon representing the desired connection.

   The Connect To dialog box appears.

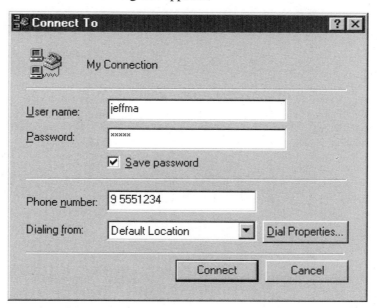

Figure 24.11 The Connect To dialog box

   Verify that the information is correct. If the information is not correct, enter the appropriate information.

   2. Click the Connect button.

   Dial-Up Networking dials the number indicated.

Figure 24.12 Dialing status

Once the connection is made, the display changes to indicate the speed of the connection and how long you have been connected.

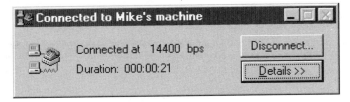

Figure 24.13 Connection status

If you want additional details about the connection, click the Details button. The dialog box expands to indicate the server type and the protocols that are available.

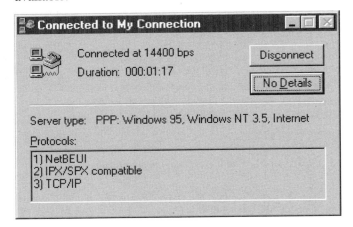

Figure 24.14 Server types

This information is useful when troubleshooting Dial-Up Networking connections. Both ends of the connection need to have at least one protocol in common.

Dial-Up Server

Microsoft Plus! for Windows 95 includes the option of using your computer as a Dial-Up server.

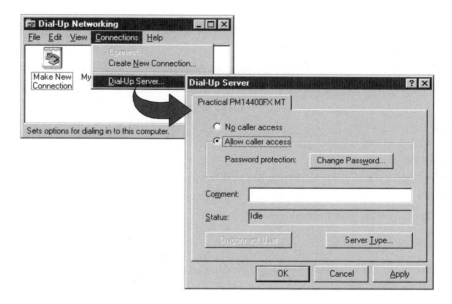

Figure 24.15 Dial-Up Server

The Dial-Up Networking administrator can either allow or not allow callers to access the computer. This is done through the Dial-Up Server choice on the Connections menu of the Dial-Up Networking window as shown in figure 24.15. This configuration is specific to each computer.

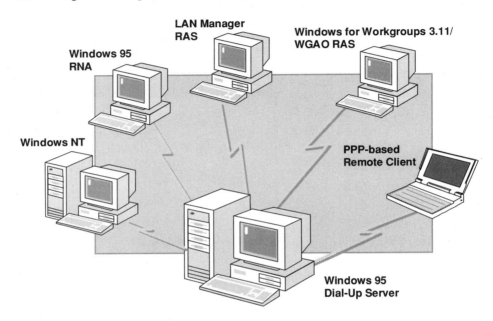

Figure 24.16 Connections available to Dial-Up Server

A Windows 95 Dial-Up Server cannot act as a gateway to a SLIP or IPX network. It can act as a gateway to Windows 95, LAN Manager RAS, Windows for Workgroups 3.11, Windows NT, and PPP-based clients.

Server Types

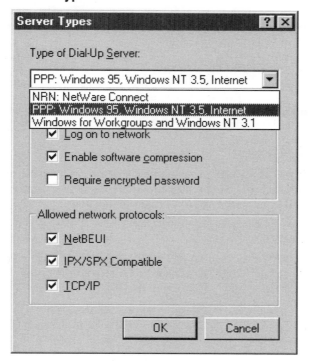

Figure 24.17 Dial-Up Server types

The Windows 95 Dial-Up Server supports the following remote access clients:

- Windows 95 Dial-Up client
- Windows for Workgroups
- Point-to-Point Protocol
- Windows 3.1 RAS client
- Windows NT version 3.1 (RAS)
- Default—Allows for negotiation of protocols.

Lesson Summary

Dial-Up Networking allows you to connect as a client to remote networks.
Microsoft Plus! for Windows 95 has the software that allows your computer to
become a Dial-Up network server.

Lesson 4: Dial-Up Networking Issues

Dial-Up Networking brings up several issues you need to consider before implementing it on your corporate network. This lesson discusses these issues.

After this lesson you will be able to:
- Determine the level of Dial-Up Networking security appropriate for a given site.

Estimated lesson time 10 minutes

Security Issues

Whenever you allow for dial-up access, you always have the possibility that someone may try and enter your computer without authorization. There are steps you can take to minimize the risks of this happening.

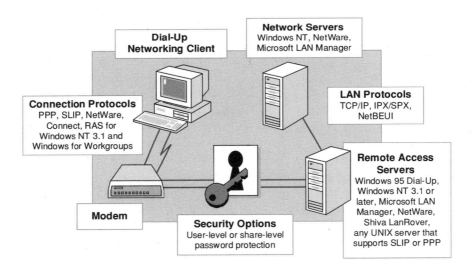

Figure 24.18 Security options

When setting up a dial-up access, there are several security issues you should consider.

- On the server side, you should be using user-level security.

- If you determine that you need additional security, Windows 95 supports hardware security tools from other vendors for dial-up access, and authentication protocols such as Challenge-Handshake Authentication Protocol (CHAP) and Shiva Password Authentication Protocol (SPAP).

Note The CHAP server sends a random challenge to the client. The client encrypts the challenge with the user's password and sends it back to the server. This prevents someone from gaining access by recording the authentication and playing it back to the server. Because the challenge is different on each call, a recorded sequence would fail.

SPAP is a version of PAP implemented by Shiva in their remote client software. SPAP allows you to authenticate with existing Shiva servers. Implementation is a reversible encryption scheme. It is not as secure as CHAP, but it is more secure than PAP.

- You can prevent users from remotely accessing computers even if a remote connection has been previously established. You can restrict access by making direct changes to a computer's dial-up support capabilities or by using System Policy Editor to create a policy file.

- Use encrypted passwords.

- If you are on the Internet, you should disable your file and printer sharing.

- Consider the use of fire walls to separate dial-up access from the rest of the Internet.

- Consider using an encryption program to encrypt your data when sent across the Internet.

Improving Data Transfer Performance

The time is takes to transfer data across phone lines may be an area of frustration. There are several things you can do to improve data transfer rates.

Software and Hardware Compression

To improve the throughput and transfer times when you use Dial-Up Networking, Windows 95 supports dynamic compression of information when you are connected to another computer that also understands compression—for example, a computer running Windows 95 or Windows NT.

You can choose to use either *software compression* (specified through the Dial-Up Server dialog box) or *hardware compression*. Software compression is performed by the remote access software; hardware compression is performed by the modem.

Choosing software compression specifies that your computer will try to compress information before sending it. Compression will occur only if the computer you are connecting to is using a compatible compression program.

Note Software compression is supported only in PPP mode, not in RAS, NetWare Connect, or SLIP modes. Software compression is enabled by default in PPP mode and is preferred over hardware compression because it reduces the amount of information that needs to be transmitted to the modem.

Use System Monitor

System Monitor can be used to help determine areas that can be improved.

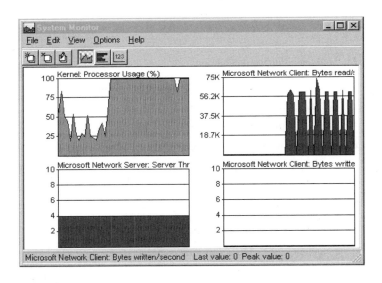

Figure 24.19 Using System Monitor to determine performance

Add the following to System Monitor to help gauge performance:

- Microsoft or Novell server threads to check performance of the server
- Microsoft Client: Bytes read/second
- Microsoft Client: Bytes written/second

Implicit Connections

Dial-Up Networking in Windows 95 can "remember" network connections in a process similar to ghosting network connections.

If you try to access a network resource when you are not connected to any network, you are prompted to select a Remote Connector. The connector you select is used to start a Remote Network session. Once the session is established, the network operation you initiated resumes to completion. If the network operation completes successfully, Windows 95 stores the connection you have chosen and recalls it in future operations that use the same network resource.

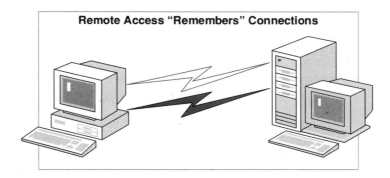

Figure 24.20 Implicit connections

Implicit connections leaves a "ghost" mapping which reconnects when you need to use the resource. If you don't need to use the resource, the connection remains inactive.

Implicit connections are basically a convenience so you don't have to keep reconnecting to resources each time you want to use them.

Lesson Summary

Before you implement Dial-Up Networking, you need to consider the security risks of allowing users to dial in to your network.

You can use System Monitor to determine if there is anything you can do to improve data transfer performance.

Lesson 5: Direct Cable Connection

The Direct Cable Connection program allows you to directly connect two computers using a serial or parallel cable. This lesson explains how to use this program to transfer data between two computers.

After this lesson you will be able to:

- Configure Direct Cable Connection as a host or guest.
- Transfer data between two computers using Direct Cable Connection.

Estimated lesson time 15 minutes

One of the programs included with Windows 95 is Direct Cable Connection (DIRECTCC.EXE). This program allows you to directly connect two computers using a serial or parallel cable. The program can be found in the Windows folder.

▶ **To prepare the Host machine**

1. Using Windows Explorer, click the My Computer icon, and then share the DOS folder.

2. On the Start menu, point to Programs, Accessories, and then click Direct Cable Connection.

A dialog box appears asking you if your computer will be the Host or the Guest.

Host—Computer that has the resources you want to use.

Guest—Computer accessing the resources.

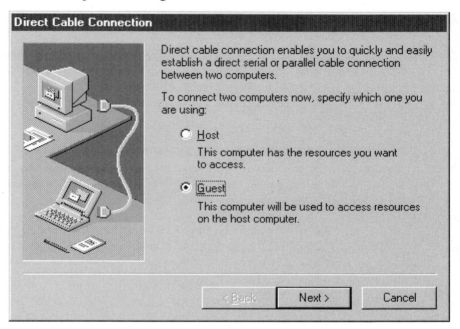

Figure 24.21 Starting Direct Cable Connection

Note You must run the Direct Cable Connection program on both the Host and Guest computers.

---

3. Click Host, and then click the Next button.

    A Configuring Ports message box appears for a few moments followed by a dialog box.

    The dialog box prompts you to select the port you want to use, a parallel cable or a serial cable.

4. Click the correct cable, and then click Next.

5. The next dialog box asks you to set up an optional password. If you decide to enter a password, just follow the on-screen directions. Close the dialog box by clicking the Finish button.

    A Direct Cable Connection dialog box appears informing you that this machine is waiting for a guest.

▶ **To prepare the Guest machine for the DIRECTCC lab**

1. On the Start menu, point to Programs, Accessories, and then click Direct Cable Connection.

   A dialog box appears asking you if your computer will be the Host or the Guest.

2. Click Guest, and then click the Next button.

   A Configuring Ports message box appears for a few moments followed by a dialog box. The dialog box prompts you to select the port you want to use, a parallel cable or a serial cable.

3. Click the correct cable, and then click Next.

4. Close the dialog box by clicking the Finish button.

   A message box appears informing you that this machine is trying to connect to a host.

5. Once the connection is established, use Windows Explorer to examine the host computer.

Once this program is running on both computers, they connect with each other. The guest computer can then access any resources on the Host computer. The resource appears as a drive, so Windows Explorer may be used to copy files.

Serial Cables

Direct Cable Connection supports two different types of serial cables:

- Standard null-modem cables
- Serial file transfer cables

The Null-Modem Connection

If you choose to use a null-modem cable, it should have the following pin-outs.

9-Pin to 9-Pin

Remote host serial port connector	Calling system serial port	Signal
Connect 3 to	2	Transmit Data
Connect 2 to	3	Receive Data
Connect 7 to	8	Request to Send
Connect 8 to	7	Clear to Send
Connect 6 to	4	Data Set Ready and Data Carrier Detected
Connect 5 to	5	Data Terminal Ready
Connect 4 to	1	Data Terminal Ready

25-Pin to 25-Pin Null-Modem Cabling

Remote host serial port connector	Calling system serial port	Signal
Connect 2 to	3	Transmit Data
Connect 3 to	2	Receive Data
Connect 4 to	5	Request to Send
Connect 5 to	4	Clear to Send
Connect 6, 8 to	20	Data Set Ready and Data Carrier Detected
Connect 7 to	7	Ground
Connect 20 to	6	Data Terminal Ready

Lesson Summary

You can transfer data between two computers using a serial or parallel cable and the Direct Cable Connection program.

Review

The following questions are intended to reinforce key information presented in this chapter. If you are unable to answer a question, review the appropriate lesson and then try the question again.

1. What are the three protocols supported by Dial-Up Networking?

2. How would a user increase security on a dial-in machine running Windows 95?

3. What is an implicit connection?

CHAPTER 25

Transitioning to Windows 95

Before You Begin

To complete the lessons in this chapter, you must have:

- Completed Chapter 1 and installed Microsoft Windows 95.

- Microsoft MS-DOS real-mode network client software.

- Some of the exercises for this lesson require the use of two computers. One computer is the server, the other is the client.

  The server computer is used to hold the installation files. Make sure there is enough space on the hard drive to hold these files (there should be at least 70 MB of available hard drive space).

- Record the following information; it will be required in the following exercises.

  Server path   _____

  Computer name for client   _____

  Path to home directory   _____

  Free disk space on local hard drive _____

Lesson 1: Planning the Transition

There are a variety of issues to consider before beginning the transition to Windows 95. This lesson describes some methods to use when planning to transition a large group of users to Windows 95.

After this lesson you will be able to:

- Create a transition plan.
- Explain how to test a transition plan.

Estimated lesson time 45 minutes

Issues and Challenges Involved in a Major Transition

Some of the key pieces to consider when planning your transition include:

- The number of users
- The variety of equipment
- The varied levels of experience
- The fear of a new environment
- Politics
- Unrealistic expectations
- The number and types of computers in the new environment
- The information routes and security issues

A Transition Model

The *Deployment Planning Guide* included with the *Microsoft Windows 95 Migration Planning Kit* suggests a nine-step plan for rolling out Windows 95 in a large organization. In all but the largest companies, you will probably want to simplify this plan, but the basic strategy is still a good guide.

These are the steps involved:

- Review resources for the transition
- Review Windows 95
- Assemble the planning team and tools
- Specify the preferred network client configuration

- Conduct the lab test
- Plan the pilot rollout
- Conduct the pilot rollout
- Finalize the rollout plan
- Rollout Windows 95

Review Resources for the Transition

The *Windows 95 Migration Planning Kit* CD-ROM includes many tools that can help plan your transition to Windows 95.

Deployment Planning Guide

The *Deployment Planning Guide* provides an introduction to Windows 95 designed to familiarize you with areas of the product that may require planning to implement optimally. It also contains the *Corporate Planning Guide* which discusses the rollout plan described in this chapter.

Windows 95 Business Analysis Tools

In case you need to analyze the business case for transitioning to Windows 95, the *Windows Migration Planning Kit* CD-ROM includes a Microsoft Excel workbook which performs the cost analysis for upgrading an organization to Windows 95. The workbook includes instructions to help you modify it to meet your site needs or to change assumptions. You need Microsoft Excel version 5.0 or later to run this model.

Windows 95 Deployment Plan

Included on the *Windows Migration Planning Kit* CD-ROM is the Business Analysis Tools set. This includes a Microsoft Project template with a full rollout plan described along with a set of Cue Cards that will step you through modifying the template for your site. You need Microsoft Project version 4.0 or later to run this model.

Review Windows 95

In addition to completing this course, there are other resources you can use to become familiar with Windows 95.

Read *Introducing Microsoft Windows 95*

This book is available from Microsoft Press and contains information about the Windows 95 interface, architecture, and so on.

Review the Business Case for Windows 95

Some items that may be worth reviewing are:

- Gartner Group, Inc. Reports
- Usability Sciences Corporation Report

Highlights of these studies are included in the *Deployment Planning Guide.*

Acquire the *Microsoft Windows 95 Resource Kit*

Although it is not likely that you will read the full resource kit, it is an invaluable reference book for technical details on Windows 95. It is available from Microsoft Press.

Read *Inside Windows 95*

Inside Windows 95 provides a look at the internal design and architecture of the operating system. This book, by Adrian King, is also available from Microsoft Press.

Assemble the Planning Team and Tools

Arrange for the personnel and test equipment.

Assign the Project Manager and Staff the Planning Team

The deployment project manager participates in the executive team and leads the planning team. This individual is usually the head of the Information Systems department; however, the executive committee may find another individual who is more appropriate to head the team, depending on the organization.

When setting up the planning team, it is important to include a set of individuals representing the groups involved in the deployment process. This includes people from the Corporate Support and Employee Training departments, the Corporate Standards Committee, and key Installation team members. Individuals from the Finance and Accounting group need to take part in planning and evaluation later on, but need not be assigned to the team for the full duration of the deployment process.

Acquire Windows 95

The CD-ROM version of Windows 95 is the preferred version. It is more convenient to work with than the floppy version and contains additional tools useful for working with Windows 95 in a larger organization.

Inventory Client and Server Hardware and Software Configurations

You need to survey a representative sample of your network to compile an inventory of hardware and software used on client and server computers. When this inventory is compiled, you can accurately simulate the organizational environment in the lab. Such a simulation helps you make broad decisions about your company's computing infrastructure, such as the choice of protocol or the default desktop configuration as it pertains to programs.

Software management tools can be used to query computers on the network for hardware and software configurations. For example, the Microsoft Diagnostics (MSD) tool can run a report for output to a text file, describing a computer's specific hardware and settings. For more detailed information about a large number of computers on a network, you can use system management programs, such as the Microsoft Systems Management Server, to conduct the inventory.

Set Up a Testing Lab and Equipment

To effectively evaluate and test the Windows 95 installation process, you need to set aside enough physical space and assemble a sufficient number of computers to test everything from Server-Based Setup to hand-tuning options for the local computer. In addition, if your network environment includes the use of portable computers that dial in to the company, or if you use additional servers or mainframe computers for business data, you want to ensure that the lab computers have full access to the network and an analog phone line. It is important that you test and implement all of the Windows 95 features comprehensively in the lab with all of your business-specific programs before moving to the pilot installation.

Installation of Windows 95 on a server requires 90 MB of disk space.

Specify the Preferred Network Client Configuration

Planning the client configuration requires that you keep several things in mind.

Configuration Layout

When deciding where to place Windows 95 files, consider how the computer will be used and evaluate the benefits of each placement option. If the computers are personal workstations, portable computers that occasionally connect to the network, or are used in workgroups that only share data and programs such as word processors, but not operating system software, then you might want to install Windows 95 program files and programs on the local hard disk and run them locally. Swapfiles and TEMP files are also located on the local hard disk. The network is used only to store commonly used data.

On the other hand, if you want to run a shared copy of Windows 95 to reduce the hardware requirements for the network computers to allow users to access more than one computer, and to provide a central location for managing users' computer configurations, then install Windows 95 files so that Windows 95 program files and programs run from the network. All data is saved on the network. Swapfiles and TEMP directories can be placed on network drives.

32-bit Protected Mode

You need to determine if all your network clients, protocols and adapter drivers are available in 32-bit protected mode versions. Even if you cannot use a full 32-bit protected mode implementation of all the components, you should try to use them wherever possible.

Features for Network Clients

Before installing a large number of client computers, it is important to determine which options will be installed and how they are to be configured.

Using System Policies

If system policies will be used in your installation, you should determine what policy choices will be used. This includes evaluating the ADMIN.ADM policy template and from there, either using it unchanged or modified, or creating your own .ADM template.

Once the question of .ADM templates is resolved, you should determine how users, computers, and groups will be set up. While a bad choice at this point is correctable with the automatic update facility, any template used should be fully tested before the rollout.

Using User Profiles

If user profiles are to be used either locally or to support roving users, this should be planned prior to the rollout as well. It is particularly important that roving user plans be done prior to the rollout to make sure that network resources are allocated and server load is planned.

Enabling Remote Administration

Because full remote administration requires the installation of additional services such as Remote Registry or SNMP agent software, you should design your Setup to enable the installation and configuration of these features.

Using Setup Scripts for Windows 95 Setup

In any installation of more than five computers, it is advantageous to customize the Setup scripts used in Windows 95 Setup to automatically install the options and configuration choices you need. This is especially critical if you are planning a "push" installation.

Using Push Installations for Windows 95 Setup

In organizations with more than 50 computers, it is advised that you design a *push installation* process.

A push installation is when the installation is sent, or *pushed*, onto the target computer from a remote site rather than being initiated from the target computer and *pulled* down from the server. There are several choices available here ranging from setting up a network login script to run a batch Setup, to using Systems Management Server to perform an intelligent push install. In any of these cases, a push install will be cost effective by reducing the hands-on time needed.

Using Peer Resource Sharing Services

If you are planning on restricting the peer sharing services on some of your computers, this should be done prior to the installation.

Using User-Level Security

In most installations large enough to need a roll-out plan, the Windows 95-based computers will be set up using user-level security so that the centralized security administration can be maintained. The choices of security type and security provider should be made prior to rollout.

Using Microsoft Exchange Mail and Microsoft Fax

If your installation site has an electronic mail system compatible with MAPI 1.0, you should consider using the Microsoft Exchange mail client, included with Windows 95 as your mail client. You should plan and test this at this stage as well so that any configuration changes needed can be built into the Setup script.

If the installation site does not have an existing electronic mail system, this is an excellent opportunity to set one up without disrupting staff computers another time.

This is also an excellent time to plan remote mail and fax support for laptop users. The Microsoft Exchange mail client supports remote preview and downloading of mail by means of Dial-Up Networking.

Using Dial-Up Networking

If you have users working from home who have an existing Microsoft Windows NT RAS or PPP, Novell NetWare Connect, Shiva NetModem or other dial-up server, or users who spend time on business trips away from the office, you may want to plan your dial-up networking. Implementing this may be a factor in determining which network protocols you decide to support.

Using The Microsoft Network

The Microsoft Network online service offers chat capability, information bulletin boards, and electronic mail. It is the best place to obtain Microsoft product information and technical support.

Using Disk Management Tools

You may also want to plan a disk compression strategy at this time. This is particularly useful when dealing with laptop computers, which often have limited ability to increase hard disk size.

Conduct the Lab Test

Before installing Windows 95 on every computer in your corporation, you should perform a lab test on smaller groups of sample equipment.

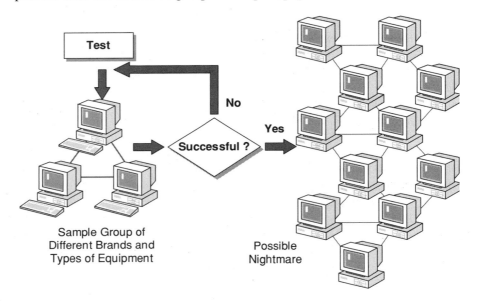

Figure 25.1 Test small, sample groups to reduce problems with larger installations

Prepare the Test Site

Preparing the site involves ensuring that the location of each computer, the computer itself, and particularly the hard disk are all ready for Windows 95 to be installed. In terms of the physical site, ensure that you have the appropriate jacks for connecting to the network.

In terms of the computer itself, ensure that it has the appropriate hard disk space, RAM of at least 4 MB, but 8 MB is recommended, and processor (386DX or higher) to run Windows 95.

In addition, run virus detection, disk scanning, and defragmentation programs on the computer to correct any problems prior to installation. Although the computer may appear to be operating properly, software upgrades often uncover hardware or software problems because of the way they read and write data to the hard disk. Correct any problems before installing Windows 95.

Lastly, when preparing the site, be sure to back up critical data and configuration files for the computer. This includes backing up .INI files such as WIN.INI and SYSTEM.INI, .GRP files, AUTOEXEC.BAT, CONFIG.SYS, and all key data files. As an added precaution, create a system startup disk and back up the Windows and MS-DOS directories, and all the files in the root directory.

It is also recommended that you run MSD.EXE from the hard disk to create a Microsoft Diagnostics (MSD) report and copy it to a floppy disk. If you need to automate the restoration, consider using a commercial backup program, instead of copying the files by hand.

Install Windows 95 on Test Computers

After verifying that the test computers are working correctly, including a full test of their network systems, you should install Windows 95 on them. Be sure to note any input and configuration changes that you may want to put into your batch .INF Setup scripts.

Test the Installation

After you set up a computer with Windows 95, you need to run a variety of tests to ensure that it runs correctly on your network and that you can still perform all of your usual tasks. Use your own testing methodology or test the following to verify correct computer operation:

- Connect to and browse the network.
- Set up a printer and test printing to local and network printers.
- Open, run, and close programs on both the client computer and the server.
- Shut down completely.

In addition to ensuring that the preferred client configuration works as expected, you may also want to conduct additional testing of the optional software features and components in Windows 95. This can help you determine whether you are running Windows 95 optimally. For this kind of testing, conduct side-by-side evaluations on two computers, changing individual features on each one, to determine the following:

- Performance in terms of responsiveness and throughput
- Ease of use

- Stability
- Compatibility
- Functionality

To evaluate network client software for Novell NetWare, run your network performance tests in the following configurations:

- Windows 95 installed with an existing 16-bit, Novell-supplied workstation client (NETX), using ODI drivers
- Windows 95 added to an existing installation of Windows 3.x and NetWare, using Microsoft Client for NetWare Networks and protected-mode networking support components (NDIS adapter drivers)
- Windows 95 as a new installation using all protected-mode components, including both Client for NetWare Networks and Microsoft Client for Microsoft Networks, plus peer resource sharing support

Perform several common tasks such as connecting to the network, administering a remote NetWare server, and so on to test for ease of use. Similarly, you need to run any business-specific NetWare programs under Microsoft Client for NetWare Networks to ensure that they run compatibly. Any stability issues should become apparent during this testing.

Test the Restoration Process

Having thoroughly tested the preferred network client, completely restore one of the test computers to the previous client configuration and document the process. The degree to which you need to test and restore the computer depends on the tools at your disposal.

Plan the Pilot Rollout

You should plan and conduct a pilot rollout on a small scale first.

Install the Source Files for Setup

You need to designate a network server that will be used as the source file installing Windows 95 over the network using custom Setup scripts. Then use Server-Based Setup to install Windows 95 source files on a server. This program is available only on the CD-ROM version of Windows 95, in the ADMIN\NETTOOLS\NETSETUP directory.

You must make choices based on your client configuration, including whether client computers will run a shared copy of Windows 95 from the server or run Windows 95 locally from the hard disk.

Automate the Installation

Automating the installation consists of creating a Setup script, setting up Windows 95 on the server, and creating a push installation process.

With a Setup script you can perform a "hands-free" installation, so that the user need not respond to any prompts or even touch the computer during Windows 95 Setup.

Setting up Windows 95 on the server requires the Server-Based Setup program (NETSETUP.EXE) from the Windows 95 installation CD-ROM. Installing Windows 95 source files on the server is a separate and distinct process from the Windows 95 Setup program (SETUP.EXE) that you ran in the initial exercise installation.

When you run Server-Based Setup to install source files on the server, you can also create a default Setup script, and you can specify whether the Windows 95 source files on the server will be used to set up Windows 95 to run locally from a single computer, or to run a shared copy from the server for client computers that require a shared installation.

In addition, you may want to manually add other files to the shared directory on the server, such as custom bitmaps for screens or a predefined WKGRP.INI file for workgroup organization, so that client computers are fully configured when Windows 95 is installed.

Creating a push installation process involves doing some final work on the server, such as editing the login script for the user, or sending a link in electronic mail to a batch file that runs Windows 95 Setup, so that the user only needs to log on or double-click an icon to start the installation. System management software such as Microsoft Systems Management Server can also be used to start the installation centrally.

Document the Logistics of a Pilot Installation

This involves determining the timing and the process for pilot installation, choosing the pilot user group, and communicating to the group about the pilot rollout.

Although you are just testing the installation process, the first pilot sets the tone and presents an example of the final rollout, so it is important to be completely prepared with all aspects of the rollout. This requires that you determine the time it will take for installation, the personnel and tools needed to facilitate the process, and the overall schedule.

When determining the installation time for the pilot rollout, base the projections on how long it takes for installation of an individual computer; remember to schedule the downtime for each user. Also, in obtaining tools for the pilot rollout, you may want to include management software that can help automate the installation.

The following list identifies critical considerations for the pilot rollout:

- Do you have a list of the target computers?
  - Has each computer been backed up?
  - Has an MSD report been run?
  - Have passwords been reset for CMOS, the network, and programs?
  - Have virus checking and disk defragmentation been performed?
  - What date, time, and location does the pilot rollout take place?

- What is the schedule for pilot installations?
- How many computers will be installed per day? Start with a conservative estimate and then increase or decrease the number, based on your experiences with the initial installations.
- At what time of day should the installations occur? You may want to schedule installations to occur on weekdays after normal business hours or on weekends.
- Who will participate in the installations? In addition to the installation team members, be sure to assign a system administrator with full rights on the server, including the right to administer mail or database server passwords.

It is important to choose a pilot user group or department that is willing and able to accommodate the rollout. Try not to select a department that is attempting to meet a schedule deadline during the rollout, or a group that is traditionally slow in adopting new technology.

Another step at this stage is informing users about the pilot rollout plan. You can use a videotape presentation, an interoffice memo, or a company meeting as the means for communicating with users about the rollout. Regardless of the form used, the message must explain to users the benefits of moving to Windows 95 and describe the overall plan and process by which each group or department will make the move. This makes it easier for your users to plan for and accept the migration to Windows 95 as part of their schedules.

Develop the User Training Plan

The first steps in developing a training plan are to acquire a training lab, set up computers in the lab, and appoint a team member as instructor. If in-house resources are not available, use outside resources to develop and conduct the training. The instructor will be responsible for creating and testing the training program.

There are a number of training approaches and a variety of tools you can use. A recommended approach is to divide the training into sessions corresponding to three distinct topics: The Basics, Corporate-Specific Applications, and Customization.

The session entitled The Basics includes the top 10 functions any user needs to know to accomplish daily work, such as the following:

Function	To do the function, use this
Launch programs, load documents, find a file	The Start button
Change settings	Control Panel
Get help on a specific topic	F1 or Help command
Switch between programs	Taskbar
Minimize, maximize, and close windows	Window buttons
Browse your hard disk	My Computer and Windows Explorer
Connect to a network drive	Network Neighborhood
Print a document	Point and Print
Move data between programs	Drag and drop; cut, copy, paste
Operate on data	Secondary mouse button

The Windows 95 online tutorial and *Introducing Microsoft Windows 95* provide the information you need to train your users in the basics. Schedule training sessions of no more than 30 minutes each; in each session, users receive information that is *just enough* to be productive using Windows 95.

The Corporate-Specific Applications session varies by the environment and the types of programs run on the network. This session should focus on the top five to ten functions that will change because of the upgrade to Windows 95.

The Customization session is intended for more experienced users. The purpose of this session is to provide information and guidance that will help these users learn on their own after the training, and teach them how to work more productively with Windows 95. Some of these topics could include:

- Adding items to the Start menu
- Adding items to the desktop (move, copy, shortcut)

- Using options of the secondary mouse button
- Adding a new device, such as a printer
- Changing the desktop, for example, screen saver settings

After creating and testing the program, schedule training sessions to occur immediately before the rollout so that the instruction is just in time, ensuring that users retain most of what they learn by putting it to use right away.

Develop the Support Plan

Similar to the training plan, the support plan must be ready to go online the first day you begin performing Windows 95 installations. Because the quality of support that is available during the pilot rollout will be seen as an indicator of the quality of the rollout as a whole, it is important that you plan carefully to ensure effective support.

Staff the support team for your pilot rollout with some of your best technicians dedicated solely to the pilot group for the first few weeks. The assigned technicians should carry pagers or be available by phone at all times to give immediate assistance to users.

And, to help users help themselves, edit Windows 95 Help with company-specific information on programs or features.

Conduct the Pilot Rollout

The pilot rollout should be conducted to simulate installations to larger groups of users.

Simulate the Installation Process

The schedule for the pilot rollout should simulate—on a smaller scale—the schedule of the final rollout. As you conduct the pilot rollout, you may find that certain tasks take more or less time than expected, that some tasks need to be added, or that some tasks can be left out. Modify the pilot rollout schedule to account for such changes, and use the pilot schedule for projecting the final rollout timetable.

Test Windows 95 Performance and Capabilities

In addition to the technicians responsible for conducting the pilot installation, extra technicians should be assigned to measure, observe, and test the installation. By tracking the time per installation, handling problems that arise, and identifying areas for improvement or automation, these individuals help ensure the success of both the pilot and final rollouts by making the installation more efficient.

In addition, after Windows 95 is installed, these technicians test computer capabilities such as remote administration for proper operation, and monitor the client computers for performance, stability, and functionality, highlighting any inconsistencies with the lab configuration.

Survey Users for Feedback

The final part of the pilot rollout involves surveying the users to gauge their satisfaction and proficiency with the new installation, and to evaluate the level of training and support provided. Test users' proficiency by having them perform a few common tasks or use several of the new features in Windows 95—for example, have these users register their survey results on the server.

When collected, combine the survey results with the ideas for improvements identified during the pilot rollout. Use this information to prepare a checklist of open issues which must be resolved prior to the final rollout. Then assign team members to take the actions necessary for solving problems or making improvements. Indicate on the checklist how and when each item was resolved, adjusting the deployment plan if appropriate.

Finalize the Rollout Plan

Once all the testing has been successfully completed, use the results and finalize the rollout plan.

Document, Budget, and Carry Out the Logistics

As you prepare for final rollout, estimate the length and scope of the overall installation process. Also plan for all tools needed to complete the process within the stated time frame. If necessary, propose a formal budget for the company-wide implementation and present it to management for approval. Your budget should include the costs for personnel and resources such as system management software.

After obtaining any necessary approval, purchase the resources required to facilitate the installation. If you need additional staff, be sure to hire experienced and qualified individuals for the team, and train them extensively before getting started.

Complete your training, communication, and staffing plans for the final rollout at this time.

Update the Policies and Practices Guidelines

Prior to final rollout, update all company policies regarding the use of the network and computers by employees. Be sure to cover items such as password length and expiration requirements, and the level of approval needed to obtain remote dial-up privileges.

In addition, update the corporate standards lists for software usage; use these lists as a reference for bringing all computers into compliance during the rollout process. Because Windows 95 enables the use of many new 32-bit Windows-based programs and of Plug and Play-compliant hardware, these new products should be added to the list, and their older counterparts should be deleted.

Create a Template for the Rollout Database

A template is used to create a central database for monitoring the progress of the rollout and to document any areas requiring further action. During preparations for the final rollout, create the template using appropriate database management software. Complete the template with configuration information for every computer and user in the company, and place the template on the server. Then, during company-wide installation, the installation team fills in the template for each computer and user, indicating if any additional upgrading is needed. The team can then use the template to track open items following the rollout and to measure actual progress against original objectives.

Roll Out Windows 95

Following the planning, organization, testing, communication, and training, the deployment teams and your organization as a whole should be ready for full-scale rollout of Windows 95. The extensive preparation for this event may make deployment seem almost routine for the teams involved; however, that's exactly the kind of uncomplicated rollout a systems administrator dreams of. And, soon after the installations, users may not know how they got their work done without Windows 95. If this happens in your company, then you know your rollout has been a success.

Lesson Summary

A successful transition revolves around a complete plan. The plan should include multiple tests, preliminary rollouts, training for everyone involved, and making sure sufficient personnel and resources are assigned to the transition.

Lesson 2: Transition Methods

Implementing the actual transition can be accomplished by a variety of means. This lesson explains how to perform administrative and network setups so that Windows 95 can easily be installed on a large number of computers.

After this lesson you will be able to:

- Customize a setup script to meet a specific set of requirements.
- Setup a network installation share.
- Install Windows 95 from a shared folder.

Estimated lesson time 45 minutes

There are several methods you can use to transition to Windows 95.

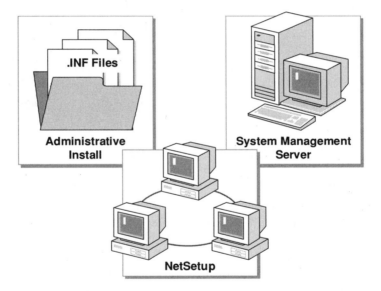

Figure 25.2 Methods of transitioning to Windows 95

The methods available to take your site from its existing environment into Windows 95 include using:

- .INF files
- Profiles
- Microsoft Systems Management Server
- Network Setup

Device Information (.INF) Files

.INF files are used by Setup to specify where information about a specific device is located.

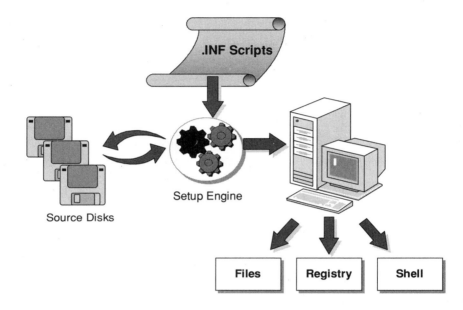

Figure 25.3 .INF files

.INF Files in Setup

The Windows 95 .INF files implement the computer's environment by telling the Setup engine which files and information to take from the source disks and where to put them. The Setup engine's primary job is to read .INF files and process the information.

An administrator can modify the .INF files to customize Setup. This is the key to setup and configuration.

The .INF files' tasks include:

- Copying files
- Setting .INI settings
- Setting registry entries
- Installing devices
- Configuring options
- Controlling other .INF files

.INF File Structure

.INF files are ASCII files that consist of several sections. Each section is assigned a different task. Its name is usually in square brackets. The syntax is:

[**section**]

keyname=value

ASCII Binary

.INF files are ASCII files. Registry files can contain binary information. To bridge the gap between the .INF files in their original form and their final form in the registry as binary files, the INF structure defines an ASCII binary which converts the original ASCII into a binary form that the registry accepts.

Types of .INF Files

There are several types of .INF files that are used by the computer.

Setup Instructions (SETUP.INF)

These tell Setup what other instructions to get. This is like a table of contents, or a list of further instructions.

Layout (LAYOUT.INF)

These list all the possible files and what disk they are on. They contain disk and version information for Setup.

Applications/Installation (APPS.INF)

If you are running MS-DOS–based programs, these .INF files recognize the programs and set up the environment for the program. They contain settings and parameters for numerous MS-DOS–based programs. MS-DOS–based programs do not have this built in. They create .PIF files.

Selective Install (Base Set in APPLETS.INF More in Various Other Optional Files)

These are parts of the installation based on features. This type of file would address the installation of optional components, for example Solitaire or Microsoft Mail. Either the user or an administrator can control the installation of these groups of components.

Device Installation and Configuration (Almost All Other .INF Files)

Each type of device has an .INF file describing the settings for specific hardware. For SCSI, for example, there is the SCSI.INF file. It lists the SCSI cards, their configuration options, and their entries in the Plug and Play hardware tree.

For legacy drivers, these *.INF files are where we get the information on their drivers. Plug and Play puts this information into the registry.

Microsoft Systems Management Server

Microsoft Systems Management Server is a set of Windows NT Services that allow a system administrator to remotely administer computers on a network. These services do not ship with Windows 95, they are included only with Systems Management Server. These administrative capabilities include:

- Collecting software and hardware inventory
- Distributing software
- Troubleshooting hardware and software problems

Although Systems Management Server itself runs with Windows NT Server, it does not require that you use Window NT for your servers or desktops.

Systems Management Server provides a desktop management solution for these network operating systems:

- Novell
- LAN Manager
- Microsoft Windows NT Server

Systems Management Server supports the following network clients:

- Microsoft MS-DOS
- Microsoft Windows
- Microsoft Windows NT
- Microsoft Windows 95

Network Setup

Windows 95 may be installed from a central network location in a variety of configurations. The basic difference in configurations is how much of the system is stored and run from the local hard drive versus how much is stored and run from a shared location.

Local

The most private configuration for Windows 95 stores and runs all program files and programs on the local hard disk. Swapfiles and TEMP files are also located on the local hard disk. The network is used only to store commonly used data.

Typically such stand-alone computers are used for personal workstations, laptop computers that occasionally connect to the network, and workgroups that only share data, not software.

The benefits of a stand-alone installation include the following:

- Faster performance
- The user can customize the system
- The system can start and continue running whether or not the server is available
- Less network traffic is generated

Shared

The most public configuration stores and runs all Windows 95 program files and programs from the shared folders. All data is saved on the network. Swapfiles and TEMP directories can be placed on network drives.

Typically, such shared installations are used where there may be roving users who need to access various computers for tasks such as point of sale data-entry. Shared installations are also typically used on enterprise networks with many thousands of similar computers.

The benefits of a shared installation include the following:

- Easier to customize and manage multiple desktops
- More secure because each user has to log on to the network to use the computer
- Easier to upgrade, especially for multiple computers
- Safer for novice users, because access to system files is controlled
- Requires less local system requirements

Windows 95 provides support for installing and running a shared copy of Windows 95 from a server, including support for the following kinds of shared installations.

- Computers that start from the local hard disk and then run a shared copy of Windows 95 from the server.
- Computers with single floppy drives that start locally from a floppy disk and then connect to a server to run a shared copy of Windows 95.
- Diskless workstations that remotely boot (sometimes called remote initial program load or RIPL) from Novell NetWare 3.*x* and 4.*x* servers and run a shared copy of Windows 95. This option is available only for diskless workstations on Novell NetWare 3.*x* or 4.*x* networks.

  After installing Windows 95 source files on a server, you can create and manage one or more home directories for shared installations. Home directories contain the specific configuration information for the client computers.

Required Files

Network Setup is not installed automatically with Windows 95. The files that make up Network Setup are uncompressed files in the \ADMIN\NETSETUP folder on the Windows 95 installation CD-ROM.

NETSETUP.EXE

▶ **To run Network Setup**

1. Insert the Windows 95 compact disc in the CD-ROM drive, and then make the CD-ROM drive the active drive.

    For example, at the command prompt, type **f:** if the F drive is the CD-ROM drive, or switch to that drive in Windows Explorer or Network Neighborhood.

2. Switch to the CD-ROM \ADMIN\NETTOOLS\NETSETUP directory.

3. At the command prompt, type **netsetup** and the press ENTER.

    –Or–

    In Windows Explorer, double-click NETSETUP.EXE.

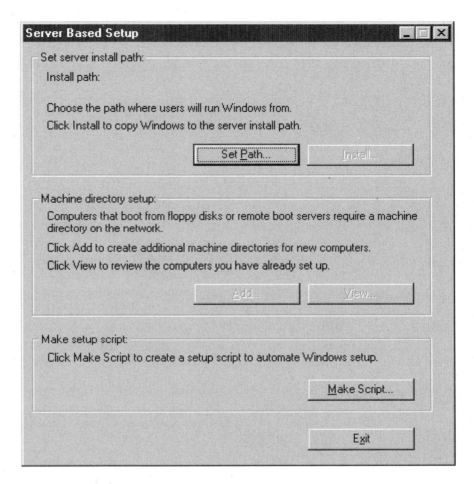

Figure 25.4 Server-Based Setup dialog box

▶ **To install Windows 95 source files on a server**

1. In the Network Setup dialog box, click the Set Path button and then specify the name of the share where you want to store the installation files. Click OK when the path is entered.

2. In the Network Setup dialog box, click the Install button.

   The source path dialog box appears.

3. Type the current location of the source installation files, such as CD-ROM, floppy disk, or network.

4. Specify how the users are allowed to install Windows 95. Depending on requirements, the files may be copied in compressed format or they may require expansion, which takes longer. Select one of the following:

    Server—Install Windows to run from a server. Most files are copied to the server in expanded format.

    Local—Install Windows to run from a local computer. Most files are copied to the server in compressed format.

    Users choice—User determines how they want to use Windows, either from the server, or locally. All files must be copied to the server in their expanded format.

5. Click the OK button.

    The installation files are copied to the specified server.

6. If you want to create a script file based on the current settings, click the Create default button.

    If you do not want to create a script file, click the Don't create default button.

The files are copied to the specified server location in the required format.

Specifying a Home Directory

Home directories are used by computers that use a shared copy of Windows 95. The home directory contains the following type of information:

- Appropriate initialization and configuration files, including WIN.INI and SYSTEM.INI
- The version of WIN.COM to be used to run Windows 95 by computers using that configuration
- SYSTEM.DAT and USER.DAT files that make up the registry for the shared installation
- Files that define the desktop, Start menu directories, and other programs
- The spool directory for printing

▶ **To create one or more home directories**

1. From the Network Setup dialog box, click the Add button.

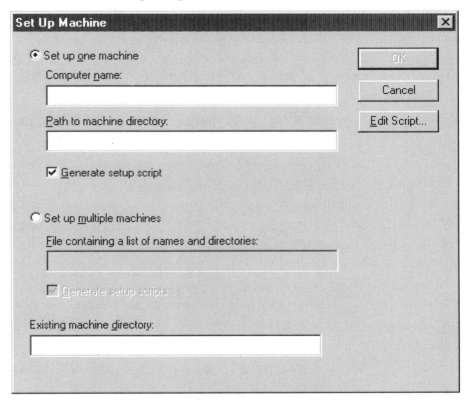

Figure 25.5   Creating a home directory

2. From the Create Home Directory dialog box, click an option to select the mode for installing Windows 95 on computers from the currently specified server.

3. If you want to add a single computer to the current server, click Set up one machine. Then specify the name of the computer and the path to its home directory.

    In this case, you can type the name of a directory on the current server or type the universal naming convention (UNC) path name to a directory on another server.

    If you want to add home directories in a batch, click Setup Multiple Machines, and then type the path and filename to the text file that contains the list of computer names and home directories.

4. If you want Network Setup to generate a batch script based on the values set in this dialog box, check the related Create Script check box.

   A Setup script for each computer is generated based on the default script created in the previous section.

5. After you have specified all options for home directories, click OK.

After Network Setup creates the specified home directories, it stores the Batch Setup script in the home directory, if you specify that a script should be created.

Installing Windows 95 from a Network Location

In this exercise, you will install Windows 95 from the network location you just created.

▶ **To install a stand-alone computer**

1. Restart using the F8 function, and select command prompt only.

2. From the command prompt, type **net use** *<drive>*: **\\server\share**, specifying the share that contains the installation files. Press ENTER.

Note If you have already installed Windows 95 on both of your computers, you need to remove it off of the computer you are going to use to test your network installation. You can follow the Uninstall instructions included in Chapter 1, "Installation and Configuration," to make sure that Windows 95 is completely removed.

---

3. If the files were installed to a shared folder, type *<drive>*: (from step 2) and then press ENTER.

4. Type **setup** and then press ENTER.

5. Complete the installation of Windows 95 onto your local hard drive.

Note A complete version of Windows 95 is required in the following exercises and lessons. If you require any information to complete the setup of Windows 95, refer to Chapter 1, "Installation and Configuration."

Creating a Setup Script

In addition to creating a default Setup script during the Network Setup process, you can create a Setup script at any time using the NETSETUP.EXE program.

▶ **Creating a Setup script**

1. In the Network Setup dialog box, click the Make Script button.

   The Server-Based Setup script dialog box appears.

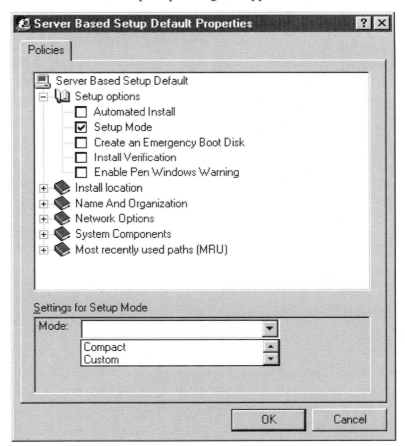

Figure 25.6 Server-Based Setup script dialog box

In the Server-Based Setup script dialog box, select the policies and configuration information that is required for a specific setup.

2. Click the OK button.

   The script is created and stored in the specified location.

Installing with a Batch Setup Script

Batch Setup scripts can be used to install Windows 95 on the hard disk of a stand-alone computer, or to set up client computers to run a shared copy of Windows 95 from a server.

▶ **To run Windows 95 Setup using a batch Setup script**

1. Log on to the network, running the existing network client software.

   The client computer must already be connected to the network to run Windows 95 Setup from the shared directory.

2. Connect to the server that contains the Windows 95 source files.

3. At the command line, run Windows 95 Setup by specifying the batch file with the installation settings, using this syntax:

   setup *msbatch.inf*

   For example, type **setup e:\wfwbatch.inf** to run Setup using an .INF file named WFWBATCH.INF on drive E. Or, you could type **setup \\nwsvr1\scripts\myscript.inf** to use the script stored in the SCRIPTS directory on a server named NWSVR1.

When Windows 95 Setup runs with a batch Setup script, Setup performs the following for both stand-alone and shared installations:

- Looks for MSBATCH.INF in the current directory. If this file is found, Setup knows it is running from a server.

- Runs detection and configures the hardware, storing the configuration in the home directory.

- Prompts the user to specify or change any settings that are not defined in the batch Setup script.

- Copies the settings in MSBATCH.INF to be used by Control Panel and the Run-Once process in Setup.

For shared installations, Setup performs the following additional tasks:

- Prompts the user for the path to the home directory, if it isn't specified in the script.

- Sets the home and shared directories in the registry.

- Formats the startup disk and the copies files to the startup disk.

   If a protected-mode network client is used, Setup configures the network for transition from the real-mode network, using settings from the Setup script or by prompting the user.

Lesson Summary

Installing Windows 95 on a large number of computers can be made easier by using various methods. .INF files help you make sure that all the computers are set up using the appropriate information. Microsoft System Management Server can automate most—if not all—of the upgrade process. Installing from a central network location helps ensure that all computers receive the same information. Setup scripts and batch files can also be used to automate the Setup process.

Lesson 3: Automating Program Installation

Program installation can be automated in Windows 95. This lesson explains how to specify installation servers for programs.

After this lesson you will be able to:

- Modify the registry to allow automated program setup.

Estimated lesson time 10 minutes

Similar to the convenience of creating an installation server for Windows 95, you can also specify installation servers for programs. This feature is added to the Add/Remove Programs function in the Control Panel.

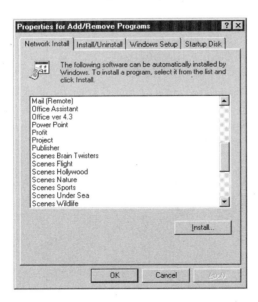

Figure 25.7 Network Install tab on the Add/Remove Programs property sheet

To add this feature, you need to add entries in the registry. This can be done by editing the registry, which is not a particularly safe choice, or by merging a registration entries file that would perform the modification.

The existing registry entry that needs new information is:

```
HKEY_LOCAL_MACHINE\SOFTWARE\Microsoft\Windows\CurrentVersion
```

The new entry added to the existing registry is called AppInstallPath. This key specifies a path that points to the APPS.INI file containing the program Setup information.

For example, if you were to create an install menu called APPS.INI and put it on the share \\INSTRUCTOR\APPS, the AppInstallPath key must point to \\INSTRUCTOR\APPS\APPS.INI.

The registration entries file is an ASCII file with a .REG extension. To continue with the same example, the registration entry file is called INSTALL.REG and contains the following information:

```
REGEDIT4
[HKEY_LOCAL_MACHINE\SOFTWARE\Microsoft\Windows\CurrentVersion]
"AppInstallPath"="\\\\INSTRUCTOR\\APPS\\APPS.INI"
```

The first line, REGEDIT4, indicates that this is a Windows 95 registry file.

Next comes the existing registry key that needs to be modified. This key is placed in square brackets to indicate it as a new section.

The final line is the change you want made. This is in the normal .INI file format of

```
keyname=value
```

with both parts inside quotation marks. Note that the backslashes in this line need to be doubled. This needs to be done because the backslash character is also used to tag special characters.

Save this file as INSTALL.REG. When you double-click this file (or if Merge is selected from the menu that appears when the secondary mouse button is pressed), the AppInstallPath is entered into the registry.

With the AppInstallPath pointing to the \\INSTRUCTOR\APPS\APPS.INI, you need to create that file.

Because APPS.INI is a Windows .INI file, it is also ASCII in the .INI file format. The .INI must begin with the section name **[AppInstallList]** in square brackets. After this, each program you want on the menu is listed in the following format:

```
menu Choice=UNC Name of the setup utility
```

For example, if you were going to install Microsoft Access 2.0 from the \ACCESS folder of the \\SOFTWARE\SOURCES server, your line would look like this:

```
Microsoft Access 2.0=\\software\sources\access\SETUP.EXE
```

In some cases, programs cannot be installed using a UNC name. If the setup list is tagged with an asterisk, the installation share is mapped to the first available drive letter. This connection remains through the rest of the session but is not reconnected automatically in the next session.

For example, a program which uses a setup that does not support UNC names would look like the following:

```
Our old application=*\\software\sources\oldapp\SETUP.EXE
```

With both of these entries, our completed APPS.INI file looks like this:

```
[AppInstallList]
Microsoft Access 2.0=\\software\sources\access\SETUP.EXE
Our old application=*\\software\sources\oldapp\SETUP.EXE
```

Of course in a real example, this list could contain dozens of entries. It is also important to note that because the actual .INI file is kept on a server and shared by the users, any changes made by a network administrator to the list would take effect on all the computers the next time they opened the Add/Remove Programs function in the Control Panel.

Lesson Summary

Automating the installation of programs can be accomplished by specifying the installation server and listing the appropriate files in the registry.

Lesson 4: Troubleshooting Shared Installations

There are some common issues that may occur when you use shared installations of Windows 95. This lesson describes these issues and what can be done to alleviate any potential problems.

After this lesson you will be able to:

*   Diagnose and solve problems related to shared installations.

Estimated lesson time 5 minutes

MS-DOS Mode Is Disabled for Shared Installations

When you start a program that runs in MS-DOS mode, Windows 95 shuts down and exits back to MS-DOS to run the program. When the program exits, Windows 95 starts again. This mode exists as a last resort mode for compatibility with existing software. The problem is that computers that run a shared version of Windows 95 lose their network capabilities when Windows 95 exits. Because of the related problems, MS-DOS mode is not available for computers running Windows 95 over the network. When a user tries to run a program in this mode, Windows 95 warns that the mode has been disabled.

Hot Docking for Plug and Play Network Adapters Is Not Supported for Shared Installations

When Windows 95 starts over the network, real-mode drivers control the network adapter card. If the network card is a Plug and Play card, the driver is responsible for setting the computer to the active state. Computers that run over the network do not support hot Plug and Play disconnects, because the operating system is on the network.

Safe Mode Start for Network Computers Always Runs Configuration Files

To perform a Safe Mode start on a network computer, the network must be started. Therefore, IO.SYS always runs AUTOEXEC.BAT, CONFIG.SYS, and NETSTART.BAT, even in a Safe Mode start. This allows the network computer to detect the data in the home directory that describes how and when to perform a Safe Mode start.

Swapfiles for Shared Installations Have Special Considerations

- The swapfile is stored on the local hard disk for a client computer that starts from the hard disk.
- The swapfile is stored in the home directory for a client computer that starts from a floppy disk and runs protected-mode network software.

  Client computers that start from a floppy disk and run real-mode network software do not have a swapfile.

Lesson Summary

There are some common issues that occur when using shared installations. By checking for these issues you can isolate problems with shared installations.

Review

The following questions are intended to reinforce key information presented in this chapter. If you are unable to answer a question, review the appropriate lesson and then try the question again.

1. What are the benefits of running a shared copy of Windows 95?

\
\

2. What is the best way to set up and test computers for the transition to Windows 95?

CHAPTER 26

Implementing Windows 95 Multimedia

Before You Begin

To complete the lessons in this chapter, you must have:

- Completed Chapter 1 and installed Microsoft Windows 95.
- A sound card and microphone installed on the computer.

Lesson 1: Multimedia in Windows 95

Windows 95 has built-in support for various multimedia features and functions. This lesson describes the multimedia programs and services included in Windows 95.

After this lesson you will be able to:

- Describe Microsoft Windows 95 multimedia services.
- List the types of hardware that Windows 95 multimedia supports.

Estimated lesson time 15 minutes

Usually, multimedia files are maintained in one of the formats described in the following table.

Format	Corresponding filename extension
Digital-video	.AVI
Waveform-audio	.WAV
Musical Instrument Digital Interface (MIDI)	.MID

Multimedia files can be stored on a compact disc, a local hard disk drive, a network file server, or other storage mediums. The playback quality is constrained by the amount of data that the storage medium can continuously supply to the file system.

A multimedia data stream such as an .AVI file generally contains multiple components, such as digital-video data, audio data, text, and perhaps other data, such as hot-spot information, additional audio tracks, and so on. As multimedia information is read from the CD-ROM drive, the multimedia subsystem determines what the data stream contains, and then it separates and routes the data accordingly.

Windows 95 multimedia features, accessible through the Control Panel and the Accessories folder, include:

- Compression services for audio, video, and image compression. These services have an open interface so that software developers can add their own service providers, and hardware vendors can implement the services in their hardware.
- Video for Windows run time. This feature makes it possible for users to play a digital video sequence on any Windows 95-based computer to incorporate digital video into existing Windows-based programs. In Windows 95, run-time video simply becomes another data-type that users can take advantage of without additional hardware.

- Improved MIDI support.
- Control for video disc devices. Microsoft is expanding the ability to control such media from the computer, allowing users to stop, start, and pause with frame accuracy from a Windows 95-based computer.

Multimedia Programs

The multimedia programs that are part of Windows 95 include:

- Improved Sound Recorder, MIDI, and Media Player programs.
- OLE for drag-and-drop capabilities in all multimedia programs.
- Media Control Device, Mixer, and Volume Control programs that are independent of the specific computer hardware.
- CD Music Player

Multimedia Services

In order to handle the rapidly changing needs of multimedia programs, Windows 95 implements multimedia using a layered approach.

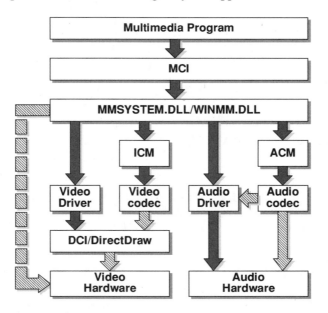

Figure 26.1 Multimedia services architecture

A multimedia program sends its commands and data using the Media Control Interface (MCI) specification. MCI data includes not only the data but also commands and data type information. These MCI data streams are handed off to the Multimedia system library, WINNMM.DLL is the 32-bit version and MMSYSTEM.DLL is the 16-bit version, for processing. Audio commands and data are sent to the appropriate driver. If the audio stream is not compressed, it is sent directly to the driver. If it is compressed, the data is sent to the Audio Compression Manager (ACM) which determines which Compressor/
Decompressor (codec) is to be used. If the codec is a software codec, the audio stream goes to the audio driver and then to the hardware. If the codec is a hardware codec, the stream goes directly to the hardware.

Video commands and data are handled in a similar way. The data is either sent directly to the driver or, if it is compressed, it is sent to Video Compression Manager (VCM) which passes the compressed data to the appropriate video codec. Depending on the codec, Video data may be sent to the video driver first or directly to the video hardware using the Microsoft/Intel Display Control Interface (DCI) or DirectDraw interface (both of these are supported), which allows for high-speed direct access to the frame buffer.

Audio Services

Audio services provide the means for integrating sound into programs. These services range from high-level playback functions that play files of waveform data to low-level functions that control playback of compressed sound.

WINMM.DLL and MMSYSTEM.DLL

The audio functions in WINMM.DLL (32 bit) and MMSYSTEM.DLL (16 bit) allow programs to play or record audio data. To maintain device-independence, WINMM.DLL and MMSYSTEM.DLL use device drivers to communicate with the various audio devices in a computer, rather than communicating directly with each device.

WINMM.DLL and MMSYSTEM.DLL provide a standard interface for device drivers written for use in the Windows-based environment. The services available through WINMM.DLL and MMSYSTEM include basic audio-processing functions.

Wave Mapper

WINMM.DLL and MMSYSTEM uses a module called a *wave mapper* to select installed devices. When a program wants to play or record audio data, it sends a device-request message to WINMM.DLL or MMSYSTEM. The wave mapper responds to this request by sending a message to a device driver, requesting the associated device be opened.

The device driver—not WINMM.DLL or MMSYSTEM.DLL—is responsible for deciding whether to accept or refuse the request from the wave mapper.

Once a suitable, available device is found, the wave mapper returns to the program, identifying the selected device.

Audio Compression Manager (ACM) Services

The services available through the ACM support compression and decompression of audio data during recording or playback. The ACM can decode or encode audio data before passing it to a device driver. The ACM also provides explicit functions for compressing, decompressing, and filtering audio data.

The ACM includes compressor/decompressor (codec) modules, format converter modules, and filtering modules.

Compressor/Decompressor

Compressor/decompressor modules change one format type to another. For example, a compressor or decompressor module can change a PCM file to an ADPCM file.

Format Conversion

Format converter modules change the format but not the data type. For example, a converter module can change 44 kHz, 16-bit data to 44 kHz, 8-bit data but can't change a PCM file to an ADPCM file. Filters don't change the format, but may change the data by adding a special effect, such as a change in volume, an echo, or reverberation.

Sound Mapper

In addition to the functions and services the ACM adds to WINMM.DLL and MMSYSTEM, the ACM is accessible through the Sound Mapper in the Control Panel. This means that programs using the Sound Mapper to choose or activate a device are using the ACM mapping services.

When WINMM.DLL or MMSYSTEM.DLL loads the ACM, the ACM attempts to install any converters or drivers that are already defined. In addition, the ACM can load converters and drivers dynamically when they are identified by a program.

Identifying Converters and Drivers

The ACM uses the following resources to identify converters and drivers for installation:

- SYSTEM.INI entries—The ACM installs any converter previously installed by the Drivers option in the registry. When a driver is installed, it adds an entry to the SYSTEM.INI file.

- Self-registration—The ACM provides functions to register converters and drivers dynamically. This lets programs install custom compression routines while they are running. Converters can be registered as task-local to protect proprietary algorithms.

- Default converters—The ACM always installs a set of default converters for converting between different PCM formats.

Most audio drivers do not directly compress or decompress audio data. Instead, they simply transfer data, a buffer at a time, to or from the device being used to play or record the audio. The ACM inserts a compressor/decompressor (codec) into the process, choosing the best available codec for the data currently being processed.

Windows 95 MIDI Capabilities

The MIDI features in Windows 95 allow programs to:

- Access raw MIDI data
- Time stamp MIDI messages
- Send and receive buffers of time-stamped MIDI data

Windows 95 MIDI also includes device-capability flags to indicate whether installed MIDI devices are compatible with the new buffered architecture.

Video Compression

Windows 95 includes various services that enhance the displaying of digital video. These services include:

- Decompressing compressed video
- Controlling the playback

Reading and Play-back

The Windows 95 multimedia video feature can read different types of video formats or compression standards. The Windows 95-based multimedia video play-back method depends on the format's header.

Lesson Summary

Windows 95 includes complete support for multimedia programs.

For more information on	See
Media Control Interface drivers and commands	*Microsoft Windows 95 Device Development Kit*
Microsoft/Intel Display Control Interface (DCI)	*DCI Level 2 Specification* available through the Microsoft Developer Network (MSDN); to obtain it, call (800) 759-5474, or from outside the United States and Canada, call (402) 691-0173.

Lesson 2: Configuring Multimedia

This lesson describes how to configure the various multimedia functions.

After this lesson you will be able to:

*   Configure multimedia for a given program.

Estimated lesson time 30 minutes

Most of the multimedia configuration programs in Windows 95 are built into the Control Panel.

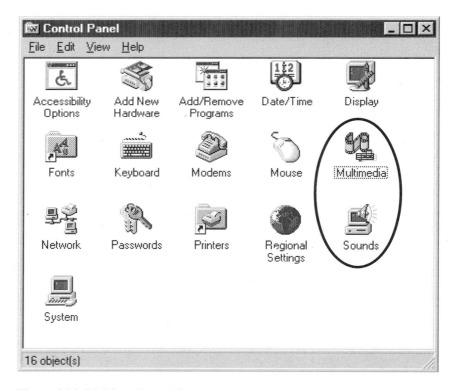

Figure 26.2 Multimedia and Sounds icons in the Control Panel

The Multimedia option includes property sheets for the following:

*   Audio
*   MIDI
*   Video
*   CD Music

In addition, there is an Advanced property sheet that allows you to configure the following.

- Audio, MIDI, mixer, video, and other control devices
- Image compression
- Video compression

Audio

The Audio property sheet allows you to configure the default settings for devices that play and record audio.

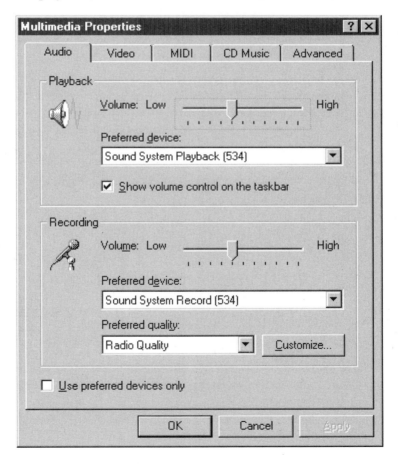

Figure 26.3 Audio tab on the Multimedia property sheet

Playback

You can adjust the initial playback volume and the default device used to play sounds.

This allows you to select a specific device for wave audio if you have more than one.

Recording

In addition to setting the recording volume and device defaults, you can select the default quality.

Windows 95 has three basic descriptions for the Preferred audio recording quality. These settings relate to format and attributes of the recorded sound. There is usually a direct trade-off between the quality of the sound and the size of the file that stores the sound. The basic settings are:

- CD Quality—The best of the basic settings. The CD quality setting records sounds with the highest sampling rate and in stereo. The disadvantage of using this level of quality is that it requires more storage for a specific recording than the other quality levels.

- Radio Quality—The intermediate setting. Sound recorded at this level is a compromise between the best quality and a reasonable file size.

- Telephone Quality—The lowest quality setting, however, this level usually takes considerably less space than the others.

If the basic settings do not meet your requirements, you may create your own settings by using the Customize button. This option allows you to set specific recording formats and attributes and save these settings in a file.

Supported Audio Devices

Windows 95 supports a variety of devices. To view a list of devices, in the Control Panel, use the Add New Hardware wizard and select to install a sound, video, or game controller. A list of manufacturers and models appears.

For hardware that is not on the list, consult the hardware compatibility list (HCL) to determine if Windows 95 supports a specific sound component.

MIDI

MIDI (Musical Instrument Digital Interface) is a serial interface standard that makes it possible to connect musical instruments and synthesizers to computers.

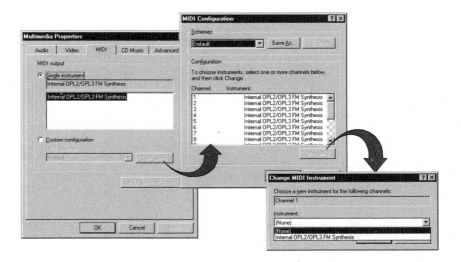

Figure 26.4 Configuring MIDI

The MIDI standard is based partly on hardware and partly on a description of the way music is encoded and communicated between MIDI devices. It is a description of musical notation for electronic devices.

The Windows 95 MIDI configuration allows you to create configuration schemes. Depending on the hardware installed in your computer, you may select any one of the 16 MIDI channels and assign it an instrument or several instruments.

CD Music

The CD Music player is configured using the CD Music property sheet.

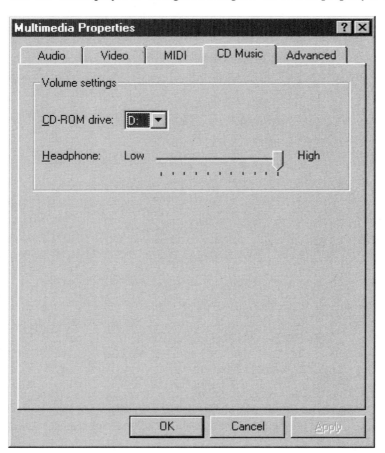

Figure 26.5 CD Music tab on the Multimedia property sheet

This sheet allows you to set the default volume levels for the headphone and line out channels.

Advanced Multimedia Properties

Most users find that the settings on the first four tabs are sufficient for their uses. However, some users may want even more control over the various multimedia devices on their Windows 95-based computer.

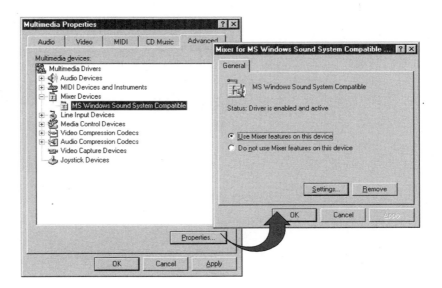

Figure 26.6 Advanced settings tab on the Multimedia property sheet

The Advanced property sheet shows a hierarchy of multimedia devices. Not all of these are necessarily installed in the computer. Which devices are enabled depends on the specific hardware and software installed in a computer. Each class of device has one or more devices below it. By selecting the device, you can change its properties. Note that some devices such as codecs are not configurable.

One of the supported codecs is the DSP Group, Inc. Truespeech™ software codec. Truespeech allows for very highly compressed storage for voice recording. The algorithm used, however, is not suitable for recording non-speech sounds.

All devices have an Enable/Disable selection. This allows for drivers to be installed but inactive in the computer.

Customizing MIDI

Standard MIDI mappings assign certain numbers to popular instruments. In Windows 95 MIDI, however, the musician can customize the numbering scheme by writing over it to create original compositions or arrangements.

Video

The Windows 95-based video services provide the software resources needed to integrate video clips into programs. This sheet allows you to specify the default display size for digital video clips. The video may be shown full screen, sized to fit in a window, or sized to fit a specified percentage of the screen.

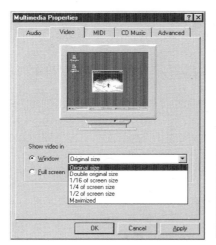 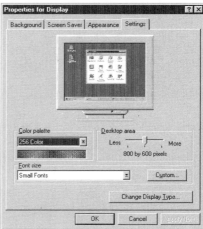

Figure 26.7 Configuring video

Video Installation

Versions of the following Microsoft video drivers may conflict with previous Windows releases:

- MCIAVI.DRV
- MSVIDC.DRV
- MSVIDEO.DLL

If you have any of these on your computer they will be replaced with the newer versions.

Monitor Settings in Windows 95 Multimedia

When Windows 95-based video runs for the first time, it profiles the display and configures the default settings for a particular multimedia computer by calculating how fast images can be presented to create the sharpest display.

As a general rule, the more color and depth in your picture, and the larger it is, the slower your video presentation will be.

The following information can help in adjusting the display to produce the best multimedia presentation possible in your computer.

Display Settings Control Panel

This dialog box allows you to select any screen resolution or color palette settings supported by your display adapter, without specifying a different display driver type. This dialog box can also be used to select font type.

Faster Performance

The Windows 95-based drivers run faster when your computer includes graphics accelerators.

Video Compression Schemes

The Windows 95 Add New Hardware dialog box can be used to add other vendor video compression schemes. These compression schemes are treated as sound, video, and game controllers.

Sounds

The Sounds property sheet lets the user assign sounds onto system events. (In the Control Panel, double-click the Sounds icon to access the Sounds property sheet.)

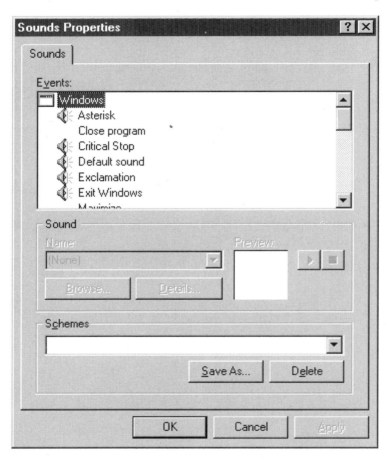

Figure 26.8 Assigning sounds to events

You can determine which sounds are played for which events. If, for example, you have favorite sound bites from cartoon characters, you can configure those sounds to play during particular events. Opening a certain program, for example, could launch a lion's roar or trigger the sound of a human voice greeting the user.

This function is similar to setting color schemes.

Additional CD-ROM Support

In addition to improving conventional CD-ROM support, Windows 95 has several features for new CD-ROM technologies.

AutoPlay

Windows 95 incorporates a feature called AutoPlay. An AutoPlay-enabled CD-ROM contains a file (AUTORUN.INF) which contains instructions for handling the CD-ROM. These instructions are run by Windows 95 when the CD-ROM is inserted into the drive. This allows programs to install or run automatically with no additional user intervention.

Support for New Formats

In addition to Red Book audio and Yellow Book CD-ROM support, Windows 95 supports Type 2 and XA format CD-ROMs, Orange Book recordable CD-ROM and Kodak PhotoCD formats. Additionally, Windows 95 supports the new Enhanced CD format that allows mixed audio, video, and interactive formats on the same disk. An Enhanced CD (Green Book) will play Red Book audio when used in a home stereo, and full video and interactive multimedia on a multimedia computer.

Lesson Summary

Multimedia programs can be configured to meet specific needs. This includes adjusting audio quality, support for various compression algorithms, and other configuration options.

Lesson 3: Multimedia Tools

This lesson explains how to use multimedia programs to record and play multimedia programs.

After this lesson you will be able to:
- Use Media Player to run a short video clip.

Estimated lesson time 20 minutes

There are several tools included with Windows 95 that allow you to control multimedia recording and playback.

CD Player

The CD Player is a program that allows you to play music CDs in your CD-ROM and have the music routed through your multimedia speakers. Of course, you must have the required hardware to use this tool.

Figure 26.9 CD Player dialog box

This program allows you to control music CD-ROMs (play, pause, stop, search, fast forward, rewind, and eject) in your CD-ROM drive. You may determine the play order, record the artist, title and track titles, and so on.

▶ **To edit the play list**

1. On the Disc menu, click Edit Play List.

    The Disc Settings dialog box appears.

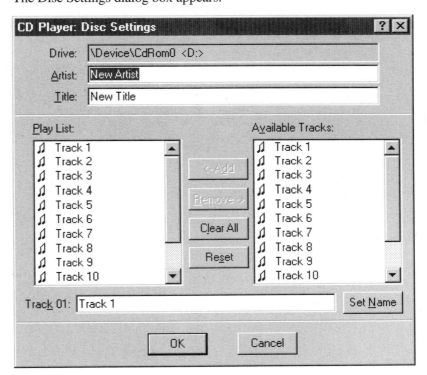

Figure 26.10 CD Player Disc Settings dialog box

2. If preferred, enter the artist and title of the disc.

The play list is the order in which the tracks are played. This dialog box allows you to determine that order.

▶ **To modify a play list**

1. Select the track to play.

2. Move it up or down to the preferred sequence.

You may also name each track, remove tracks from the play list, add the same track multiple times, and otherwise experiment with this user interface.

Windows 95 uses the total length of the CD-ROM and the number and length of each track to create a unique identifier for each music CD-ROM you enter. Windows 95 uses this information to recognize CD-ROMs when they are placed in the computer.

This information is located in the \WINDOWS folder, stored in the CDPLAYER.INI file.

Mixer

The multimedia features in Windows 95 can control sound from multiple inputs. For example, Windows 95 can control relative volumes of MIDI input and a wave audio.

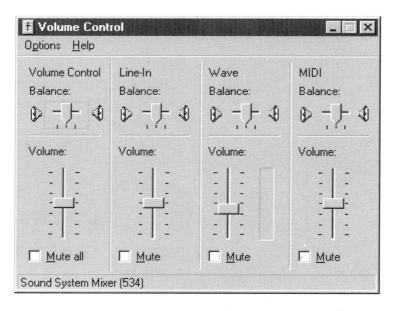

Figure 26.11 Volume Control

The mixers in the multimedia API set provide audio line routing services to manage the different audio lines installed on a computer system.

This allows you to control the volume for the different lines. These settings may be adjusted by means of the Control Panel, however specific configuration information varies for each program.

Sound Recorder

Sound Recorder allows you to record wave audio from the inputs available on your hardware. You can then package the resulting .WAV files into embeddable OLE objects.

Figure 26.12   Recorded sound playing back

Using Sound Recorder is straightforward.

To record a sound, click the record button, which is the button with the circle on it. The computer starts recording and continues until the stop button, the button with the square on it, is clicked.

To rewind, click the rewind button (<<). Clicking the fast forward button (>>) takes you to the end of the file.

To play a recorded file, press the play (>) button.

▶ **To use Sound Recorder**

1. On the Start menu, point to Programs, Accessories, Multimedia, and then click Sound Recorder to launch the Sound Recorder.

2. Start recording by clicking the Record button (the button with the large red dot).

3. Speak a short phrase into the microphone. Click the Stop button (the button with the solid square) when you are finished.

4. Listen to your voice by clicking the playback button. Try listening to your voice using different effects (echo, reverse, high speed, low speed, and so on).

5. Save your voice in a file.

6. Increase the speed of your voice by 500 percent and then reduce the speed back to normal.

   Does it sound the same?_____

   Why or why not?_____

   _____

7. Save the current contents of Sound Recorder in a second file.

   Is the size of this second file the same size as your original voice?_____

   If not, explain the differences.

   _____

   _____

   _____

Media Player

Media Player is a program that acts as the primary Windows 95 multimedia delivery program.

Figure 26.13 Media Player

Media Player presents audio or video files from inputs that support the Media Control Interface (MCI). Typical MCI sources include:

- Wave audio
- CD-ROM audio
- Video
- MIDI

The Media Player in Windows 95 is an OLE server.

Media Player Objects

Windows 95 multimedia treats presentations as OLE objects.

When you edit a Media Player OLE object, the menus from the container and from Media Player merge, giving you full access to Media Player commands.

Synchronization

All multimedia has to be time synchronized. The Media Player starts and stops playback, acting as a front end to your computer's multimedia drivers that do the actual synchronization work.

In presenting video, for example, Media Player profiles your computer and figures out how fast it should present images in that computer.

Presentation

The Windows 95 multimedia presentation options include settings depending on how an OLE media object is going to be represented. This varies from medium to medium.

Lesson Summary

Included with Windows 95 are tools that allow you to play audio CD-ROMs, record sounds, mix sounds from different sources, and play multimedia files.

Review

- John recently bought a new Pentium computer running Windows 95. He decided to take the Microsoft Windows Sound System card out of his old computer and install it in the Pentium machine. Should he also install the Windows Sound System software that came with the card?

_____

_____

C H A P T E R 2 7

Troubleshooting and Tools

Before You Begin

To complete the lessons in this chapter, you must have:

- Completed Chapter 1 and installed Microsoft Windows 95.

Lesson 1: Basic Troubleshooting Strategy

This lesson provides an overview to a basic troubleshooting strategy.

After this lesson you will be able to:

• Use a logical approach to diagnose and isolate problems.

Estimated lesson time 5 minutes

Troubleshooting is a logical, iterative process that involves isolating potential problems.

Gather Symptoms

- What hardware and software is involved?
- Does the problem occur in just one program?
- Does sequence of steps make a difference?
- Has it ever worked?
- What changed?
- What did you change?

Note Always make backups of the SYSTEM.DAT and USER.DAT configuration files. It is a good idea to have a startup disk. Test your startup disk before you need it.

Decide on Problem Area

Decide what you think the cause and solution are. Make the modifications and then test. Make only one change before you retest.

Test

Test each modification to determine whether it fixed the problem.

Write It Down

Note all symptoms, causes, and solutions. This makes an excellent reference for future troubleshooting.

Return System to Original State

Before you leave, return the computer to a state that is as close as possible as you found it. Obviously you will have made changes that affect the computer, but you should make sure the user still has all the programs that were on the computer when you started.

Lesson Summary

Troubleshooting involves gathering enough data to be able to eliminate some areas and concentrate on others. Once the symptoms of the problem are completely determined, you can start testing areas to isolate the problem.

Lesson 2: Remote Troubleshooting

There are times when you do not have direct access to computers that are having problems. This lesson covers the remote troubleshooting functions supported by Windows 95.

After this lesson you will be able to:

- Troubleshoot problems on remote computers.
- Use remote monitoring tools to locate problems on remote computers.

Estimated lesson time 15 minutes

Many of the tools used on a local computer may also be used remotely. However, these functions do need to be enabled on the remote computer before you can access them remotely.

To access these functions, select the remote resource, click the secondary mouse button, point to Properties, and then click the Tools tab.

Remote Net Watcher

Net Watcher can be used to monitor connections to a remote computer.

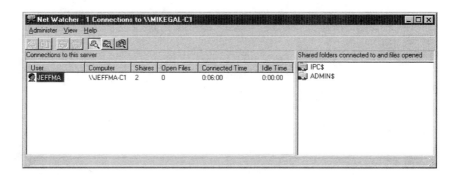

Figure 27.1 Example of remote Net Watcher

When you click the Net Watcher button, you are prompted for a password. Once you enter the password, you receive the Net Watcher dialog. The remote Net Watcher performs the same functions as the local net watcher, as discussed in Chapter 19, "System Policies and Templates." In addition, there are two hidden shares that you can observe:

- Admin$—Administrative access to the Windows folder.
- IPC$—Handles RPC calls for remote administration.

The remote Net Watcher allows you to view:

- Other remote users that are currently connected to the remote computer; you will be listed as one of the users.
- Folders that are shared for remote access.
- Files that are currently opened by remote users.

Remote System Monitor

System Monitor is designed to identify the majority of performance problems by allowing you to track most of the system components and programs running on the system. The program measures system responsiveness and the use of system components to help you determine the root cause of a problem.

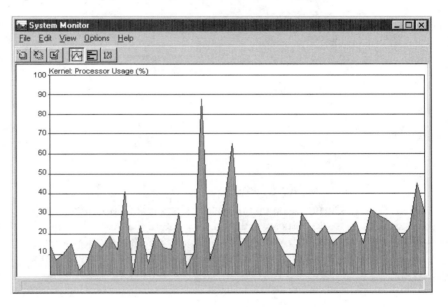

Figure 27.2 Example of remote System Monitor

To use System Monitor remotely, both computers must be set up with user-level security and have the Remote Registry service running.

When you make changes to the computer, System Monitor shows you the effect they have on overall system performance. The program can also be used to show others why the computer behaves the way it does, and to justify system upgrades.

System Monitor views computer components as objects. When using the program, you select specific features of these objects, called *counters*, that you want System Monitor to track. The counters, which are maintained by the kernel, can be monitored to determine where performance bottlenecks may be occurring.

System Monitor can be used to:

- Monitor real-time computer performance.
- Identify areas where resource limitations are affecting performance.
- Monitor the effects of computer configuration changes.
- Determine system capacity.

The following table describes some of the categories of items tracked by System Monitor. These vary based on computer configuration.

Category	Function
32-bit file system	Information about the 32-bit file system, including number of bytes read, written, and other information.
IPX/SPX-compatible protocol	Tracks various data about IPX/SPX packets (sent/received).
Kernel	Information about the kernel, including approximate processor usage, number of threads, and number of virtual machines.
Microsoft Network Server	Various information about read and writing bytes, memory, and so on.
SMB redirector	Bytes read/write, transactions.
VMM32 Memory Manager	Details of the memory management system including paging and working set information.

Processor Spikes

During some operations such as initialization of a program, a compile, or a worksheet recalculation, the system may experience spikes that approach 100 percent. Even if such a spike occurs and is followed by a return to a more reasonable level between 0 percent and 80 percent for most normal operations, the processor is not the likely bottleneck in the system.

Processor Time

The Processor Usage counter indicates how busy a processor is. It shows the percentage of elapsed time that a processor is busy executing non-idle threads.

Processor Limiting Performance

The processor does not limit performance until the total processor sustains nearly 80 percent utilization. When processor use consistently approaches 100 percent, it may indicate that the processor is not adequate for the tasks the user is trying to perform. However, acceptable processor usage may depend on computer activity.

Sustained processor utilization above 80 percent would indicate the need for an upgrade. However, percentages may vary depending on expected computer performance and processor type.

Use the System Monitor to chart Kernel: Processor Usage for all processes. If more than a couple of processes are contending for the majority of the processor time, then a faster processor should be considered.

Remote Administer

Administer functions can be used to access a remote computer and manipulate resources on the computer.

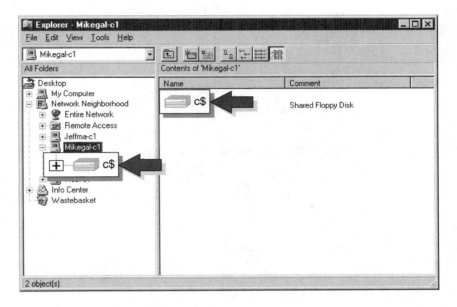

Figure 27.3 Example of remote Administer

Clicking the Administer button allows you to access the remote computer. It opens a hidden directory for the root of designated drive. For example, the root of the C drive is designated C$.

You can then use Windows Explorer to access everything in the remote computer, whether or not it has been shared. You can also manipulate the folders and other resources the same as you would on a local computer.

You can create, delete, and share any resource available to the remote computer.

Remote Registry Editor

The registry contains dynamic information and should not be edited manually. There may be times when a required device is not Plug and Play-compatible and you need to make manual modifications to the configuration. These modifications are best performed by using the appropriate user interface.

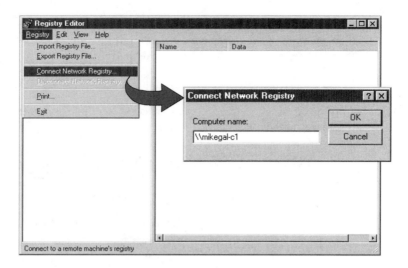

Figure 27.4 Example of remote Registry Editor

However, if nothing else works, you may need to access the registry of a remote computer. The computer being monitored must have the Microsoft Remote Registry service installed.

Note Before you can use Remote Registry on a computer, the computer must have the Remote Registry Network service enabled. The Remote Registry service requires that the computer be running with user-level security.

▶ **To access a remote registry**

1. Start the RegEdit program.

2. From the Registry menu, click Connect Network Registry.

3. Enter the name of the remote computer.

   You can now manipulate the registry of the remote computer.

Lesson Summary

With the appropriate permissions, the remote troubleshooting tools included with Windows 95 give you the capability to completely control a remote computer.

Lesson 3: Log Files

Successfully isolating a problem usually depends on having sufficient information about the problem. Windows 95 creates several log files that can be used to determine where a problem is occurring. This lesson describes the various log files that are created by Windows 95.

After this lesson you will be able to:

- Use the log files to identify problems.

Estimated lesson time 5 minutes

Microsoft Windows 95 can maintain a variety of logs. The information in these logs can be valuable when troubleshooting a problem.

The following logs are created automatically.

Log filename	Location of log	Contents	Useful for...
BOOTLOG.TXT	Root directory (this is a hidden, system file)	Record of boot (similar to Windows 3.1 BOOTLOG.TXT)	Diagnosing setup and boot time errors
DETLOG.TXT	Root directory (this is a hidden, system file)	List of devices detected during setup	Determining hardware detection problems
SETUPLOG.TXT	Root directory (this is a hidden, system file)	List of messages received during setup	Viewing setup errors, and for verifying the integrity of files installed during setup*
IOS.LOG**	Windows folder	Error message location from file system drivers (SCSI)	Tracking down errors from disk controllers and drives

*If you rerun Microsoft Windows 95 Setup after Windows 95 is installed. Setup examines the SETUPLOG.TXT and verifies the integrity of files installed during setup. If the integrity check fails due to a missing or corrupted file on the computer, Setup automatically reinstalls the file.

**IOS.LOG is only created on computers with a SCSI card that has generated errors.

In addition the following log files can be created at any time. You may give them different names and they must be enabled before they start logging information.

Log filename	Enabled from	Contents	Useful for...
MODEMLOG.TXT	The Advanced Connection Settings dialog from the Modems icon in the Control Panel	A log of responses to and from a modem when a connection is being made	Finding communications errors and modem configuration problems

Lesson Summary

The log files that can be created and maintained by Windows 95 can help isolate problems.

Lesson 4: New Devices

When new devices are added to a computer that has Windows 95 installed, setup and configuration of the new device is automated. This lesson explains the procedures to follow when installing new devices on a Windows 95-based computer.

After this lesson you will be able to:
- Use the Add New Hardware wizard to configure new hardware.

Estimated lesson time 30 minutes

Windows 95 uses Plug and Play and other detection routines to detect and configure new devices during installation and startup. If the new device is not detectable, you may need to use the Add New Hardware installation wizard to install and configure it.

▶ **To install a new device**

1. In the Control Panel, click the Add New Hardware icon.

   The Add New Hardware wizard appears.

Figure 27.5 Starting the Add New Hardware wizard

2. Click the Next button.

   You are prompted to choose either automatic or manual installation.

Figure 27.6 Selecting manual hardware configuration

3. If Windows 95 can detect and configure the device automatically, click Yes, and let Windows 95 handle the installation and configuration of the device.

   If you need to configure the device manually, click No.

4. Click Next.

5. Click the type of device you want to install and then click Next.

The Manufacturers and Models list boxes appear.

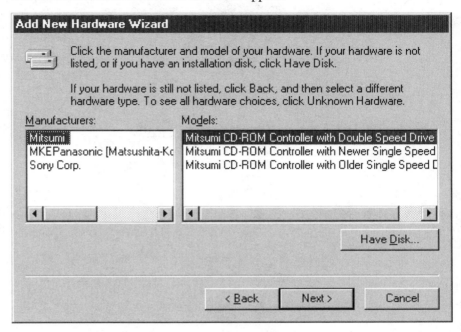

Figure 27.7 Selecting hardware manufacturer and model

6. Click the manufacturer and model of the device that you are installing.

Depending on the resource requirements for the new device, you may be finished at this point, or a property sheet for the specific device may appear.

If resources are required, Windows 95 detects the resources and configures the device. If you must, you may change these assignments. However, it is not recommended that you do this as it may interfere with other Plug and Play-compliant devices already installed. Windows 95 can adjust resources when required, but the computer works best if allowed to arbitrate and assign resources automatically.

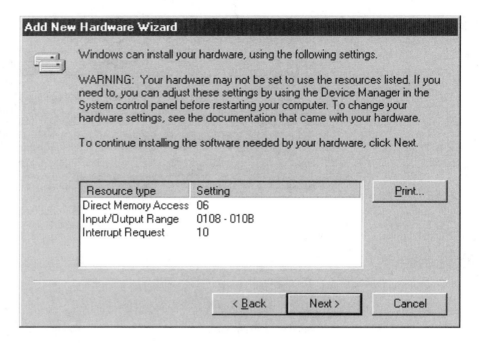

Figure 27.8 Completing hardware configuration

7. To complete the installation, click Next, and then click Finish.

Device Configuration

The registry contains dynamic information and should not be edited manually. There may be times when a required device is not Plug and Play-compatible and you need to make manual modifications to the configuration. These modifications are best performed by using the appropriate user interface. This interface is usually the Device Manager.

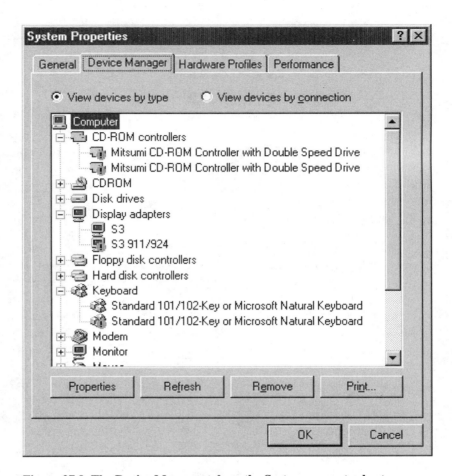

Figure 27.9 The Device Manager tab on the System property sheet

Device Manager

Device Manager is a user interface that allows you to access the hardware tree. It shows you how all devices in the computer are configured. The devices are displayed in tree fashion. If a + appears in the tree before the device, this indicates that more detailed device information is available. Clicking the + expands the tree below that device.

To use Device Manager, highlight the device you need to change and then click the Properties button. This brings up a property sheet for that device. Just as there are several levels of devices, there are corresponding levels of property sheets. The property sheets range from generic information about the device to specific user interfaces for changing the device configuration.

▶ **To change the configuration of a port (optional exercise)**

1. In the Control Panel, double-click the System icon.

   The System property sheet appears.

2. Click the Device Manager tab.

   The Device Manager property sheet appears. Make sure that the View devices by type radio button is selected.

3. Expand the Ports tree by either clicking on the + next to Ports, or by double-clicking the Ports name or icon.

4. Click the first Communications Port once, and then click the Properties button.

   The Communications Port property sheet appears.

   Several common devices have at least two property sheets; General and Resources. If the device uses a specific driver, a tab for that appears.

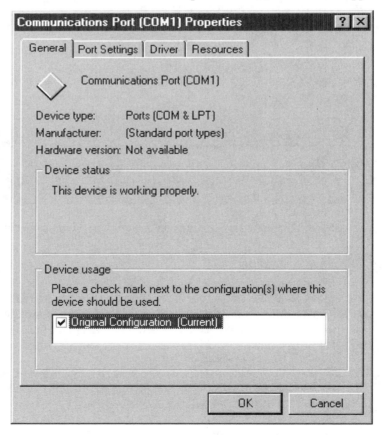

Figure 27.10 Changing the configuration of a communications port

The General tab on the property sheet may contain descriptive information about the device, device settings, and driver information. You may also be able to change drivers from this sheet, depending on the device.

5. Click the Driver tab.

The Driver property sheet appears.

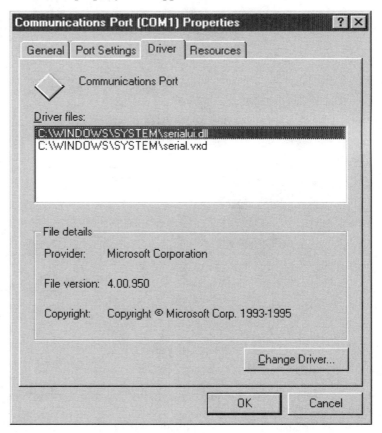

Figure 27.11 Driver tab on the Communications Port property sheet

The Drivers sheet lists what drivers are associated with that device. You may change drivers by clicking the Change Driver button and indicating which driver, and if necessary, where, to use with the device. This property sheet also provides you with some details about the driver file, if these details are available.

6. Click the Resources tab.

The Resources property sheet appears.

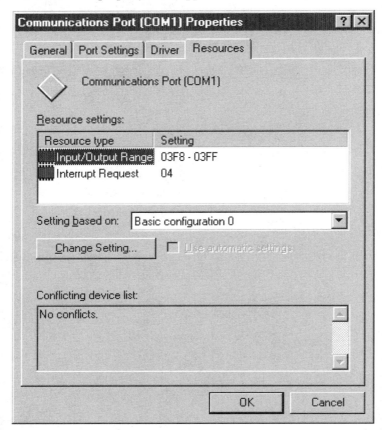

Figure 27.12 Resources tab on the Communications Port property sheet

The Resources sheet indicates what resources are currently assigned to that device. You may manually change these assignments, but be sure that the new assignments do not conflict with other assignments; you may have to change the settings on the device. Conflicts are indicated by an asterisk appearing beside the resource.

7. Click the Cancel button.

8. Click the Close button to close Device Manager.

Rebuilding Default Groups

If required, you can rebuild the default groups by running a simple command.

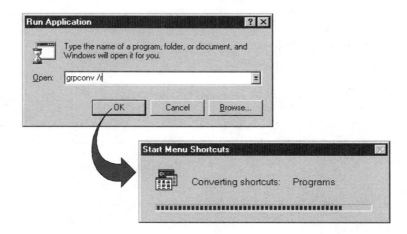

Figure 27.13 Default groups can be rebuilt

▶ **To rebuild the default groups**

1. On the Start menu, click Run.
2. In the Run text box, type **grpconv** and then press ENTER, or click OK.

The default groups are rebuilt without affecting any new groups, shortcuts, and so on that you had already created.

Another method is to select the .GRP file and open it, or double-click the file. This converts the group to a Windows 95 folder. While this must be done on individual GRP files, it is not limited to the default groups.

Note Custom groups will not be rebuilt.

Lesson Summary

Windows 95 support of Plug and Play and the other detection routines greatly automates the configuration of new devices. If absolutely required, you can manually configure new devices using Device Manager.

Lesson 5: Resources for Troubleshooting

Staying current with new information is crucial to supporting and troubleshooting computers. This lesson describes some of the commonly available information resources and how to utilize them.

After this lesson you will be able to:

- Use various resources to locate answers to troubleshooting problems.

Estimated lesson time 45 minutes

There are sources that you can use to get information about Microsoft products. These sources can be very valuable when troubleshooting.

- TechNet—A monthly CD-ROM that is available by subscription.

- CompuServe—An online service that contains information on a variety of subjects, including several forums dedicated to Microsoft and its products.

- Internet—Microsoft maintains an FTP site that contains information about Microsoft products, drivers, and so on.

- The Microsoft Network—An online service that contains information on a variety of subjects including several forums dedicated to Microsoft and its products.

- Microsoft Download Libraries (MSDL)—An electronic bulletin board service (BBS) operated by Microsoft. This contains the latest drivers and other information.

Much of the information contained by each of these sources is duplicated on the other sources. For example, the TechNet information is also on CompuServe, the latest drivers can be found on all of these sources, and so on. If you have problems accessing one particular source, try one of the other sources.

TechNet

The TechNet CD-ROM is produced by Microsoft. It contains technical information that is useful for supporting Microsoft products.

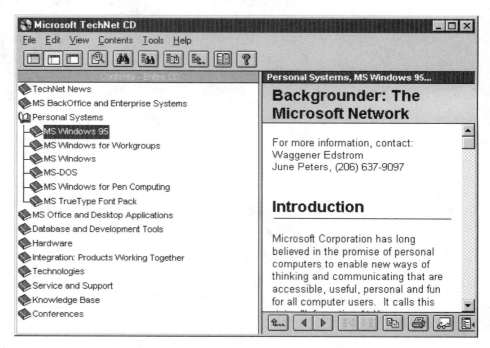

Figure 27.14 Example of TechNet contents screen

The CD-ROM installs just like any other program. Once installed, it adds choices to the Programs folder.

▶ **To use the TechNet CD-ROM**

One of the keys to using the TechNet CD-ROM is being able to find the information you need. There are several methods to locating data on the CD-ROM; the following method uses the Find tool to search for a phrase. Refer to the Help menu for more information on using the various features of the TechNet CD-ROM.

1. On the Start menu, point to Programs, and then click Microsoft TechNet.

2. Click the TechNet CD-ROM selection.

3. On the Tools menu, click Find.

   The Query text box appears.

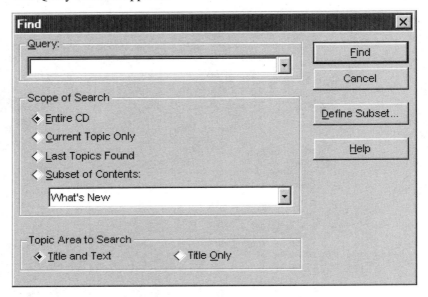

Figure 27.15 The TechNet Find function

4. Type the subject on which you need more information.

   For example, if you want to find out how set up an MS-DOS network client, you might type network client in the query box. To assist in an accurate search, you can be more specific in your query.

Note You could enter fewer words and still get find what you need, but the more precise you can be the faster you will locate what you need. For example, if you entered Microsoft Network Client Software in the query text box instead of entering network client, the search may reduce the number of found topics from over 1,000 to just 10.

The results of your search appear.

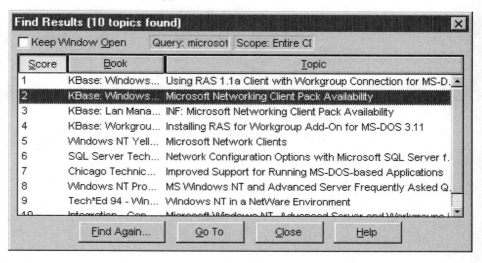

Figure 27.16 Results of a TechNet search

5. On the list of topics, select an appropriate article.

In this case, you are searching for article 2.

6. Click the Go To button.

The article appears.

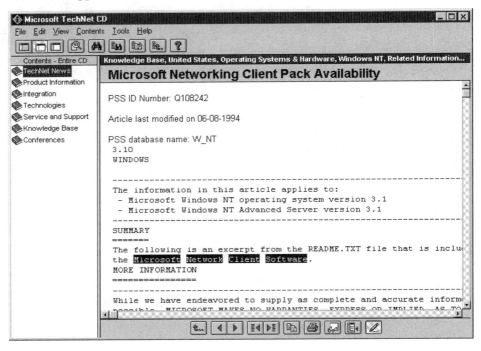

Figure 27.17 Example of a TechNet article

The TechNet CD-ROM is full of valuable information. You can subscribe to TechNet by calling:

1-800-344-2121

or

Mail your subscription request to:

Microsoft Corporation
P.O. Box 10296
Des Moines, IA 50336-0296

You can also access the TechNet information from CompuServe by typing GO TECHNET.

CompuServe

CompuServe is an online service that contains a variety of information. Microsoft maintains several forums where you can obtain information about Microsoft products.

To use CompuServe, you must first have an account. You can get an account by calling:

1-800-848-8199

The CompuServe representative will explain the various fees and options.

There are a variety of methods of accessing CompuServe. WinCIM is an interface that is included on the TechNet CD-ROM and other sources. HyperTerminal, which is included with Windows 95, can also be used to access CompuServe.

CompuServe consists of many different forums. A forum is a grouping of related information. The actual structure and permissions for a forum vary, but a forum usually consists of the three main components:

- Threads—Locations where you can post questions and answers. This is not real-time, interactive responses. Anyone may ask the question, anyone may answer.

- Libraries—Locations where you can download and, if you have the appropriate permissions, upload files.

- Conferences—Real-time, online discussions with two or more people. Anyone may submit a question or a response.

To locate a particular forum, type GO INDEX at a prompt. In WinCIM, the results should look something like the example in Figure 27.18.

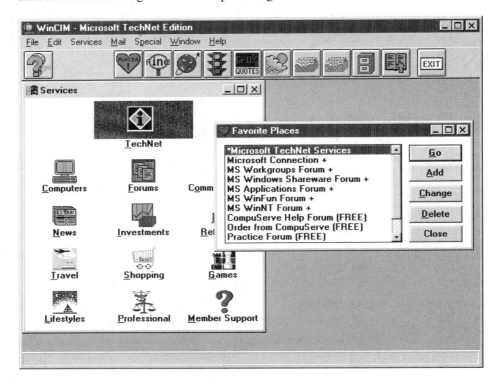

Figure 27.18 Example of WinCIM screen

Microsoft maintains a series of forums relating to Microsoft products. To see a list of the Microsoft forums, from the Index, click option 1, type Microsoft, and then press ENTER.

You receive a series of screens, listing the available Microsoft forums.

Figure 27.19   Examples of Microsoft-related CompuServe forums

To access one of these forums, type the number of your choice and then press ENTER.

If you know the name of the forum you want to enter, you may go there directly by typing GO *<FORUMNAME>* and then pressing ENTER.

Internet Site

Microsoft maintains an FTP site with product information, drivers, and so on. To access this site, you need an Internet service provider. There are many different providers, all with varying types of services.

Once you have service with an Internet provider, you can access the Microsoft FTP site.

▶ **To access the Microsoft FTP site**

1. From an FTP prompt, type **ftp.microsoft.com** and then press ENTER. You can use the IP decimal address of 198.105.232.1 instead of the friendly name IP address.

A log in screen appears.

Figure 27.20 ftp log in screen

2. At the command prompt, type **anonymous** and then press ENTER.

3. At the password prompt, type your full Internet electronic mail name (for example, *yourname.companyname.com*), and then press ENTER.

   The Welcome screen appears, and you have access to the server.

Once you are logged on, you may access any of the files on the server. But like all the other sources of information, you need to be able to find the files that you want.

There are two files that are useful for finding files.

- INDEX.TXT—Contains a list of the files in the root and the first level directories.

- DIRMAP.TXT—Contains a list of the first and second level directories of ftp.microsoft.com. The following was the contents of the of the DIRMAP.TXT file as of September 1994.

  This file is to help you find your way around ftp.microsoft.com. This file only covers the directory structure two levels deep. If you see a *KB* directory in a second level directory, it contains all of the information regarding that second level directory. For example, the /DEVELOPER/WIN32DK directory has a KB directory in it. This KB directory contains all of the articles for any 32-bit development kit.

Root directory	Subdirectory	Contents
ADVSYS		Advanced Systems, Networks, Mail
	LANMAN	LAN Manager and other networks
	MAIL	Microsoft Mail and Schedule+
	MSCLIENT	Microsoft Networking Client
	SQL_ODBC	SQL and ODBC
	WINNT	Microsoft Windows NT
	WINSOCK	Windows Sockets information
DESKAPPS		Desktop programs
	ACCESS	Microsoft Access
	DOSWORD	Microsoft Word for MS-DOS
	EXCEL	Microsoft Excel
	GAMES	Entertainment Packs Microsoft Flight Simulator, and so on
	HOMEAPPS	Home programs (Microsoft Fine Artist, Microsoft Creative Writer)
	MISCAPPS	Other programs
	MMAPPS	Multimedia titles
	OFFICE	Microsoft Office
	POWERPT	Microsoft PowerPoint®
	PROJECT	Microsoft Project
	PUBLISHER	Microsoft Publisher
	WORD	Microsoft Word for Windows and the Macintosh
	WRKS_MNY	Microsoft Works and Microsoft Money
DEVELOPR		Developer tools and information
	BASIC	Microsoft Quick Basic and other Basics
	DEVCAST	DevCast information
	DEVUTIL	MS Test, Delta, EXEMOD, EXEPACK, and LIB utilities
	DRG	Developer Relations Group
	FORTRAN	FORTRAN and FORTRAN POWERStation™
	FOX	Microsoft FoxBASE® and Microsoft FoxPro®
	MAPI	Messaging API information

(continued)

Root directory	Subdirectory	Contents
	MASM	Macro Assembler
	MSDN	Microsoft Developer Network
	MSJ	Microsoft Systems Journal
	OLE	OLE
	TAPI	Telephony API information
	VB	Microsoft Visual Basic
	VISUAL_C	Microsoft Visual C++™, MFC, and other C products
	WIN_DK	Microsoft Windows SDK, DKs, and Microsoft At Work™
	WIN32DK	32-bit Development Kits
MSEDCERT		Microsoft Education and Certification
	EDUCATIO	Microsoft Education information
	CERTIFIC	Microsoft Certified Professional information
MSFT		Microsoft shareholder information
	ANNREPT	Microsoft Annual Report
	BACKGRND	Background information on Microsoft
	PRESSREL	Microsoft press releases
	SEC	Recent filings with the Securities and Exchange Commission
SOFTLIB		Instructions and index for software library
	MSLFILES	Software library files (> 1500 files)
PEROPSYS		Personal Operating Systems and hardware
	HARDWARE	Mouse and other hardware
	MSDOS	MS-DOS
	WINDOWS	Microsoft Windows (all versions)
	WIN_NEWS	Information on Windows 95
TECHNET		Information on TechNet
	SERVDIR	Microsoft Services Directory

To manipulate the files, you need to use certain commands. These are UNIX commands and are case-sensitive. You should type the following common commands in lowercase.

- **ls -l**—Lists all of the available files.
- **show** *filename*—Displays the contents of a file; this is similar to the MS-DOS **type** command.
- **get** *filename*—Copies the file to the local provider.
- **help**—Lists the commands available.
- **help** *command*—Lists the function and syntax of a command.
- **close**—Disconnects your provider from ftp.microsoft.com.
- **bye**—Shuts down your session to the Internet.

Note   You must have TCP/IP protocol stack loaded to access the Internet site.

Microsoft Download Library (MSDL)

The Microsoft Download Library is an electronic bulletin board service maintained by Microsoft. You can download the latest drivers and other software from this service. You cannot upload, ask questions, or anything else with this service; MSDL is for downloading information only.

To access the MSDL, you can use the HyperTerminal program included with Windows 95.

▶ **To access MSDL with HyperTerminal**

1. On the Start menu, point to Programs, Accessories, and then click HyperTerminal.

   The HyperTerminal program starts.

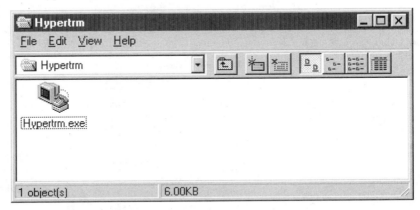

Figure 27.21 Example of a HyperTerminal screen

2. Double-click the HyperTerminal icon.

   The Connection Description dialog box appears.

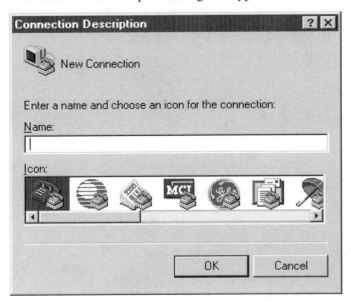

Figure 27.22 Connecting with HyperTerminal

3. Type **MSDL** in the Name text box, click an icon to represent MSDL, and then click OK.

The Phone Number dialog box appears.

Figure 27.23 Specifying a phone number with HyperTerminal

4. Enter the following:

Country code—United States of America (1)

Area code—206

Phone number—936-6735

5. Click OK.

When you click OK, the Connect dialog box appears.

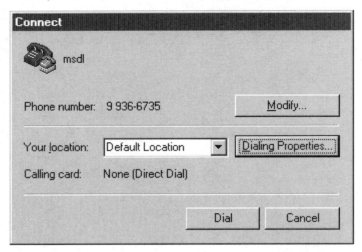

Figure 27.24 Connect dialog box in HyperTerminal

6. Enter the following settings:

Bits per second—MSDL accepts modem speeds between 2400 and 9600.

Data bits—8

Parity—None

Stop bits—1

Flow control—None

When you click OK, HyperTerminal places a call to MSDL and connects. You can then select files and download them to your computer.

Once you set up MSDL in HyperTerminal, to call again you simply double-click the MSDL connection icon.

Lesson Summary

TechNet, CompuServe, MSN, the Internet, and the Microsoft Download Library are just some of the information resources you can use to stay current with Windows 95 and other Microsoft products. Staying current can help you prevent problems you might otherwise have to resolve.

Questions and Answers for Volume 2

Chapter 13: Communications

Lesson 3, page 591 ▶ **To start the Phone Dialer**

- On the Start menu, point to Programs, Accessories, and then click Phone Dialer.

Note For this exercise, the examples use the 206 area code. Please use your own area code where 206 is shown.

Before continuing, make sure that your modem is *not* connected to the telephone line to prevent making unwanted telephone calls.

If you travel with your computer, you may need to dial from hotels. Generally, each hotel has a different telephone system with different dialing rules. In this exercise, you will set up a hotel location.

▶ **To dial a call in your home area**

1. On the Phone Dialer Tools menu, click Dialing Properties, and then click Default Location in the I am dialing from text box.
2. Click OK to close the dialog box.
3. Type 1 (206) 555-1234 as the number to dial.

   (Remember to substitute your area code for 206.)
4. Click the Dial button.

   What number was used to dial?

   555-1234

   You will get an error message after a few seconds because your modem is not connected to the telephone lines. If you didn't write down the number dialed, close the error message dialog box and dial again.

▶ **To set up a second location**

1. On the Phone Dialer Tools menu, click Dialing Properties.

   The Dialing Properties dialog box appears.

2. Click the New... button.

3. Type **hotel** in the text box as the new location name, and then click OK.

4. Use Dialing Properties to configure the second location according to the following scenario.

   This example assumes the hotel is in New York City, so the area code is 212. (If your normal location is in the 212 area code, substitute Los Angeles (213) for 212 in the examples.)

   To access an outside line, you must dial 9 for a local call and 8 for long distance.

   You use an AT&T calling card; its number is 20655512349876. Make sure to select AT&T via 1-800-321-0228 in the Change Calling Card dialog box.

   The hotel has call waiting that can be disabled by dialing 70#.

5. When you have made these changes, click OK to close the Dialing Properties dialog box.

6. Type 1 (206) 555-1234 as the number to dial.

   (Remember to substitute your area code for 206.)

7. Click the Dial button.

   What number was used to dial?

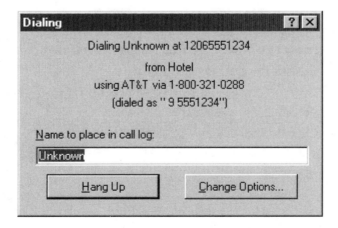

▶ **To dial an extension**

1. On the Phone Dialer Tools menu, click Dialing Properties. In the I am dialing from text box, click Default Location.

2. Click OK to close the Dialing Properties dialog box.

3. Enter 5551 as the Number to dial. Assume that this is a valid internal extension in your company.

4. Click the Dial button.

   What number was used to dial?

   5551

5. Exit Dial Helper.

Page 593

Review Questions

1. What is the central communications component in Windows 95?

   The central communications component in Windows 95 is the virtual communications driver, VCOMM.VXD.

2. Name the two types of device drivers needed for modems and describe the function of each.

   Unimodem—Main device driver provided by Microsoft which contains most of the functionality needed by the modem.

   Mini-driver—Written by the manufacturer which provides hardware-specific information for each modem.

3. What is TAPI?

   The Windows Telephone Application Programming Interface (TAPI) provides a standard way for programs to control telephony functions.

Chapter 14: Printing

Page 614

Review Questions

1. Describe the different types of printer driver combinations used in Windows 95.

    1. Microsoft universal driver + vendor provided mini-driver—For all printers except PostScript and HP Color Inkjet.

    2. Microsoft PostScript mini-driver + vendor provided mini-driver—For all PostScript printers.

    3. Monolithic driver—For HP Color Inkjet printers.

2. How do you check the status of the print queue in Windows 95?

    Open the Printers folder and double-click the icon of the printer you want to check.

Chapter 15: Network Printing

Page 653

Review Question

- After installing a printer using the Point and Print method on your desktop, how is this printer referenced by Windows 95?

    A. Using a mapped letter, for example, P:

    B. Using a mapped port, for example, LPT3:

    C. Using the UNC name, for example, *server**printer*

    D. Using a dynamically loadable printer reference. This is possible because of the new dynamically loadable device drivers that come with Windows 95.

    Answer: C, also B if you choose to print from MS-DOS–based programs.

Chapter 16: Programs and the Windows 95 Architecture

Page 668

Review Questions

1. Why does Windows 95 have both 16-bit and 32-bit system code?

    The 16-bit code was needed for three reasons: compatibility, memory usage, and performance.

2. A client calls and complains that after closing a 16-bit Windows-based program that had stopped responding, the system resources remain low. Why?

    16-bit Windows-based programs may use resources that are not tracked by the operating system, or these programs may share resources with other 16-bit Windows-based programs. The resources are not released until all 16-bit Windows-based programs are closed.

3. A customer complains that after closing various programs, the available resources are still reported lower than they were before the programs were started. No problems are occurring, the complaint is just that the resources are reported lower. Why?

    Windows 95 caches frequently used resources. If the resource is cached, it is not unloaded from the cache until system resources become low.

Chapter 17: Tuning an MS-DOS-Based Program

Lesson 2, page 675 ▶ **To modify program properties**

1. Explore My Computer and use the Find function to locate MEM.EXE.
2. Click the secondary mouse button on **mem**.
3. Click Properties on the menu.
4. Click the Program tab.
5. Click Close on Exit.
6. Click OK.
7. Start **mem** by double-clicking it or opening it.
8. According to the display, what is the total amount of Extended memory? Were you able to read it? Why or why not?

    You would be unable to read the amount of Extended memory. As soon as the program finished, that is, as soon as it prints to the screen, it exits and the window closes because of the Close Window on Exit setting.

9. Without changing the settings in the .PIF, start a command prompt and run **mem** in it.
10. Were you able to read the total amount of extended memory? Why or why not?

    Yes, you were able to run the Extended memory. The Mem program is not opening the window. The window belongs to COMMAND.COM and Mem is being run in the COMMAND.COM window.

Lesson 6, page 689 ▶ **To change command window miscellaneous attributes**

1. Shut down all programs.

2. Start two command prompts and put each in a window on your desktop.

3. Arrange the MS-DOS windows so that both are viewable at the same time and one is positioned above the other.

4. In each MS-DOS window, type the following command:

   **cd ** and then press ENTER

   cls and then press ENTER

   This brings you to the root directory and clears the screen.

5. In each of the command windows, type in the following commands:

   c:\labs\piftest

   This starts a counter on the upper-left corner of the windows screen. You may have to scroll up to see the counter running.

6. In the top MS-DOS window, click the MS-DOS icon in the upper-left corner, and then click Properties.

7. Click the Misc tab, and then click the Background Always suspend check box.

8. Click the Apply button, and then click the OK button. Look at both counters— what happened?

   Both counters are running.

9. Click the bottom MS-DOS window to bring it to the foreground. What happened?

   The counter in the top window stopped because it is suspended in the background.

10. Return to the top MS-DOS window. What happened to the counter in the bottom MS-DOS window?

    Both counters resume counting.

11. Stop the **piftest** counters by pressing the SPACEBAR while in the active window.

12. Deselect all of the changes you made in this exercise before shutting down the two command windows.

Page 691

Review Questions

1. A user calls and says, "When I try to switch between my MS-DOS–based program and Windows by using ALT+TAB, nothing happens. I have to quit the program to get back to Windows." How do you help this user?

   On the user's machine, open the properties list for that program. Click the Misc tab and make sure that all the Windows shortcut keys are reserved.

2. A user wants a special batch file to run before she runs her favorite MS-DOS–based program. How can this be set up?

   Open the properties list for that program and click the Program tab. Look for the Batch file: label and type in the appropriate path.

3. A user complains that he can no longer get an MS-DOS session to work properly. Each time he tries to start an MS-DOS session from the Programs menu, the system shuts down Windows and goes into MS-DOS mode. A quick glance at the Properties list for the C:\WINDOWS\COMMAND.COM file shows that the MS-DOS mode option is cleared. How do you fix this problem?

   Open the properties list for the following program: C:\Windows\Start Menu\Programs\MS-DOS Prompt (this is the PIF file). Click the Program tab, click the Advanced... button, and then clear the MS-DOS mode option.

Chapter 18: Display

Page 711

Review Questions

1. What is the DIB engine?

   The DIB engine contains common display device driver code. In earlier versions of Windows, independent hardware vendors (IHVs) were responsible for supplying this code. With Windows 95, the IHV only has to write the hardware specific code and call on the DIB engine for software calls.

2. What is a display mini-driver?

   An IHV has a choice between writing the entire device driver or taking advantage of the common code that Microsoft has supplied with the DIB engine. If the IHV decides to use Microsoft's DIB engine, then the software that the IHV supplies is called a display mini-driver. The display mini-driver contains hardware-specific code for the IHV's device and the software calls to the DIB engine.

3. Match the component with the appropriate definition.

Component	Definition
A. mini-VDD	1. Generic VxD used by the mini-VDD to virtualize the video hardware; supplied by Microsoft.
B. virtual display device (VDD.VXD)	2. Hardware-specific DRV to draw output on a video display; written by IHV. IHVs need to write only if they cannot write a display mini-driver.
C. VFLATD.VXD	3. Generic VxD to virtualize frame buffers larger than 64K; supplied by Microsoft.
D. full display driver	4. Hardware-specific VxD to virtualize the video hardware so that more than one virtual machine (VM) can share the same display; written by the IHV.

A = 4

B = 1

C = 3

D = 2

4. Which components of the Windows 95 display system handle virtualizing video graphic services for MS-DOS–based programs running in a Virtual Machine?

   The VDD and the grabber (VGAFULL.3GR).

5. Why is it important for the correct monitor type to be selected in Windows 95?

   If the wrong monitor is chosen, then it is possible to drive it beyond it's capacity. Driving a monitor beyond it's capacity can permanently damage the device.

6. You receive the following support call from a user. The user states: "I was adjusting my display settings when I was distracted. I accidentally installed the wrong card and monitor and then clicked OK. The system asked me if I wanted to restart the computer and I hit the ENTER key so it would restart. As it was restarting, I realized that I had installed the wrong display and video card and so I shut off the computer." What is the next step to take to help this user?

   Turn on the machine and wait. If the video card and monitor are not compatible with the user's hardware, Windows 95 will run in VGA fallback mode. VGA fallback mode will provide a usable VGA display so that the user can keep working until the correct hardware is installed.

Chapter 19: System Policies and Templates

Lesson 2, page 731

Using a Template

4. Complete the right side of this table by examining the template and the System Policy Editor.

Template	System Policy Editor
CLASS USER	**Default User**
CATEGORY !!ControlPanel	**Control Panel**
CATEGORY !!CPL_Display	**Display**
POLICY !!CPL_Display_Restrict	**Restrict Display Control Panel**
PART !!CPL_Display_Disable CHECKBOX	**Disable Display Control Panel**
PART !!CPL_Display_HideBkgnd CHECKBOX	**Hide Background Page**
PART !!CPL_Display_HideScrsav CHECKBOX	**Hide Screen Saver Page**

Lesson 2, page 732

Modifying the Templates

4. Open the Properties box for the default user, click Desktop, and then put a check mark next to Wallpaper.

   Is there a default wallpaper name listed, or is the entry blank?

   No, the entry is blank.

   What is the name of the default wallpaper, if there is one?

   The entry is blank.

Lesson x, page 732

8. Open the Properties box for the default user, click Desktop, and then put a check mark next to Wallpaper.

   Is there a default wallpaper name listed, or is the entry blank?

   Yes

   What is the name of the default wallpaper, if there is one?

   The default wallpaper is THATCH.BMP.

Lesson 2, page 733   12. Open the Properties box for the default user, click Desktop, and then put a check mark next to Wallpaper.

Is there a default wallpaper name listed, or is the entry blank?

Yes

What is the name of the default wallpaper, if there is one?

The default wallpaper is THATCH.BMP.

13. What other differences do you notice about the MINIMAL.ADM file?

All the other restrictions that were available with the original file (ADMIN.ADM) are gone.

Lesson 2, page 733   ## Creating a Template (Optional)

Your template should look like the following:

```
CLASS MACHINE

CATEGORY !!Network
KEYNAME Software\Microsoft\Windows\CurrentVersion\Policies\Network

    CATEGORY !!Logon
        POLICY !!LogonBanner
        KEYNAME Software\Microsoft\Windows\CurrentVersion\Winlogon
            PART !!LogonBanner_Caption EDITTEXT
            VALUENAME "LegalNoticeCaption"
            MAXLEN 255
            DEFAULT !!LogonBanner_DefCaption
            END PART

            PART !!LogonBanner_Text EDITTEXT
            VALUENAME "LegalNoticeText"
            MAXLEN 255
            DEFAULT !!LogonBanner_DefText
            END PART
        END POLICY
    END CATEGORY    ;Logon

    CATEGORY !!RemoteAccess
        POLICY !!RemoteAccess_Disable
        VALUENAME "NoDialIn"
        END POLICY
    END CATEGORY ; Remote Access
END CATEGORY ; Network
```

```
CLASS USER

CATEGORY !!Desktop
KEYNAME "Control Panel\Desktop"
    POLICY !!Wallpaper
        PART !!WallpaperName COMBOBOX REQUIRED
        SUGGESTIONS
            256color.bmp arcade.bmp argyle.bmp cars.bmp castle.bmp
Windows 95.bmp
            egypt.bmp honey.bmp leaves.bmp redbrick.bmp rivets.bmp
squares.bmp
            thatch.bmp winlogo.bmp zigzag.bmp
        END SUGGESTIONS
        VALUENAME "Wallpaper"
        END PART

        PART !!TileWallpaper CHECKBOX DEFCHECKED
        VALUENAME "TileWallpaper"
        VALUEON "1" VALUEOFF "0"
        END PART
    END POLICY  ;Wallpaper
END CATEGORY ;Desktop

CATEGORY !!Network
KEYNAME Software\Microsoft\Windows\CurrentVersion\Policies\Network
    CATEGORY !!Sharing
        POLICY !!DisableFileSharingCtrl
        VALUENAME NoFileSharingControl
        END POLICY

        POLICY !!DisablePrintSharingCtrl
        VALUENAME NoPrintSharingControl
        END POLICY
    END CATEGORY  ; Sharing
END CATEGORY  ; Network
```

```
[strings]
Network="Network"
Logon="Logon"
LogonBanner="Logon Banner"
LogonBanner_Caption="Caption:"
LogonBanner_Text="Text:"
LogonBanner_DefCaption="Important Notice:"
LogonBanner_DefText="Unauthorized logon is prohibited."
Sharing="Sharing"
RemoteAccess="Remote Access"
RemoteAccess_Disable="Disable dial-in"
Desktop="Desktop"
Wallpaper="Wallpaper"
WallpaperName="Wallpaper name:"
TileWallpaper="Tile wallpaper"
DisableFileSharingCtrl="Disable file sharing controls"
DisablePrintSharingCtrl="Disable print sharing controls"
@
```

Page 735

Review Questions

1. Is it possible to restrict a user from starting a single mode MS-DOS session? If so, how?

    Yes, this can be accomplished using the System Policy Editor and then setting this policy for the user.

2. What would be the best way to restrict all users from starting single-mode MS-DOS sessions?

    Set the default policy to restrict this feature.

3. You are the network manager of a 1000-node, twelve hundred user network—some users share machines—with 950 of these nodes running Windows 95 and the rest running Windows NT. There are 24 different departments sharing resources on the network, and you would like to restrict access to various programs to different groups of users using the following guidelines:

    Group A: No Restrictions

    Group B: Disable Registry Editing tools

    Group C: Group B restrictions + Restrict Network Control Panel

    Group D: Group C restrictions + Restrict Passwords Control Panel

    Group E: Group D restrictions + Restrict Printer Settings

    Group F: Group E restrictions + Restrict System Control Panel

Because these groups are set up on the Windows NT server, there will be users in more than one group. Make sure that if a user is listed in both Group F and in Group C that Group F's restrictions will take effect. How can this be accomplished?

The simplest way is to use group policies, then arrange the groups with the appropriate priorities. The following dialog box indicates how the priorities should be arranged.

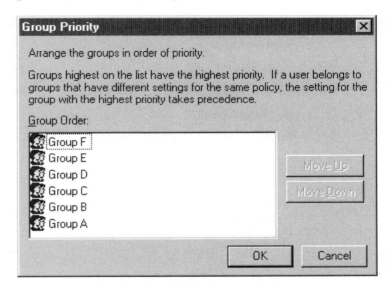

Chapter 20: Disk Utilities

Lesson 2, page 748

Back Up Local Drives

▶ **To back up local drives**

8. In the left pane, double-click My Computer, the C drive, and then the Windows folder to explore which directories are included in the Full Backup file set.

Each folder and drive in the dialog box is preceded with a box. An empty box means no files and folders within the folder will be backed up. A checked box indicates that *all* files and folders within the folder will be backed up. A grayed checked box indicates that *some* files and folders within the folder will be backed up.

What is *not* included in the Full Backup set?

Other drives.

Lesson 2, page 749   17.   Click the backup set you just created and then click the Next Step button.

Did Backup prompt you for a password? **Yes**

Lesson 2, page 752
Backup Individual Files (Optional)

▶   **To restore backed up files**

12.   Did Backup recreate the Test Delete directory?

Yes

13.   Did Backup restore the deleted Delete.doc and Remove Directory.doc files?

Yes

14.   Did Backup overwrite the Overwrite.doc file in the Test Directory folder with the original, older file?

Yes

15.   On the Settings menu in Backup, click Options.

Which setting prevents Restore from overwriting newer files?

Overwrite older files only.

How does enabling incremental backup affect making backups?

A Full backup makes a backup of all selected files. A Differential backup makes a backup of selected files which have changed since the last backup.

Page 774

Review Questions

1. When is it most important to run ScanDisk?

   1. After the system crashed (due to a power outage, turning off the computer without shutting down Windows 95 properly, rebooting the computer while Windows 95 is running, and so on).

   2. Before the Disk Defragmenter utility is run.

2. When is it important to run Disk Defragmenter?

   1. Any time a large number of files and or directories have been removed.

   2. When the system seems sluggish or when there seems to be an excessive amount of hard disk activity.

3. List the different media types that Windows 95 Backup can use.

   1. Tape

   2. Floppy disk

   3. Server

   4. Local hard disk

Chapter 21: The Boot Sequence

Lesson 5, page 797

Examine the Boot Process

In this exercise, you will single-step through the boot process, recording what happens during each step.

▶ **To single-step boot (note: read all instructions first)**

1. Restart your computer.

2. After the POST, the Starting Windows... message appears. As soon as this message appears, press F8. Highlight Step-by-Step confirmation, and then press the ENTER key.

3. Windows 95 prompts you to confirm each startup command. The following is a sample of what you may see. In this example, Windows 95 was installed in the default C:\WINDOWS directory. If you installed Windows 95 in another location, your path will vary.

```
Load DoubleSpace driver [Enter=Y,Esc=n]?
Process the system registry [Enter=Y,Esc=N]?
Create a startup log file (BOOTLOG.TXT) [Enter=Y,Esc=N]?
Process your startup device drivers (CONFIG.SYS) [Enter=Y,Esc=N]?
DEVICE=C:\WINDOWS\HIMEM.SYS [Enter=Y,Esc=N]?
LASTDRIVE=Z [Enter=Y,Esc=N]?
DEVICE=C:\WINDOWS\IFSHLP.SYS [Enter=Y,Esc=N]?
DEVICE=C:\WINDOWS\SETVER.EXE [Enter=Y,Esc=N]?
Process your startup command file (AUTOEXEC.BAT) [Enter=Y,Esc=N]?
PATH C:\WINDOWS;C:\DOS [Enter=Y,Esc=N]?
C:\WINDOWS\COMMAND\doskey [Enter=Y,Esc=N]?
WIN [Enter=Y,Esc=N]?
Load all Windows Drivers [Enter=Y,Esc=N]?
```

4. Restart your computer as often as necessary to answer the following questions. If any of the following prevents Windows 95 from loading, cold boot your computer by turning it off, waiting five seconds, and then turning it back on.

5. Will Windows 95 start without creating a BOOTLOG.TXT file? **Yes (answer No to the prompt Create start-up log file and answer Yes to all other prompts.)**

   Does Windows 95 have full functionality? **Yes**

   Why or why not? **BOOTLOG.TXT records errors encountered during the boot process and is not required for Windows 95 to run**

6. Will Windows 95 start without running the CONFIG.SYS file? **Yes (answer No to the prompt Process start-up device drivers and answer Yes to all other prompts.)**

   Does Windows 95 have full functionality? **Yes**

   Why or why not? **CONFIG.SYS is not required to run Windows 95.**

7. Will Windows 95 start without loading HIMEM.SYS? **No (answer No to the prompt C:\WINDOWS\HIMEM.SYS and Yes to all other prompts.)**

   Does Windows 95 have full functionality? **No**

   Why or why not? **Windows requires HIMEM.SYS**

8. Will Windows 95 start without running IFSHLP.SYS? **No (answer No to the prompt DEVICEHIGH=C:\WINDOWS\IFSHLP.SYS and Yes to all other prompts.)**

   Why or why not? **The Microsoft Installable File System Manager (IFSMGR) requires the helper driver IFSHLP.SYS.**

9. Will Windows 95 start without running the AUTOEXEC.BAT file? **Yes - (answer No to prompt Process start-up command file and Yes to all other prompts.)**

   Why or why not? **The AUTOEXEC.BAT file is not used by Windows 95.**

10. Will Windows 95 start without loading all Windows-based drivers? **No (answer No to the prompt Load all Windows drivers and Yes to all other prompts.)**

    Why or why not? **No network functionality in Windows 95.**

11. Can you break out of the boot process into MS-DOS? **Yes.**

    If yes, how? **Answer No to the prompt Win? and Yes to all other prompts**

    Why or why not? **If you do not process WIN.COM you receive a command prompt**.

Page 800

Review Questions

1. What are three functions of the POST?

   1. Test RAM

   2. Test and initialize various system devices (display, drives, and so on)

   3. Locate the boot drive

2. What additional capabilities does a Plug and Play ROM BIOS provide beyond a legacy ROM BIOS?

   The Plug and Play ROM BIOS identifies all Plug and Play-compliant devices and initializes them before booting the computer.

3. List the sequence of events during protected-mode Plug and Play initialization.

   1. Initialize existing VxDs

   2. Arbitrate resource conflicts

   3. Initialize devices

4. What is the registry? What is its purpose?

   The registry is a centralized configuration database. The purpose of the registry is to consolidate all the configuration information that used to be stored in separate .INI files.

Chapter 22: Microsoft Exchange

Page 835

Review Questions

1. What is MAPI?

   A set of common commands that allow programs to communicate with electronic mail systems and other MAPI-compliant programs.

2. What is the purpose of a message profile?

   A message profile contains service configuration information. It can contain generic settings, locations, delivery order, and other message settings.

Chapter 23: File Synchronization

Page 848

Review Questions

1. What is the purpose of Briefcase?

   The purpose of the Briefcase is to synchronize files that may be used in different locations or folders.

2. What is an orphan file?

   A file copied into the Briefcase that no longer synchronizes to a master file. The master file may have been deleted, moved, or otherwise lost.

Chapter 24: Dial-Up Networking Functions

Page 880

Review Questions

1. What are the three protocols supported by Dial-Up Networking?

   NetBEUI

   IPX/SPX

   TCP/IP

2. How would a user increase security on a dial-in machine running Windows 95?

   Enable the Require encrypted password option when setting up Windows 95 as a dial-in server.

3. What is an implicit connection?

   The ability of Windows 95 to restore a connection to a network resource quickly without having to start a new remote connection.

Chapter 25: Transitioning to Windows 95

Page 915

Review Questions

1. What are the benefits of running a shared copy of Windows 95?

   Easier to customize and manage multiple desktops

   More secure (each user has to logon to the network to use the computer)

   Easier to upgrade software

   Safer for novice users because access to system files is controlled

   Requires less local system requirements

2. What is the best way to set up and test computers for the transition to Windows 95?

   Install Windows 95 on a small group of computers.

   Test this small group until all the bugs are worked out.

   Repeat the procedures on another small group of computers until done.

Chapter 26: Implementing Windows 95 Multimedia

Lesson 3, page 937 ▶ **To use Sound Recorder**

1. On the Start menu, point to Programs, Accessories, Multimedia, and then click Sound Recorder to launch the Sound Recorder.

2. Start recording by clicking the Record button (the button with the large red dot).

3. Speak a short phrase into the microphone. Click the Stop button (the button with the solid square) when you are finished.

4. Listen to your voice by clicking the playback button. Try listening to your voice using different effects (echo, reverse, high speed, low speed, and so on).

5. Save your voice in a file.

6. Increase the speed of your voice by 500 percent and then reduce the speed back to normal.

   Does it sound the same? **No**

   Why not?

   Because the sampling rate does not change when you increase the speed, data gets dropped. When you decrease the speed, the data is not returned. The system adds duplicates of the remaining data to expand the space.

7. Save the current contents of Sound Recorder in a second file.

   Is the size of this second file the same size as your original voice? **Yes**

   If not, explain the differences.

Page 940

Review Question

- John recently bought a new Pentium computer running Windows 95. He decided to take the Microsoft Windows Sound System card out of his old computer and install it in the Pentium machine. Should he also install the Windows Sound System software that came with the card?

  Plug and Play support in Windows 95 will detect the card and install the updated drivers. The Windows Sound System utilities will need to be installed separately.

A P P E N D I X   A

Tips to Using the Windows 95 User Interface

Note When the terms *right mouse button* or *right click* are used, these terms refer to the secondary mouse button—the right mouse button when configured for right-hand use, and the left mouse button when configured for left-hand use.

Shell

Right Mouse Drag Operations (from Program to Shell)

Many OLE-aware programs including Microsoft WordPad, Microsoft Word for Windows version 6.0, and Microsoft Excel version 5.0 support right mouse button drag and drop operations. This allows for the following shell and programs interoperability.

1. Start Microsoft Excel and then minimize it.

2. Open a Word for Windows or WordPad document.

3. Drag some text out of the document and onto the desktop.

   This creates a *scrap*. A scrap is a file that is created when you drag part of a document onto the desktop.

4. Drag the scrap icon over the Excel button on the taskbar. Hold the mouse button down until Excel opens.

5. Release the mouse button to drop the scrap.

   The text is inserted into an Excel spreadsheet.

6. Open an Excel spreadsheet.

7. Find an important cell in the spreadsheet, one that requires you to scroll to the a distant portion of the spreadsheet, and use the right mouse button to drag it to the desktop.

8. When you release the mouse button, you have several options. Click Create Document Shortcut here.

   This creates a shortcut that points *into* the spreadsheet, to the selected cell.

9. Close the spreadsheet and then double-click the shortcut.

   Excel opens to the specific cell.

Dragging from One Window to Another with Maximized Windows

You can drag and drop from one window to the other by dragging from one window and lingering over the icon on the taskbar for the other window. The other program activates, allowing you to drop the contents of the first window. This can be accomplished when dragging from one program to another, including from one Windows Explorer window to another.

Cut/Copy/Paste

In any standard edit box, the right mouse button can be used to bring up a context menu allowing the user to cut, copy, paste, or delete information. The user can also use the keyboard equivalents, but the context menu makes it so the user doesn't have to remember them.

Taskbar

Set Date/Time from Taskbar

Double-click the clock located on the taskbar to set the time.

Hiding the Taskbar

If the taskbar is taking up too much space on the screen, you can hide it by choosing Taskbar properties (on the Start button or by clicking the taskbar with the right mouse button) and enabling the Auto Hide feature from the Taskbar Options property sheet. When the mouse moves near the taskbar area, the taskbar appears.

Moving the Taskbar

The default location of the taskbar (at the bottom of the screen) can be changed by dragging the taskbar to one of the other three (top, left, or right) sides of the desktop area.

Displaying the Date

The time is displayed on the taskbar, but the date can be made visible by placing the mouse cursor over the time display—the tool tip will show the current date.

Start Button

Opening the Start Menu

You can open the Start Menu folder by clicking the Start menu with the right mouse button and then either choosing Open to view in folder view, or choosing Explore to use Windows Explorer.

Adding Items to the Programs Menu on Start Button

To add items to the Programs menu on the Start button, you can either use the Start Menu Programs property sheet to customize the Start menu (click Taskbar properties from the Start button or right-click the taskbar) or you can directly add new items by dragging and dropping items onto the Start menu button.

Access to Frequently Used Programs/Documents

You can drag an icon for a program or document to the Start button to put a shortcut to that item at the top of your Start menu.

Keyboard Access By Numbering Start Menu Items

You can improve keyboard access to the items at the top of the Start menu by numbering the icons you put in there (rename them with a number at the beginning of the name). Once renamed, you can press CTRL+ESC followed by the number to launch your most commonly used programs.

Keyboard Access By Using Accelerator Keys

You can improve keyboard access to the Start menu or Programs menu on the Start button by placing an ampersand ("&") before a unique letter in the name of items (rename them with an ampersand within the name.) Then, you can press CTRL+ESC followed by a **p** (for Programs) and the accelerator key letter to quickly launch an item. For example "&MS-DOS Prompt" allows the user to type CTRL+ESC+P+M to quickly launch a command prompt using the keyboard.

Desktop

Access to Desktop Properties

Right-clicking the desktop brings up the display properties. You can then change the desktop background, screen saver, appearance, or settings.

File Operations

Selecting Multiple Files in My Computer/Windows Explorer

Selecting multiple files in My Computer with Large Icon view enabled produces a different behavior than when you are in List view. For example, when in Large Icon view, click the beginning of the list of files. If you press SHIFT+CLICK in the middle of the file list to select all files, the result would be the same as if you highlighted all files by clicking and then dragging the mouse pointer over them. The highlighted area will not extend to the right as it did with Windows 3.x File Manager. The selected area only goes over as far as the file at which you started the Shift + Click.

When in List view, group selection functionality is similar to Windows 3.x File Manager. The items are selected from left to right all the way across the window.

To select all files in a folder, use the CTRL+A keys.

Copy Files into Different Windows

1. Select the files or folders that you want to copy.
2. Right click on the files, click Copy (or Cut if you want to move the files).
3. Click on the Start menu, click the Run option (or **CTRL+ESC R**), then type in the target drive or folder.
4. Right click in the target and click Paste. The files are copied or moved.

Creating a New File or Folder

Create a new file by right clicking on the desktop or inside a folder and clicking New, then select the type of document to create.

Create a New Folder While Saving a File

When doing a File Save As using the common dialogs, you can create a new folder to store the document. Right click in the dialog box and click New Folder to create the folder where you want to store the document.

Deleting Files Without Moving them to Recycle Bin

To permanently remove files (without first storing them in the Recycle Bin), hold the SHIFT key down when clicking Delete on the File menu, or by pressing the DELETE key if you are using the keyboard. The selected items are permanently removed from the computer and are not moved to the Recycle Bin.

Sending Files to an Object

You can drag any shortcut into the Send To folder under the Windows directory. This provides a quick way to send data to an object. The object can be a printer, fax, network drive, or Windows-based program. On the object's context menu you will always have the device on the Send To available then without having to find the object on the desktop. For example, putting Notepad or WordPad into the Send To folder gives you a quick way to edit text files regardless of their extension.

Using Other Programs with a File

Select the document you want to open, hold down the SHIFT key, right-mouse click, and then click Open. You can then select which program you want to use to edit the document.

Copying Files

Select the files you want to copy, right-mouse click and click Copy. Open the destination location, right-mouse click and click Paste.

Keyboard Shortcuts

The following is a list of the various keyboard shortcuts and their functions.

Keystrokes	Function
F2	Rename
F3	Find
CTRL-X,C,V	Cut, Copy, Paste
Delete key	Delete
SHIFT+DELETE	Immediate Delete without placing file in Recycle Bin
ALT+ENTER	Properties
CTRL+Right click	Put alternative verbs on context menu for *Open With*
SHIFT+Right click	Change the default command to the next one in the list

General Control Folders/Windows Explorer

Keystrokes	Function
F4 (Windows Explorer)	Drops down the combo box and puts focus on it
F5	Refresh the screen
F6	Tabs between panes in Windows Explorer
CTRL-G (Windows Explorer)	Go to
CTRL-Z	Undo
CTRL-A	Select all
Backspace	Goes to the parent folder
SHIFT-<close>	On folders this closes this folder and all its parent folders

The Windows Explorer Tree

Keystrokes	Function
Num *	Expands everything under selection
Num +	Expands selection
Num -	Collapses
Right Arrow	Expands current selection if it is not expanded, otherwise goes to the first child
Left Arrow	Collapses current selection if it's not expanded, otherwise goes to the first parent

Property Sheets

Keystrokes	Function
CTRL+TAB	Selects each property sheet from left to right
SHIFT+CTRL+TAB	Selects the sheets in the opposite direction

Open/Save Common Dialog

Key	Function
F4	Drops down the location list
F5	Refresh the view*(works globally)*
Backspace	Go to parent folder if focus on view window

General Keyboard Commands

Keys	Function
F1	Help
F10	Goes to menu mode
SHIFT+F10	Context menu for selected item
CTRL+ESC	Bring up Start Menu/Sets taskbar focus
CTRL+ESC, ESC	Focus rests on taskbar, now you can press TAB then SHIFT+F10 for the context menu, or press the arrow key to change tasks, or press TAB to go to the desktop
ALT+TAB	Switch to the next program in the Z-Order

Accessibility Shortcuts

Keystrokes	Function
SHIFT five times	Toggles StickyKeys On/Off
Hold down Right SHIFT for 8 seconds	Toggles FilterKeys On/Off
Hold down NUMLOCK for 5 seconds	Toggles ToggleKeys On/Off
Left ALT+Left SHIFT + NUMLOCK	Toggles MouseKeys On/Off
Left ALT +Left SHIFT +PRINTSCRN	Toggles High Contrast On/Off

MS Natural Keyboard Keys

Keystrokes	Function
Win+R	Run Dialog
Win+M	Minimize All
SHIFT+Win+M	Undo Minimize All
Win+F1	Help
Win+E	Windows Explorer
Win+F	Find Files or Folders
CTRL+Win+F	Find Computer
Win+TAB	Cycle Through taskbar buttons
Win+BREAK	System Properties Dialog

Running a File

You can start a program from within any folder by opening that folder and then choosing Run... from the Start menu. This takes the place of the File Run menu option in the Windows 3.x File Manager. The open folder identifies the current working directory from which to run the program or open the document.

Viewing Files

Find Files of a Specific Type

On the Start menu, click Find. Click Files or Folders, and then click the Advanced tab.

Enter the file type in the Of Type text box.

Sorting File View

When you are looking at the contents of a folder in details view, you can click the column headers to sort automatically. To reverse the sort order, click the header a second time.

Manipulating Windows

Closing Multiple Windows

If you are using multiple window browse and you want to close all the windows you have open at the same time, hold the SHIFT key and then click the Close icon button (the box with an X located in the upper-right corner of the dialog box) of the window that is active.

Cycling Through Open Programs

Pressing ALT+TAB repeatedly cycles you through all open programs.

Cycling Through Open Windows and Property Sheets

Pressing ALT+ESC repeatedly cycles you through all open windows and property sheets.

Minimizing All Active Windows

Right-click the taskbar, and then click Minimize All Windows. All the windows are minimized to the taskbar.

You can restore the windows to their original size and position by choosing Undo Minimize All.

Note When using the Microsoft Natural Keyboard™ for MS-DOS and Windows, pressing the Windows key and the letter M minimizes all active windows. Pressing the Windows key, and SHIFT+ M restores the windows to their original size and position.

Tiling/Cascading Windows

Right-click the taskbar, and then click Cascade, Tile Horizontally, or Tile Vertically to organize the open windows to your preferences.

If you do not like the arrangement you selected, you can restore the windows to their original size and position by right-clicking the taskbar and then choosing the Undo operation.

Operations on Windows from Taskbar

You can Restore, Move, Size, Minimize, Maximize, or Close a window and program by right-clicking the button for the window on the taskbar.

Simulating Windows 3.x Program Manager

Create a shortcut to the Programs folder. (\WINDOWS\START MENU\PROGRAMS). This shortcut may be placed anywhere convenient, such as on the desktop, in the Start menu, or in the Startup group.

By creating this one shortcut, the user has an easy, familiar way to access most of their programs.

My Computer

Access to Computer Properties

Right-clicking the My Computer icon and selecting Properties displays the system properties. The user can then view and change the computer settings.

Changing the Name of My Computer

Click My Computer. Click a second time (or press F2) to rename My Computer.

Access to Screen Saver from the Desktop

Drag the .SCR file of your favorite screen saver from the folder it is stored in to the desktop. This creates a shortcut to your favorite screen saver.

Using the Cursor Keys Instead of a Mouse

You can operate the cursor without using the mouse by turning the MouseKeys feature on. It is located in the Accessibility Options in the Control Panel.

Networking

Search for a File on a Server

On the Start menu, point to Find, and then click Files or Folders. Enter the filename of the file. In the Look in text box, enter a server name. This causes a search of *every* share on the server for the matching filename.

Access to Network Information

Populate the Network Neighborhood (Windows\NetHood folder) with shortcuts to network locations. The shortcuts remain when you are logged off the network and automatically invoke the Dial-Up Networking features (as long as these features are installed).

Connecting to a Network Server and Share

On the Start button, click Run and then type the name of the server (and optionally, share name and paths) using universal naming convention (UNC) names. For example, typing *server* opens a window showing shared resources on that server. Typing *server**share*\dir opens the specified directory on the server\share path. In addition, if you have a Windows 95 aware Internet browser, you can enter Universal Resource Locator (URL) names (such as http://www.microsoft.com) in the same way to access Internet resources.

Access to Network Properties

Right-clicking the Network Neighborhood brings up the network properties. This dialog box allows you to change the network settings.

Changing the Name of Network Neighborhood

Click Network Neighborhood. Click a second time (or press F2) to rename Network Neighborhood.

Multimedia/CD-ROM

How to Change the Default of AutoPlay CD Player when an Audio CD-ROM Is Inserted

1. Open a folder, for example, My Computer.

2. Click View, Options.

3. Click the File Types tab.

4. Click Audio CD, and then click Edit...

5. Click the Play from Action list box.

6. Click Set Default (this actually toggles the default).

   If the word Play is bold, then the audio CD-ROM will play when inserted in the CD-ROM drive. If the word Play is not bold, the audio CD-ROM will not automatically play.

Custom Playlists in the Audio CD Player

1. On the Disc menu, click Edit Play List.

   The Disc Settings dialog box appears.

2. If preferred, enter the artist and title of the disc.

The play list is the order in which the tracks are played. This dialog box allows you to determine that order.

▶ **To modify a play list**

1. Select the track to play.

2. Move it up or down to the preferred sequence.

You may also name each track, remove tracks from the play list, add the same track multiple times, and otherwise experiment with this user interface.

Windows 95 uses the total length of the CD-ROM and the number and length of each track to create a unique identifier for each music CD-ROM you enter. Windows 95 uses this information to recognize CD-ROMs when they are placed in the system.

This information is located in the \WINDOWS folder, stored in the CDPLAYER.INI file.

Opening Media Player

When an AVI file is playing, you can open Media Player by double-clicking the title bar for the AVI. Double-clicking the Media Player title bar will close it.

Printing Offline

Windows 95 allows you to print when not connected to a printer (for example, from a portable computer removed from its docking station). The files are spooled to the default printer folder and printed when the printer is back online.

Mobile Computing

Creating a Second Undocked Configuration

To create a second, undocked configuration for your portable computer (for example, if one configuration has a printer available and the other does not) with your computer in the configuration you want to create, right-click My Computer and then click Properties. Click the Hardware Profiles tab and then select your undocked configuration. Click Copy. Select the new configuration and rename it to whatever you want to call it. Click the Device Manager tab and then click Refresh. This re-enumerates all of the hardware devices on your computer and builds the new configuration including available printers and so on.

Viewing Remaining Battery Life of Laptop

For computers with APM functionality, clicking the battery icon in the taskbar status area displays a more detailed battery meter.

MS-DOS Command Prompt

Opening a Command Prompt Using Default Directory

To open a command prompt from the desktop in Windows 95, on the Start menu, click Run, type **command** in the text box, and then click OK or press ENTER. The MS-DOS Prompt window opens in the folder that is active.

Visual Display of Directory from Command Prompt

If you are at a command prompt and want a visual display of a folder, type **start .**, **start ..**, or **start c:***foldername* and an open folder starts on the desktop.

Drag/Drop Filenames to Command Prompt

You can drag filenames from the shell and drop them in a command prompt. The filename is placed into the keyboard buffer of the running MS-DOS–based program.

Copy/Paste Information between Command Prompts

Moving information between a command prompt and an MS-DOS–based program is easy. Activate the toolbar in the MS-DOS–based program window to gain access to copy, cut, and paste operations from a Windows-based program to an MS-DOS–based program. For example, copy the output from a **dir** command on the screen and paste it into electronic mail.

Starting Windows-Based Programs from a Command Prompt

You can start Windows-based programs from a command prompt by typing the name of the program you want to run, and then specifying any parameters as needed. For example, to start Notepad, type **notepad** at a command prompt and then press ENTER—you can also start Windows-based programs in batch files. To open a data file with its associated program, use the **start** command.

Using the Start Command

From a command prompt (or from Run on the Start button), you can use the **start** command to start a program or open a document. In addition, you can specify options to use when starting the program.

Control Panel

Access Individual Control Panels from the Start Menu

1. Right-click the Start menu, and then click Explore.
2. Create a new folder in the Start Menu folder (named Control Panel or something else you prefer).
3. On the Start menu, point to Settings, and then click Control Panel.
4. Select all the icons and right drag them into your new folder.
5. Click Create a shortcut.

   This makes an alias for the Control Panel.
6. Close everything.
7. Click the Start menu.

   The newly created folder appears in the Start menu.
8. Select the new folder.

   A hierarchical list appears with all of the Control Panel functions.

A P P E N D I X   B

Configuring Printers

This appendix covers the information you may need to configure specific printers. The types of printers included in this appendix are:

- HP PCL
- HP Plotter
- Generic
- PostScript

Configuring a HP PCL Type Printer

All Hewlett-Packard LaserJet and compatible PCL printer drivers are based on the UNIDRV/Mini-driver format under Microsoft Windows 95.

Paper Property Sheet

This screen is generally the same among all PCL printers. It is used to determine size and type of paper used when printing.

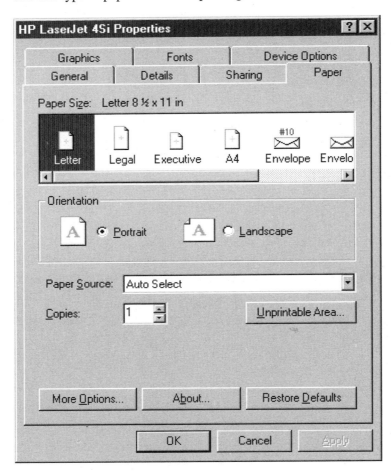

Figure B.1

Paper size selection is icon-based. The available paper sizes and sources depends on the printer model.

Clicking More Options on the Paper property sheet brings up the following dialog box on PCL printers which support one or more of these options for Duplex printing.

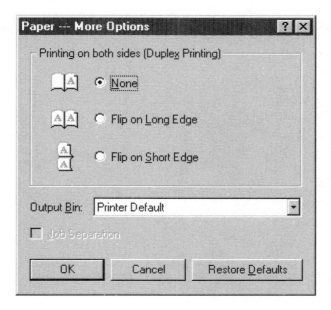

Figure B.2

Graphics Property Sheet

The Graphics property sheet controls how graphics are printed on a PCL printer.

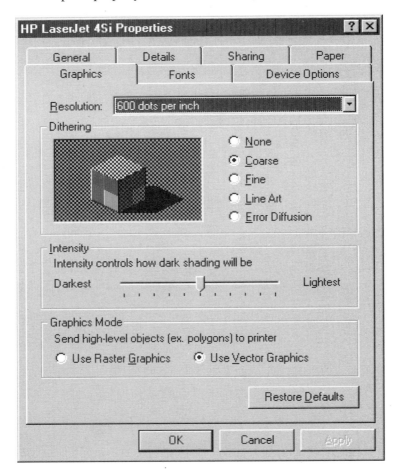

Figure B.3

The resolution in dpi (dots per inch) as well as options for dithering can be set here.

The available Dithering options are:

- None—This option completely disables dithering. The graphics are printed in black and white only with no gray shading.
- Coarse—Dithering is done with a coarse shading pattern. This option should be used for even dithering with resolutions of 300 dpi or above.

- Fine—Dithering is done with a fine shading pattern. This option should be used for even dithering with resolutions below 300 dpi. Do not use this option with higher resolutions or the images will be too dark.

- Line Art—This option should be used with vector graphics such as metafiles (clip art, graphs, or documents containing only paragraph shading).

- Error Diffusion—This option uses error diffusion to make images look less patterned. This option is best used for photographic images.

- Intensity controls the darkness of the printed images.

- Graphics Mode is available on printers which support HPGL/2 (Hewlett-Packard Graphics Language/2 commonly used on plotters)—This option is the same as the Raster versus HP-GL/2 setting on the Windows 3.1 HP LaserJet 4 series drivers. Use Raster Graphics rasterizes all graphics before sending them to the printer. Use Vector Graphics sends any vector images (metafiles, graphs, clip art, and so forth) as HP-GL/2 code and let the printer do its own rasterization. Generally, vector graphics is the fastest option while raster may give a more accurate printout. Use this setting as a troubleshooting step if there are problems with printing some kinds of documents such as those containing overlaid objects.

Fonts Property Sheet

The Fonts property sheet controls what cartridge fonts will be available and how TrueType fonts will be printed.

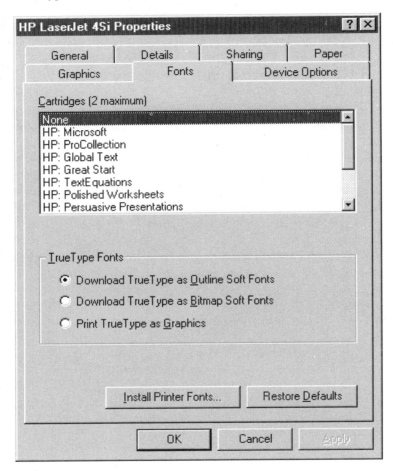

Figure B.4

Cartridges

Allows the user to choose up to two installed cartridges. If the printer supports cartridge fonts, the Cartridges list appears in the printer setup dialog box. This list indicates the cartridge fonts that are built into the printer driver for the printer. You can make these fonts available for use with Windows-based programs.

▶ **To make cartridge fonts available to Windows-based programs**

1. Make sure that the font cartridges are properly inserted into the cartridge slots on the printer.

2. From the printer's Fonts property sheet, select the cartridge fonts you want to use.

   If you want to use cartridge fonts that are not in the Cartridges list, you need to install them. You can either use the installation program that came with the cartridges, or if you are using a Hewlett-Packard LaserJet or DeskJet® (PCL) printer, you can use the Install Printer Fonts button. If you use Install Printer Fonts button to install cartridge fonts, the fonts appear in the Cartridges list. If you use another method, the fonts do not appear in the Cartridges list but are available to your Windows-based applications.

▶ **To install cartridge fonts by using Install Printer Fonts button**

1. From the printer property sheets choose the Fonts property sheet.

2. Use the Add button to add the cartridge fonts you want. Refer to the disk which came with your cartridge.

3. Choose the Exit button.

   The cartridges with the fonts you installed now appear in the Cartridges list.

4. Select the cartridges you want to use from the list.

Options for Printing TrueType Fonts

Windows 95 users can select from three options how to print TrueType fonts:

- **Download TrueType as Outline Soft Fonts**—This option downloads the TrueType font as a scaleable outline font. The printer does all rasterization. This option is only available on PCL printers which can rasterize TrueType fonts such as the LaserJet 4 series printers.

- **Download TrueType as Bitmap Soft Fonts**—This option downloads the TrueType fonts as bitmap soft fonts. Each set of characters for each font size used is rasterized and sent to the printer as separate bitmap fonts. This is the default method used for PCL printers which cannot rasterize TrueType fonts such as the LaserJet II and III series printers.

- **Print TrueType as Graphics**—This option rasterizes the whole page of TrueType fonts as a graphic. This option is used for PCL printers which cannot accept the format that we use for Bitmap Soft Fonts such as the original LaserJet and LaserJet Plus. This option is also handy for troubleshooting font printing problems.

Device Options Property Sheet

The Device Options property sheet controls device-specific settings.

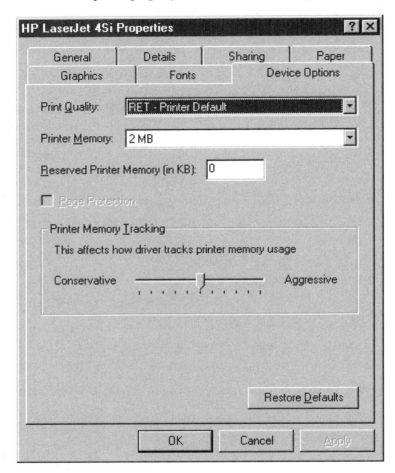

Figure B.5

Print Quality refers to the RET (Resolution Enhancement Technology) setting on the printer. RET is a method used by HP to increase the quality by inserting partial dots into an image to make it appear as if it were printed at a higher resolution.

This option can be set to:

- Printer Default—Setting is not be changed from what the user has set on the printer's control panel.
- On—RET is turned on.
- Off—RET is turned off.

- Printer Memory is the amount of memory installed in the printer—If the printer is Plug-and-Play capable and is directly connected, this option is set automatically upon installation. To verify the amount of memory in the printer, the user can use the printer's control panel to print a self-test page.

- Reserved Printer Memory is an option available on the LaserJet 4Si MX—This option allows a small amount of memory to be set aside for soft fonts and macros that are not be erased when the printer is reset by a change in settings such as language, resolution, and so forth.

- Page Protection is an option which reserves some of the printer's memory for rasterizing the page. If a complex page is printed to a LaserJet, sometimes the area that the printer uses to process the data overflows into the area it uses to draw the page image. When this occurs, the printer may show an error 20 Out of Memory or error 21 Print Overrun.

  Page Protection eliminates this problem by reserving memory for the page image. However, this option requires additional printer memory. Two megabytes are required for letter size paper at 300 dpi. Five megabytes are required for Letter or A4 at 600 dpi. Six megabytes are required for Legal size paper at 600 dpi.

- Printer Memory Tracking affects how the driver will track the amount of memory used. When set to Conservative, it closely monitors the printer memory, however, printing is slower. When set to Aggressive, the monitoring of memory usage is less and printing is faster.

Configuring a HP Plotter

The Hewlett-Packard Plotter driver from Windows 3.1 was modified to work under Windows 95.

Paper Property Sheet

The Paper settings are essentially the same as that of the Windows 3.1 driver.

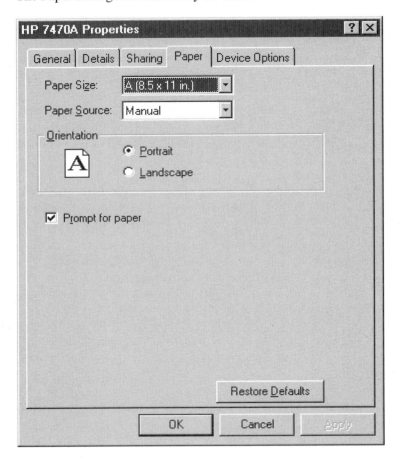

Figure B.6

The Prompt for paper option will cause the driver to prompt for each sheet of paper as needed.

Device Options Property Sheet

The Device Options property sheet for the HP Plotter are essentially the same as that of the Windows 3.1 driver.

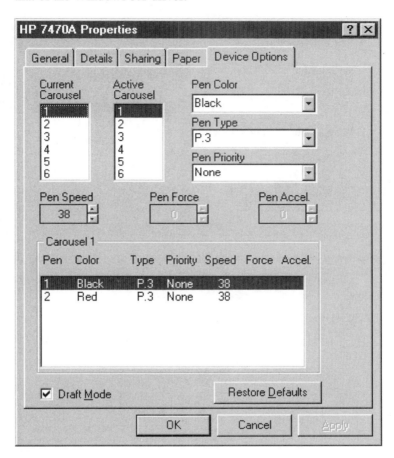

Figure B.7

The user can configure each carousel of pens.

Configuring a Generic / Text Only Printer

Windows 95 has a new Generic / Text Only driver based on UNIDRV.DLL.

Generic / Text Only Paper Property Sheet

The Paper settings are essentially the same as the other UNIDRV-based drivers.

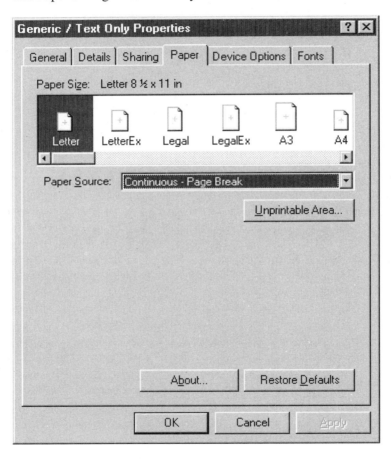

Figure B.8

Paper Source allows a choice of Cut Sheet for cut-sheet printing, or Continuous with or without page break. Use the Continuous - No Page Break setting when printing to a file and no Form Feed character will be inserted between pages. Use the Continuous - Page Break setting when setting the paper length manually on the printer.

Device Options Property Sheet

The Generic Text Only Device Options property sheet allows the user to create custom Printer Models to specify printer control codes for different printers.

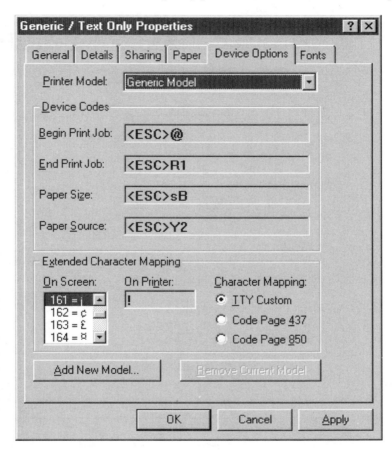

Figure B.9

Use the Add New Model... button to add a new custom model, then fill in the control codes for the supported commands. Use the CTRL key or ALT+ numeric pad to enter control characters—for example, CTRL or ALT+027 will give the Escape character. Please note that these device code fields are empty by default.

Extended Character Mapping allows mapping of extended characters to printer characters. This is useful for supporting international characters. There are also built-in options for supporting the standard character sets, Code Pages 437 and 850.

Font Property Sheet

The Generic / Text Only driver can support printer font commands. You can enter the printer control codes here to change CPI (characters per inch), double-wide, bold, and underline.

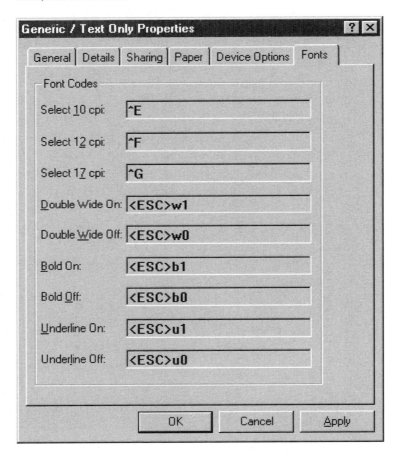

Figure B.10

To use these options, simply format your text for the desired effect in your program. Again, these fields are blank by default.

Configuring a PostScript Printer

Windows 95 has a new PostScript printer driver. The property sheets for PostScript printers contains a number of addition device options specific to PostScript printers.

Paper Property Sheet

The Paper settings are essentially the same as the other UNIDRV based drivers, with a few additions.

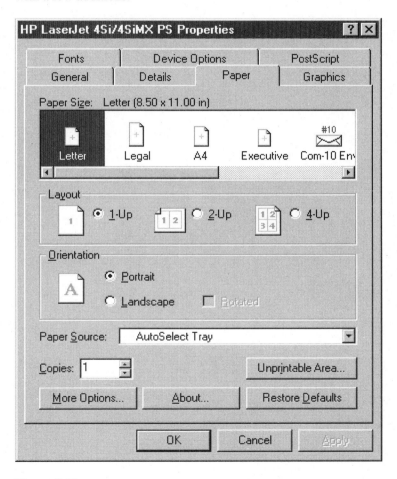

Figure B.11

The Paper Sizes and Sources available are dependent on what model printer is being used. Some optional paper sources—such as an optional envelope feeder—may not be available for selection if they have not been installed on the printer. These can be installed through the Device Options property sheet.

Layout allows automatic layout of one, two, or four pages per printed sheet of paper. Pages printed from the application will automatically be scaled and positioned on the paper.

The Rotated check box will rotate landscape orientation to 270 degrees. This eliminates the need for the LandscapeOrient=270 setting in WIN.INI.

More Options brings up a dialog box with options such as duplex, media types, or output bins if the printer supports those options.

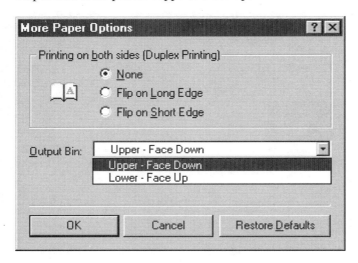

Figure B.12

Graphics Property Sheet

The Graphics property sheet controls how graphics are printed on a PostScript printer.

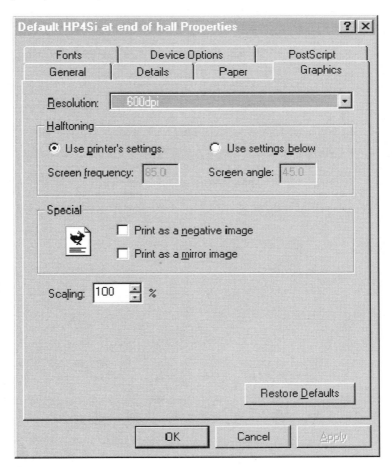

Figure B.13

The Resolutions available depend on the printer model.

Halftoning options determine how halftoning is performed on the printer. The user can choose to either use the settings set on the printer or to use the settings in the driver.

- Screen Frequency—The number of lines per inch used for the halftone screen. If this number is set too low, the graphics look as grainy as if they were printed at a very low resolution. If this setting is too high, the graphics print too dark. Generally, 60 is a good setting for 300 dpi, 85 for 600 dpi.
- Screen Angle—The angle of the halftone patterns.

Special options cause the graphic to print with special effects.

- Negative Image—Prints a negative image reversing black and white.
- Mirror—Prints a mirror image. Useful for iron-on transfers.

Scaling scales the page to the set percentage.

Fonts Property Sheet

These settings determine when the printer will use TrueType fonts.

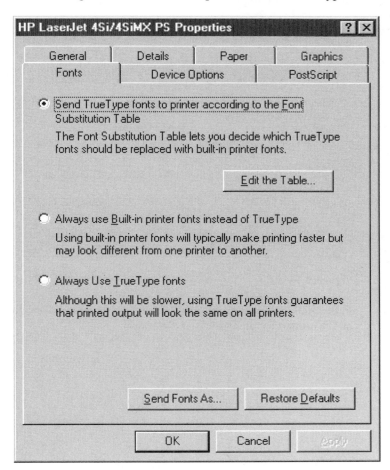

Figure B.14

Because TrueType fonts are metrically equivalent to PostScript fonts, some fonts can be substituted directly. Clicking the Edit the Table button brings up the Font Substitutions dialog box:

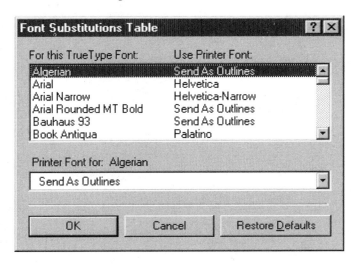

Figure B.15

In this dialog box, each available TrueType font can be assigned to be downloaded or substituted for an available printer font.

The Send Fonts As button brings up the dialog box to choose in what format the TrueType fonts will be sent to the printer.

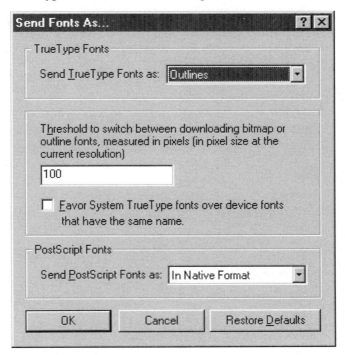

Figure B.16

- Outline sends the TrueType font as a Type 1 PostScript font.
- Bitmap will send the TrueType font as a Type 3 PostScript font.
- Don't Send will force printer fonts to be used instead.

■ Because it is more efficient to send bitmap fonts at smaller sizes, you can customize the threshold at which the driver switches to sending outlines instead of bitmaps.

■ The Favor System TrueType fonts... check box allows you to specify whether to use the system TrueType font or the printer's internal font if they have the same name. For example, if you have a TrueType font called Helvetica® installed in Windows 95 and your printer also has a font internally called Helvetica, when you format text for Helvetica by default it will print in the printer's font. If you check this box, the driver downloads the Helvetica TrueType font from your system.

■ If you have PostScript Type 1 fonts installed on your system, you can choose to send them in native format to the printer or not have them sent at all.

Device Options Property Sheet

The Device Options property sheet allows for device-specific settings.

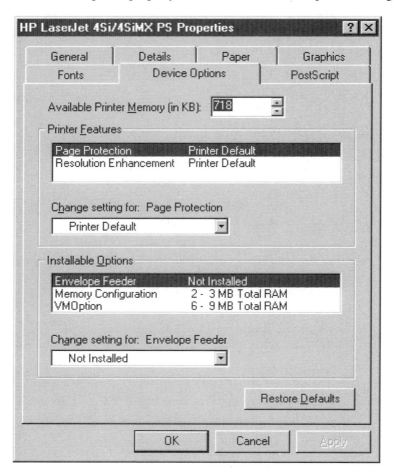

Figure B.17

In the example in Figure B.17 you can set Printer Feature options for Page Protection and Resolution Enhancement.

Installable Options allows you to specify whether any optional components have been installed in the printer, such as an Envelope Feeder.

To change either of these options, select the setting you wish to change and then use the drop-down box to choose from available settings.

PostScript Property Sheet

This property sheet is for PostScript-specific settings.

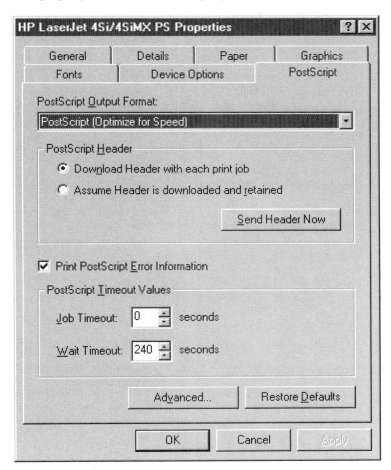

Figure B.18

PostScript Output Format allows the user to select the format of the PostScript code generated by the driver. These options include:

- PostScript (Optimize for Speed)—This is the fastest and should be used for general printing.

- PostScript (Optimize for Portability - ADSC)—Use this option if you are printing to file and want to use the file in another application which supports ADSC (Adobe Document Structuring Conventions). This option is also useful if you want to share the printed file with others, or if you want to use a printing service to print the file.

- EPS (Encapsulated PostScript)—This option should be used to create an EPS file. Use EPS only when you intend to make an EPS file for inclusion in another document. EPS is a graphics file format and does not include printer-specific information such as paper size or orientation needed to print the final output. If you want to create a PostScript print file to take to another printer, use one of the other formats.

A PostScript header is sent to the printer to define the functions used by the driver. By default, the header is sent to the printer every time a job is printed. If the header is not present, the job will not print and the printer may print an error page Windows PostScript Header Not Downloaded. You can check Assume Header is downloaded and retained and send the header manually using the Send Header Now button the first time you print. This speeds up subsequent print jobs. However, it is important to always send the header with each job in a network situation since other applications may reset the printer or other Windows driver version headers may conflict.

When Print PostScript Error Information is enabled, a PostScript error handler is downloaded to the printer. If an error condition occurs, a page prints with information about the error for debugging.

The PostScript Timeout Values allow you to set the PostScript time-out values for the print job and for how long to wait for the printer to process data.

The Advanced button brings up the Advanced PostScript Options dialog box.

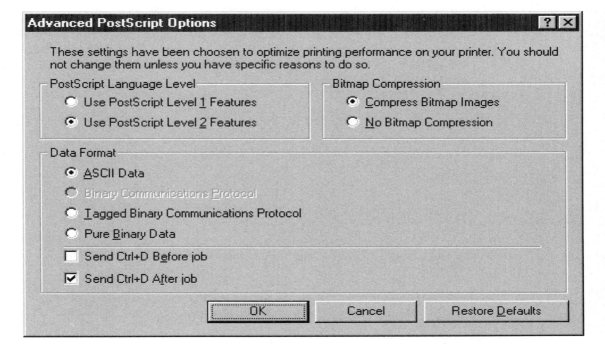

Figure B.19

- There should rarely be any need to change these settings. The PostScript Language Level, Bitmap Compression, and Data Format settings are automatically configured to give the best performance for the printer model.

- You can independently disable or enable the CTRL+D character inclusion at the beginning or end of print jobs. This is important when printing on some networks—especially UNIX—where the spooler looks for a CTRL+D to signify the end of the spooled job. This eliminates the need for the CTRLD=0 line in the WIN.INI file.

Registry Information

Support engineers should use the interface provided in the Printers folder to determine the way the printers are configured. But if it should be necessary to check elsewhere in the system, printer information can be found in the registry. The following branch shows the printer information location in the registry:

```
\\HKEY_LOCAL_MACHINE
    \System
        \CurrentControlSet
            \Control
                \Print
```

Figure B.20

Extended Capabilities Port (ECP)

An Extended Capabilities Port provides high-speed printing. If the user has an ECP port installed and has a printer which supports ECP, they can enable this option.

The ECP port is not auto-configurable. Windows 95 cannot detect the IRQ and DMA settings. The user must know these settings and configure them through Device Manager Properties to enable ECP support.

▶ **To enable ECP support in Windows 95**

1. Consult your computer (or add in card) manual to determine the IRQ and DMA settings selected for each of the ECP ports you want to use. You must have this information to enable ECP support.

2. On the Start menu, point to Settings, and then click Control Panel.

3. Double-click the System icon.

4. Click the Device Manager tab.

5. Double-click Ports (COM & LPT), and then select the Extended Capabilities Port entry.

Note You only see this entry if an Extended Capabilities port has been detected in your computer. If you have multiple ECP ports, you must repeat steps 7 and 11 to configure each port's DMA and IRQ values.

---

6. Click the Properties button on the dialog box.

7. Click the Resources property sheet tab.

   The property sheet page shows an I/O range that has automatically been detected and the Settings based On value is Basic Config 0.

8. Select the drop-down list box for Settings based On, and then choose Basic Config 2.

   An ECP parallel port has 5 possible configurations, (0->4)

   - Basic Config 0 = Std I/O ranges for LPT ports only
   - Basic Config 1 = Std I/O ranges for LPT ports + any IRQ
   - Basic Config 2 = Std I/O ranges for LPT ports + and IRQ + any DMA
   - Basic Config 3 = Any I/O ranges for LPT ports only
   - Basic Config 4 = Any I/O ranges for LPT ports + any IRQ setting

9. To view control for Interrupt Request (IRQ) and Direct Memory access (DMA) settings select Interrupt request and click the Change Settings button. This provides a dialog box where you can enter the values you noted during step 1 of these instructions. Choose OK after entering, and then select Direct Memory access and repeat these steps.

10. Choose OK to close the dialog box.

11. When prompted to use new or current files, choose Current.

12. When prompted, restart Windows 95.

   After restarting, you should be able to take advantage of the ECP specific capabilities of the port.

A P P E N D I X   C

APPS.INF Settings

This appendix lists the entries in the [**appname**] section that are valid in the Microsoft Windows 95 APPS.INF file. It is important to note that there are several settings that are ignored. These settings are included to allow easier migration of PIF settings created for earlier versions of Windows.

Settings Under [appname] Section of APPS.INF

Name	Key	Description	Default
WINDOWED	win	Open windowed instead of full screen	Y
BACKGROUND	bgd	Run in background (opposite of "Always suspend in background")	Y
EXCLUSIVE	exc	Exclusive mode	Ignored
DETECTIDLE	dit	Idle sensitivity (if N, then idle sensitivity slider is moved to low)	Y
LOWLOCKEDlml		Lock conventional memory	Ignored
EMSLOCKED	eml	Lock EMS memory	N
XMSLOCKED	xml	Lock XMS memory	N
USEHMA	hma	Uses HMA	Y
EMULATEROM	emt	Fast ROM emulation	Y
RETAINVRAM	rvm	Retain video memory	Ignored
FASTPASTE	afp	Fast pasting	Y

The following group of settings control which keyboard shortcuts should be active when the MS-DOS–based programs has focus. If the key is disabled, then pressing the key sends the keystroke to the program instead of to Windows.

Name	Key	Description	Default
ALTTAB	ata	Allow ALT+TAB to switch away	Y
ALTESC	aes	Allow ALT+ESC to switch away	Y
CTRLESC	ces	Allow CTRL+ESC to switch away	Y
PRTSCRN	psc	Allow PRINTSCRN to perform screen snap	Y
ALTPRTSCRN	aps	Allow ALT+PRINTSCRN to perform screen snap	Y
ALTSPACE	asp	Allow ALT+SPACEBAR to view the Control menu	Y
ALTENTER	aen	Allow ALT+ENTER to toggle window/full screen	Y
WINLIE	lie	Prevent MS-DOS–based programs from detecting Windows	N
GLOBALMEM	gmp	Enable global memory protection	
REALMODE	dos	Run program in MS-DOS mode	N

The following group of settings are applicable only if the REALMODE flag is set. They control which MS-DOS TSRs should be loaded in real mode.

Name	Key	Description	Default
MOUSE	mse	Mouse functionality	Y
EMS	ems	EMM386	Y
CDROM	cdr	CD-ROM driver / MSCDEX	Y
NETWORK	net	Network drivers	Y
DISKLOCK	dsk	Allow direct disk access	N
PRIVATECFG	cfg	Use custom CONFIG.SYS settings	N
VESA	vsa	Extended video (VESA) support	Y
CLOSEONEXIT	cwe	Close on exit	N
ALLOWSSAVER	sav	Allow screen saver to interrupt MS-DOS–based program	Y
UNIQUESETTINGS	uus	Run program in separate session	N

The following settings are not implemented.

Name	Key	Description	Default
DISPLAYTBAR	dtb	Display toolbar	
RESTOREWIN	rws	Restore settings on startup	
QUICKEDIT	qme	Mouse-QuickEdit mode	
EXCLMOUSE	exm	Mouse-Exclusive mode	
WARNIFACTIVE	wia	Warn if still active	

APPENDIX D

.ADM Template Keywords

The following are the keywords which may be used to define policies.

!! The double exclamation points are used to indicate that the following word is a variable defined in the [**strings**] section of the file.

```
PART !!NetworkSetupPath_Path EDITTEXT REQUIRED
Since NetworkSetupPath_Path is defined by the entry
NetworkSetupPath_Path="Path:"
This evaluates to:
PART "Path:" EDITTEXT REQUIRED
```

; A semicolon marks the rest of the line as a comment.

```
END CATEGORY   ; Printers
```

ACTIONLIST / END ACTIONLIST These keywords mark the beginning and end of a list of actions that are to be processed as a group as a response to a setting.

```
ACTIONLIST
    KEYNAME System\CurrentControlSet\Services\VxD\NWSP
    VALUENAME StaticVxD VALUE nwsp.386
    VALUENAME Start VALUE NUMERIC 0
    KEYNAME Security\Provider
    VALUENAME Address_Book VALUE nwab32.dll
END ACTIONLIST
```

ACTIONLISTOFF / END ACTIONLISTOFF These mark the beginning and end of a list of actions that are to be processed as a group as a response to a negative response to a setting.

```
ACTIONLISTOFF
    KEYNAME Security\Provider
    VALUENAME Platform_Type VALUE NUMERIC 0
END ACTIONLISTOFF
```

ACTIONLISTON / END ACTIONLISTON These mark the beginning and end of a list of actions that are to be processed as a group as a positive response to a setting.

```
ACTIONLISTON
    KEYNAME System\CurrentControlSet\Services\VxD\FILESEC
    VALUENAME StaticVxD VALUE filesec.386
    VALUENAME Start VALUE NUMERIC 0
END ACTIONLISTON
```

ADDITIVE Values will be added to existing registry entries rather than overwriting them.

CHECKBOX Indicates that a check box will be used to get the information from the user.

```
PART !!DisplayErrors CHECKBOX
VALUENAME "Verbose"
END PART
```

In this example, the value of the check box would be stored in the registry with the value name Verbose.

CLASS MACHINE Marks the beginning of the computer policies. CLASS is in effect until another CLASS entry is encountered.

CLASS USER Marks the beginning of the User policies. CLASS is in effect until another CLASS entry is encountered.

COMBOBOX Displays a combo box which is an edit field with a drop-down list for suggested values.

DEFAULT *value* Sets a default answer for a given PART.

```
PART !!LogonBanner_Caption EDITTEXT
    VALUENAME "LegalNoticeCaption"
    MAXLEN 255
    DEFAULT !!LogonBanner_DefCaption
END PART
```

The value stored in **LogonBanner_DefCaption** is the Legal Notice Caption unless the user changes it.

DEFCHECKED   Sets a default value of a check box to TRUE.

```
PART !!TileWallpaper CHECKBOX DEFCHECKED
VALUENAME "TileWallpaper"
VALUEON "1" VALUEOFF "0"
END PART
```

DELETE   If this is used as the action for a PART, the VALUENAME in the registry will be deleted rather than having its value set.

```
POLICY !!EnableUserProfiles
    KEYNAME Network\Logon
    VALUENAME UserProfiles
    VALUEON NUMERIC 1
    VALUEOFF DELETE
END POLICY
```

In this example, an ON value will set Network\Logon to a numeric value of 1. An OFF value will delete the Network\Logon entry and any previous value.

DROPDOWNLIST   Creates a drop-down list box which is used to get the value.

```
PART !!UpdateMode DROPDOWNLIST REQUIRED
VALUENAME "UpdateMode"
ITEMLIST
    NAME !!UM_Automatic VALUE NUMERIC 1
    NAME !!UM_Manual VALUE NUMERIC 2
END ITEMLIST
END PART
```

EDITTEXT   Creates a text edit box for data entry.

```
PART !!WorkgroupName EDITTEXT REQUIRED
VALUENAME "Workgroup"
MAXLEN 15
END PART
```

CATEGORY / END CATEGORY   Marks the beginning and end of a major grouping of items.

```
CATEGORY !!AccessControl

    ...
    ;Access control entries go between these headers
    ...
END CATEGORY
```

EXPLICITVALUE Modifier that forces specific name to be entered for a new value. Compare the following:

```
POLICY !!Run
    KEYNAME Software\Microsoft\Windows\CurrentVersion\Run
    PART !!RunListbox LISTBOX EXPLICITVALUE
    END PART
END POLICY
```

produces this entry box:

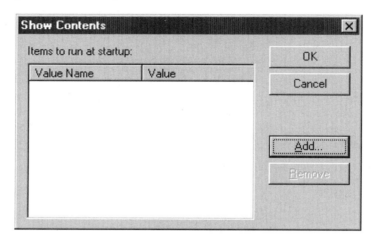

Figure D.1

where the same entry without EXPLICITVALUE produces the following:

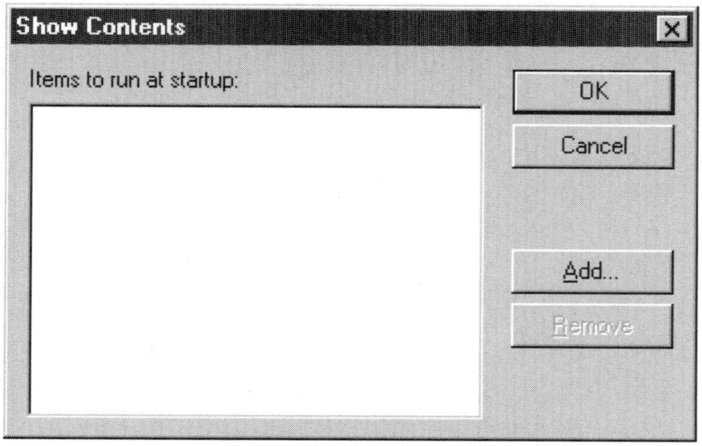

Figure D.2

ITEMLIST \ END ITEMLIST   Surrounds a group of entries entered into a list box, combo box, or drop-down list box.

```
ITEMLIST
    NAME !!UM_Automatic VALUE NUMERIC 1
    NAME !!UM_Manual VALUE NUMERIC 2
END ITEMLIST
```

KEYNAME   Specifies the registry key to be modified. This is used with a VALUENAME to get the fully qualified registry entry.

```
KEYNAME Security\Provider
```

LISTBOX   Creates a list box for the entry.

```
PART !!RunListbox LISTBOX EXPLICITVALUE
END PART
```

MAX *value*   Specifies a maximum value that can be used in this entry.

```
PART MPL_Length NUMERIC REQUIRED
MIN 1 MAX 8 DEFAULT 3
VALUENAME MinPwdLen
END PART
```

MAXLEN *value*   Specifies a maximum length for the entry.

```
PART !!LogonBanner_Caption EDITTEXT
VALUENAME "LegalNoticeCaption"
MAXLEN 255
DEFAULT !!LogonBanner_DefCaption
END PART
```

MIN *value*   Specifies a minimum value for the entry.

```
PART MPL_Length NUMERIC REQUIRED
MIN 1 MAX 8 DEFAULT 3
VALUENAME MinPwdLen
END PART
```

NAME   Allows for a "friendly" alias to be presented for a value.

```
NAME "NetWare 3.x or 4.x" VALUE NUMERIC 3
```

Allows the user to choose "NetWare 3.*x* or 4.*x*" and have the registry entry contain the numeric value 3.

NUMERIC Defines the entry as a numeric value and validates it.

```
PART MPL_Length NUMERIC REQUIRED
MIN 1 MAX 8 DEFAULT 3
VALUENAME MinPwdLen
END PART
```

PART / END PART Marks the beginning and end of a section dealing with a single question.

```
PART MPL_Length NUMERIC REQUIRED
MIN 1 MAX 8 DEFAULT 3
VALUENAME MinPwdLen
END PART
```

POLICY / END POLICY Surrounds entries that represent a minor grouping of entries.

```
POLICY Policy
    PART Part EDITTEXT
        VALUENAME UserProfiles
    END PART
END POLICY
```

REQUIRED A modifier that guarantees that the entry field cannot be blank.

```
PART MPL_Length NUMERIC REQUIRED
MIN 1 MAX 8 DEFAULT 3
VALUENAME MinPwdLen
END PART
```

SPIN *value* Specifies the increment used for values in a Spin control. SPIN 0 removes the spin control. SPIN 1 is the default.

SUGGESTIONS / END SUGGESTIONS Surrounds a group of values in a combo box that are made available to the user as possible choices.

```
PART !!WallpaperName COMBOBOX REQUIRED
SUGGESTIONS
    256color.bmp arcade.bmp argyle.bmp cars.bmp castle.bmp chicago.bmp
    egypt.bmp honey.bmp leaves.bmp redbrick.bmp rivets.bmp squares.bmp
    thatch.bmp winlogo.bmp zigzag.bmp
END SUGGESTIONS
VALUENAME "Wallpaper"
END PART
```

TEXT Displays the PART name as text. This is useful when a message must accompany a field.

```
PART !!RemoteRegistry_Txt1
TEXT
END PART
```

TXTCONVERT Writes values as strings rather than binary values.

VALUE Specifies the actual data to be entered into the VALUENAME registry entry.

```
VALUENAME ActiveBorder    VALUE "174 168 217 32"
```

Sets the ActiveBorder registry entry to the string "174 168 217 32"

VALUENAME Specifies the entry in the registry to be modified.

```
VALUENAME ActiveBorder    VALUE "174 168 217 32"
```

Sets the ActiveBorder registry entry to the string "174 168 217 32"

VALUEOFF Specifies a value to be entered or action taken when the OFF value is selected.

```
PART !!TileWallpaper CHECKBOX DEFCHECKED
VALUENAME "TileWallpaper"
VALUEON "1"
VALUEOFF "0"
END PART
```

VALUEON Specifies a value to be entered or action taken when the ON value is selected.

```
PART !!TileWallpaper CHECKBOX DEFCHECKED
VALUENAME "TileWallpaper"
VALUEON "1"
VALUEOFF "0"
END PART
```

VALUEPREFIX Defines a prefix to be used with a changing value to create the full value name. For example:

```
VALUEPREFIX "FILE"
```
would create values such as FILE1 and FILE2.

APPENDIX E

PPP Dial-Up Sequence

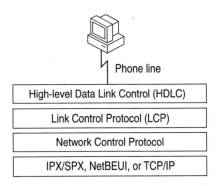

Figure E.1

PPP is designed to work with a variety of hardware, including any asynchronous or synchronous, dedicated or dial-up, full-duplex bit-serial circuit. It can employ any common serial communications protocol, including EIA-232-E (formerly, RS-232-C), EIA-422, EIA423, EIA-530, and CCITT V.24 and V. 35. PPP does not place any particular restriction on the type of signaling, type of transmission speed, or use of modem control signals.

PPP Dial-Up Sequence

When a user dials in to a PPP-compatible server, three things happen:

1. The Data Link Control Layer (HDLC) defines how data is encapsulated before transmission on the WAN. By providing a standard framing format, PPP ensures that various vendors' remote access solutions can communicate and distinguish data packets from each other. PPP uses HDLC framing for serial, integrated service digital network (ISDN), and X.25 data transfer.

    The PPP Data Link Control layer is a slightly modified version of the HDLC layer. The HDLC format, extensively used by IBM and others for synchronous data transfer, was modified by adding a 16-bit protocol field that allows PPP to multiplex traffic for several Network Control Protocol layers. This encapsulation frame has a 16-bit checksum, but the size of this field can be negotiated.

2. Link Control Protocol (LCP) establishes, configures, and tests the integrity of the data-link connection. LCP also negotiates authentication and determines whether compression is enabled and which IP addresses will be used. When LCP negotiates authentication of protocols, it determines what level of security validation the remote access server can perform and what the server requires.

    LCP can negotiate with any of these authentication protocols:

    *   Password Authentication Protocol (PAP) uses a two-way handshake for the peer to establish its identity. This handshake occurs only when the link is initially established. Using PAP, passwords are sent over the circuit in text format, which offers no protection from playback.

    *   Shiva Password Authentication Protocol (SPAP) offers encryption of PAP passwords and Novell NetWare bindery access for user account information. When Microsoft Windows 95 is set up for user-level security using a NetWare server account list, this is the security type used for remote access clients.

    *   Challenge-Handshake Authentication Protocol (CHAP) periodically verifies the identity of the peer, using a three-way handshake. The authenticator sends a challenge message to the peer, which responds with a value using a one-way encryption. The authenticator then checks this response and, if the values match, the authentication is acknowledged; otherwise, the connection is ended. CHAP provides protection against playback attack because the challenge value changes in every message. Because the password is never sent over the link, it is virtually impossible to learn it. CHAP allows different types of encryption algorithms to be used, such as DES (MS-CHAP) and MD5 (MD5-CHAP). Windows 95 doesn't support ongoing challenges with CHAP, but does implement MS-CHAP, as does Microsoft Windows NT.

3. Network Control Protocols establish and configure different network protocol parameters. The type of Network Control Protocol that PPP selects depends on which protocol (NetBEUI, TCP/IP, or IPX) is being used to establish the Dial-Up Networking connection. Windows 95 supports the following:

   - NetBIOS Frames Control Protocol (NBF CP) is used to configure, enable, and disable the NetBEUI protocol modules on both ends of the link. NBF CP is a Microsoft-proposed protocol for NetBEUI configuration. NBF CP is currently in "draft" status with the Internet Engineering Task Force (IETF). Windows 95 provides implementations for the current draft of NBF CP (as of March 1994).

   - Internet Protocol Control Protocol (IPCP), defined in RFC 1332, is used to configure, enable, and disable IP Protocol modules at both ends of the link.

   - Internet Packet eXchange Control Protocol (IPXCP), defined in RFC 1552, is used to configure, enable, and disable IPX protocol modules on both ends of the link. IPXCP is widely implemented by PPP vendors.

A P P E N D I X   F

Windows 95 and the Internet

What Is the Internet?

The Internet is the name given to a global collection of private and public networks that are connected together. These systems communicate with each other using the TCP/IP protocol suite. While there are administrative agencies that handle the distribution of IP addresses and the formats of commonly used protocols and utilities, there is no actual governing body for the Internet.

A Brief History of the Internet

The Internet grew out of an experimental wide area network called ARPAnet created by the United States Department of Defense Advanced Research Projects Agency in the 1970s. ARPAnet was created to allow military research facilities and defense contractors to share data between their facilities.

The ARPAnet was expanded in the 1980s by the addition of the US National Science Foundation's NSFNET. NSFNET was established to ease communication between universities, research centers, and supercomputer sites. Its inclusion of university sites greatly increased both the size of the Internet and the usefulness of its tools.

Toward the end of the 1980s, commercial Internet service providers began appearing. These companies offered access to the Internet for subscription fees. This began the modern growth of sites on the Internet.

One measure of the growth of the Internet can be seen through the growth of host systems connected together. In 1981 there were 213 systems on the Internet. By January of 1995, there were roughly 4,852,000 sites.

Hosts

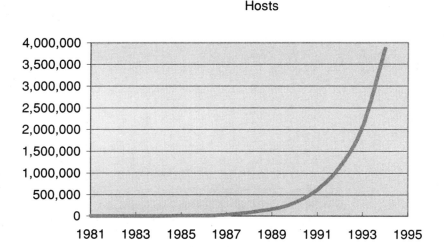

Figure F.1

While the distributed, largely unregulated nature of the Internet makes exact record keeping difficult at best, it is clear that the Internet has become a major source of communication between computers.

Common Services (Protocols)

While the Internet is, in itself, just a very large TCP/IP wide area network (WAN), there are many services that are traditionally used when communicating over the Internet. These services are generally referred to as protocols. This use of "protocol" should not be confused with the many other uses of the word; here it simply means a set of standards that have been agreed to by the various organizations in the computer industry.

Telnet

One of the earliest protocols established was Telnet. Telnet is used to act as a remote terminal to an Internet host.

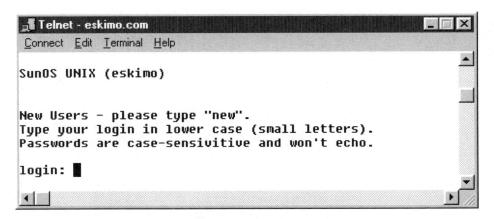

Figure F.2

This terminal/host system grew out of the preponderance of UNIX character terminal-based systems in the early days of the Internet. Windows 95 installs a Telnet program as part of the TCP/IP utilities. This program allows you to act as either a VT-52 or VT-100 terminal to a system accessible by means of TCP/IP including computers reached by means of the Internet.

ftp

The most common protocol used for sending files between computers is the File Transfer Protocol (ftp). The ftp protocol allows for transferring both text and binary files.

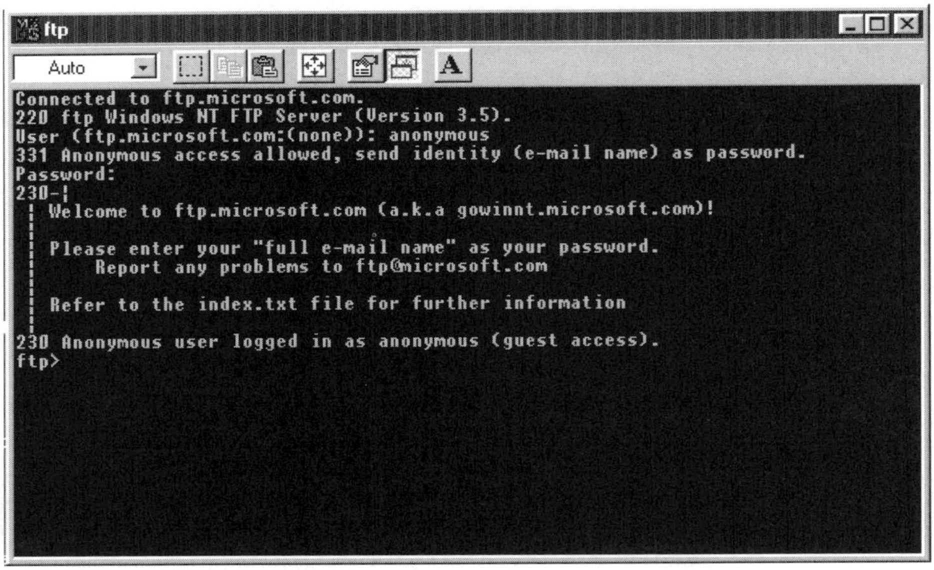

Figure F.3

The standard Windows 95 package includes the traditional character based ftp client. This is one of the utilities that is copied onto the system when the TCP/IP protocol suite is installed. In addition, most Internet browsers such as Mosaic, NetScape™, or the Microsoft Internet Explorer that comes with Microsoft Plus! for Windows 95 support the ftp protocol and use it behind the scenes when transferring files.

Because of the large number of sites that support file transfer using ftp, it has become difficult to keep track of which computer has which files. A protocol named *Archie* is commonly used to act as an interactive search facility.

Gopher

While ftp works well for transferring files, it doesn't provide a good means of dealing with file systems spread over multiple computers. An updated file transfer system called *Gopher* was developed in response to this issue.

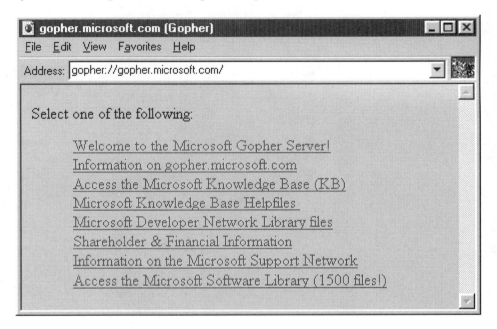

Figure F.4

Gopher computers are linked together with distributed indices into a searchable system called a "Gopherspace." Gopherspaces typically offer a menu-driven system for access and are searchable with several search engines. The most common of these are the Gopher counterpart to Archie (named *Veronica*) and the Wide Area Information Server (WAIS) index search system.

http

The protocol that has sparked the most growth in the Internet in the 1990s is the Hypertext Transfer Protocol (http).

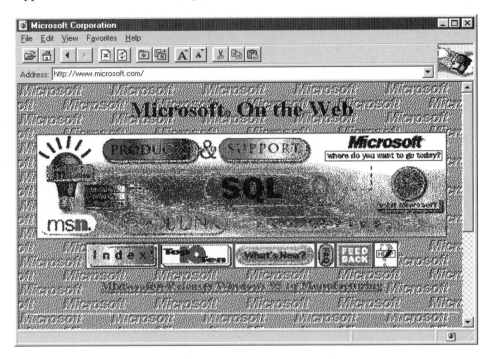

Figure F.5

This protocol is used in the World Wide Web. Web "pages" are documents formatted using the Hypertext Markup Language (html) and allow for embedding links to other documents and other files, as well as jumps within the same document.

URLs

When using a tool that supports multiple protocols, the address of the document is usually specified using a Uniform Resource Locator (URL). A URL consists of several parts. The simplest version contains:

- The protocol to be used.
- A colon.
- The address of the resource. This address begins with two forward slashes and uses the forward slash as a delimiter. Aside from using forward slashes rather than backslashes, this is very similar to the UNC format.

Here are a few simple UNC addresses.

```
http://www.microsoft.com
```
This is Microsoft's World Wide Web server. The http: shows that it should use the http protocol. //www.microsoft.com is the address of the computer.

```
ftp://ftp.microsoft.com
```
This is Microsoft's ftp server. Again, the part before the colon (ftp) shows that the protocol used is ftp.

```
gopher://gopher.microsoft.com
```
This is Microsoft's Gopher server.

Setting Up an Internet Connection

Service Provider

In order to access servers on the Internet, your computer needs to be connected to the Internet's WAN. There are several ways of doing this.

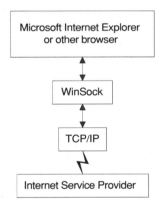

Figure F.6

Larger corporations often arrange a direct link between their local area network (LAN) or WAN and the Internet. For individuals or smaller companies, the attachment to the Internet is usually done by connecting to a commercial service provider. This can be done directly through high-speed lines or by using a dial-up connection over the telephone.

LAN

If you attach directly to the Internet or are directly attached to a service provider, the computers on the Internet are essentially a part of your WAN, which means that you can access them directly. One issue with this is that you are also accessible to them, which may lead to potential security issues. For this reason, it is common for companies using a direct connection to set up a special machine, called a Proxy Agent, to act as a gateway between their local network and the Internet. The proxy agent filters requests over the gateway and makes it more difficult for unauthorized requests to reach the local network.

Telephone

Most small networks and virtually all individual users connect to the Internet over their telephone lines. There are two types of Internet accounts generally offered for these dial-up accounts by service providers. The first of these is a *shell* account. These accounts are generally used by standard communications programs such as HyperTerminal and offer either character-based access or a proprietary graphics access.

A much more useful method of dial-up access is by way of a Serial Line Internet Protocol (SLIP) or Point-to-Point Protocol (PPP) account. With either of these, the provider gives you a temporary IP address on the Internet and you can run any WinSock program on it. This includes graphical Web browsers such as Mosaic, NetScape, or the Microsoft Internet Explorer.

Commercial online services such as The Microsoft Network and CompuServe often make a WinSock/PPP access method available either as part of their service or as an additional fee supplemental service.

While many providers offer SLIP access, the newer PPP access is generally preferable. In addition to the increased flexibility of PPP, it also offers a dynamic allocation of IP addresses similar to DHCP, which makes logging on to the service simpler. With a SLIP account an automated script is generally used to make logon more automatic.

Utilities in Windows 95 and Plus! for Windows 95

Microsoft Windows 95 includes several utilities that can be used on the Internet. These are installed when you choose TCP/IP as a network protocol.

Telnet

A Telnet client is part of Windows 95. The Telnet client is a simple VT-100 or VT-52 terminal emulator that works over the network. To connect to an Internet computer by means of Telnet, you can type **telnet** *computername* from the command line, or on the Windows 95 Start menu, click Run and then type **run** in the text box, or start Telnet without a computer name and start the connection from Telnet's Connect/Remote System... menu. Once you have made the connection, you can log in to the remote computer as if you were using a locally attached terminal.

ping

If you are unsure of whether you are having communication problems with the Internet, you can test the connection by using the ping command. Ping will send test message to the remote system and time how long it takes to get a reply. By default ping will do this four times. If you get a time-out error all four times, you are not communicating with the remote computer. If, on the other hand, you do get a reply but still cannot use one of your other programs, the problem most likely lies with that program.

ftp

Windows 95 also includes a character-based ftp file transfer utility. With this, you can send and receive files from sites that support the ftp protocol. Be sure when you send or receive a file that you specify whether the file is text or binary. If you use the wrong setting, ftp may not transfer the file accurately. The text/binary setting is necessary to preserve line endings in text messages transferred between computers that use different end-of-line character sequences.

Utilities in Microsoft Plus! for Windows 95

Microsoft Plus! for Windows 95 includes three additional Internet utilities.

Internet Setup Wizard

The Internet Setup wizard is designed to assist you in setting up your connection to the Internet. It works with direct LAN connections as well as telephone dial-up accounts.

Internet Electronic Mail

Microsoft Plus! for Windows 95 adds an Internet mail service to your Microsoft Exchange client. This allows you to send and receive electronic mail using your Internet provider's electronic mail system and have the electronic mail integrated into your Microsoft Exchange mail client. To use this service, your Internet provider must support the Simple Mail Transfer Protocol (SMTP) and Post Office Protocol version 3 (POP3).

Microsoft Internet Explorer

Windows 95 fully supports the WinSock interface. This means that most "Web browsers" designed for Windows 95 will work. While there are many Web browsers available for Windows 95 systems, the Microsoft Internet Explorer that comes with Microsoft Plus! for Windows 95 offers very tight integration into the Windows 95 shell.

Internet Mail Client

Setting Up the Mail Client

Adding the Internet mail service to your Microsoft Exchange mail system follows the same procedures as other electronic mail services. In order to make installation simpler, you should first set up your Internet connection either as a direct LAN connection or by setting up a Dial-Up Networking session that connects to your Internet mail host. This can be done by using the Internet Setup wizard.

To configure the Internet mail service, double-click the Mail and Fax icon in the Control Panel.

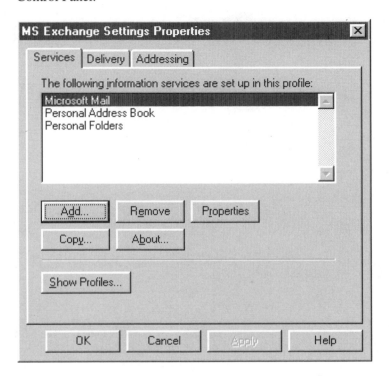

Figure F.7

Click the Add button, highlight Internet Mail, and then click OK.

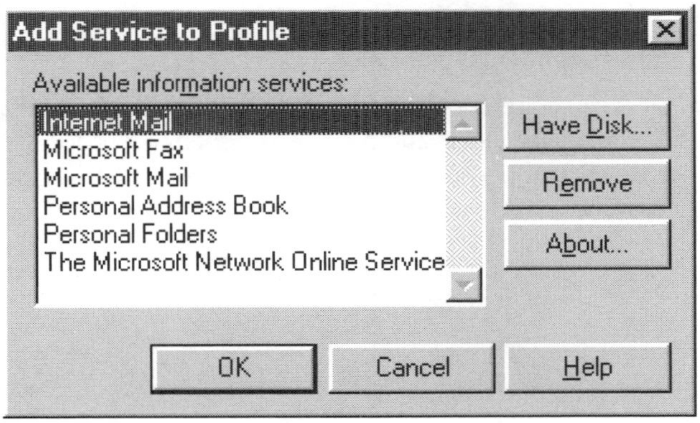

Figure F.8

The Internet Mail property sheet appears.

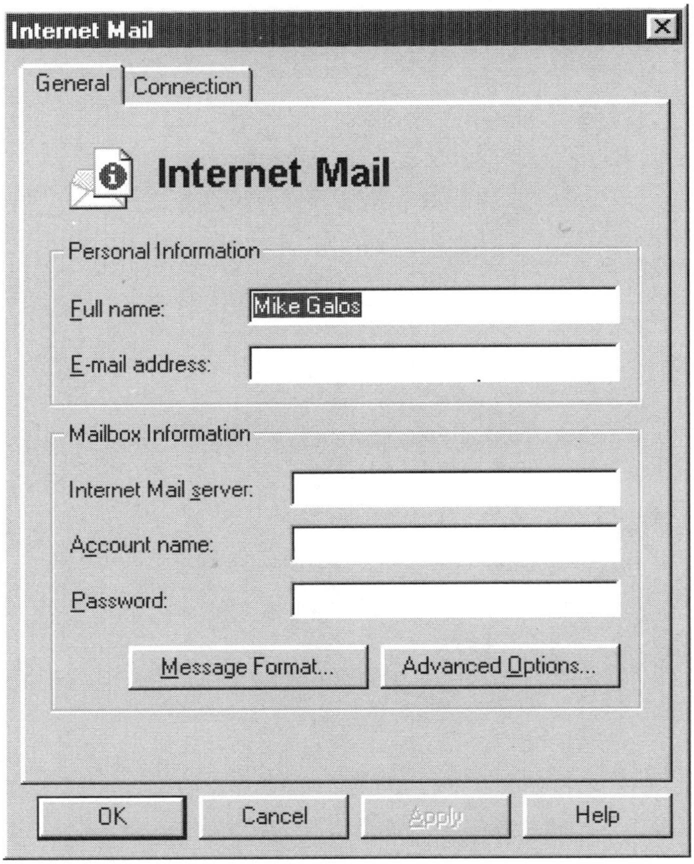

Figure F.9

On the General tab, enter your full name and electronic mail address. You will also need to specify your electronic mail server's name or address, your account name, and your password. If you do not know them, they should be obtained from your electronic mail server's administrator.

By clicking the Message Format button, you have the opportunity to use the MIME convention for embedding objects in electronic mail.

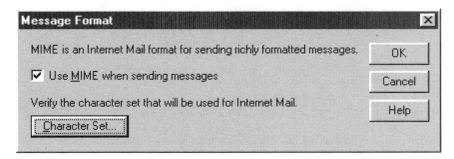

Figure F.10

If you do not choose to use MIME, any embedded objects will be encoded and decoded using the UUENCODE format.

Click the Character Set button in the Message Format dialog box to specify your character set.

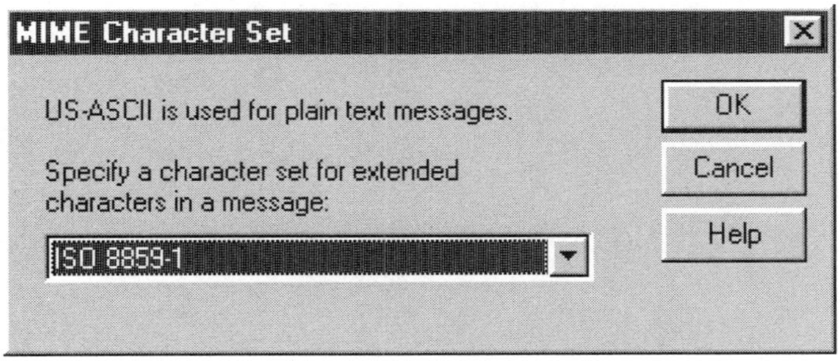

Figure F.11

The character set determines how high-order characters (above 127) will be handled. There are several possible choices but the default and most common encoding is the ISO 8859-1 standard.

If your electronic mail system uses different computers for sending and receiving electronic mail, you can specify an outbound electronic mail server by clicking the Advanced Options button on the General tab.

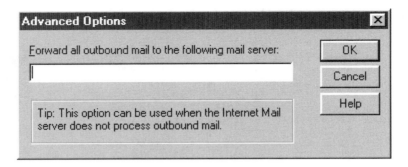

Figure F.12

The Connection tab allows you to specify whether you are connecting to your postoffice by means of your LAN or with Dial-Up Networking.

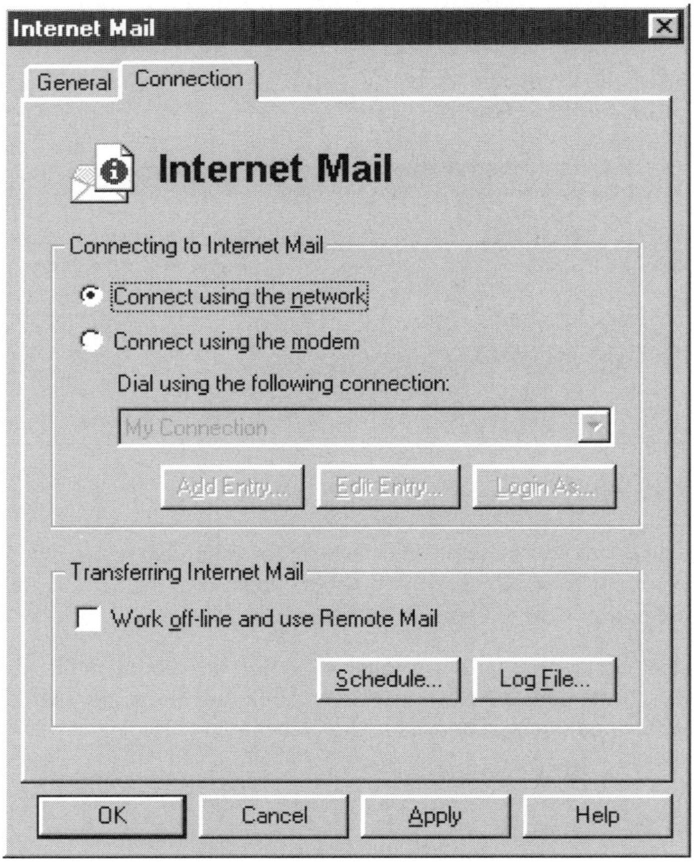

Figure F.13

You can also choose to work offline and let Microsoft Exchange call your electronic mail server on a regular basis.

Once you have set up Internet mail, it is fully integrated into the Microsoft Exchange mail client. This means that using it is no different than using any other electronic mail service provider.

The Microsoft Internet Explorer

Setup

Setting up the Microsoft Internet Explorer is done with the Internet Setup wizard which can be found on Start/Programs/Accessories/Internet Tools menu.

Figure F.14

The first decision you need to make is whether your connection will be by means of a LAN or over a telephone line. Even if you are on a LAN, you will not be able to use LAN access unless your network has its own gateway computer to the Internet. If you choose to use your LAN, you will be prompted for:

- Your IP address and subnet mask if you aren't using DHCP to configure them dynamically.
- Your DNS server and an alternate DNS server.

- The IP address of your gateway computer.

- Internet mail information if you have an Internet mail account.

If you don't know the answers to these questions, you will need to obtain them from your network administrator before accessing the Internet. Remember that having an incorrect IP address can cause significant problems for your entire network.

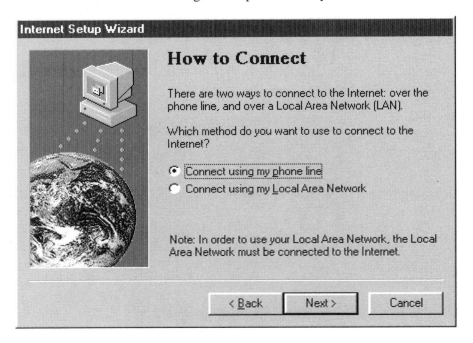

Figure F.15

If you have chosen to use your telephone lines, you will need to choose whether you want to use The Microsoft Network as your Internet provider or another service provider. If you choose a different service provider, you will be prompted for the following:

- The name of the Dial-Up Networking connection to your service provider.

- Your service provider's telephone number and whether you need a terminal window to enter login information after dialing.

- Your user name and password.

- Your IP address if your service provider doesn't provide one.

- Your DNS server's address and, optionally, an alternate DNS server.

- Internet mail information if you have an Internet mail account.

As with the direct LAN connection, you will need this information before you attempt to log in.

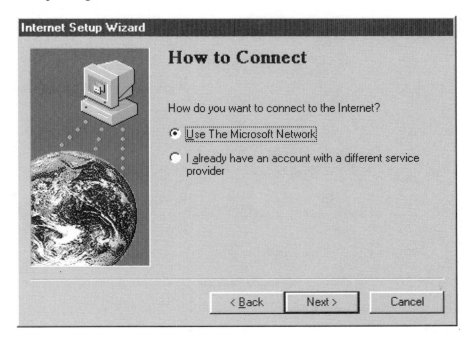

Figure F.16

If you selected The Microsoft Network as your service provider, you will need to specify whether you have an account. If you do not, you will be prompted to set up an account.

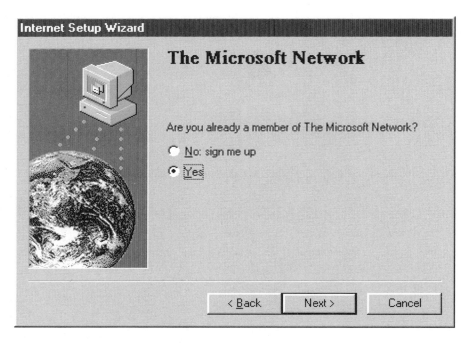

Figure F.17

After a screen showing the features of The Microsoft Network appears, you will be prompted for your area (or city) code and the first three digits of your telephone number. This information is used to obtain the nearest access line to you that has Internet support.

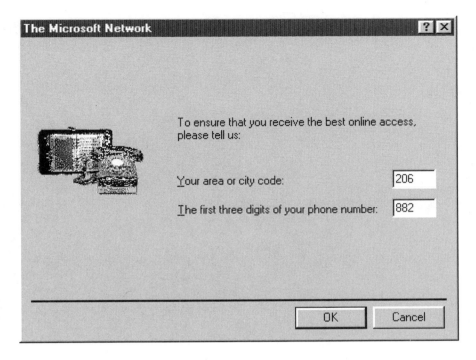

Figure F.18

After you enter your telephone information, your system will call The Microsoft
Network to obtain the local Internet and The Microsoft Network telephone number.
This number will provide access to both systems simultaneously.

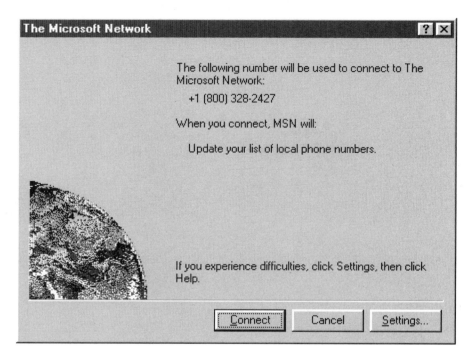

Figure F.19

Once the setup is complete, you can access many Internet services by double-clicking the The Internet icon on the desktop. This starts the Microsoft Internet Explorer.

The Internet Explorer, like most web browsers can access several types of Internet Services (or protocols). Internet Explorer can use the following protocols:

- ftp
- Gopher
- http
- text

Internet Explorer can work with the Microsoft Exchange mail client to handle electronic mail. It can also interface with a newsreader to access UseNet news. If you are using The Microsoft Network, it can act as your newsreader and your Internet mail service.

Location of Files

Microsoft Internet Explorer is installed by default in the C:\PROGRAM FILES\PLUS!\MICROSOFT INTERNET folder, which is referred to here as the Internet folder.

The Internet folder contains the Internet Setup wizard (INETWIZ.EXE), the Internet Explorer, a player for Progressive Networks' RealAudio, and various support files. There are also two folders in the Internet folder named History and Cache.

History

The History folder contains shortcuts to your 300 most recently visited Internet sites. Both the number of sites stored and the location can be changed on the View menu by clicking Options, and then clicking Advanced. It is worth noting that these Internet Shortcuts are fully contained shortcut objects that can be embedded in documents, included in electronic mail or moved to a shared folder on a network.

Cache

The Cache folder is similar to the History folder. It also contains a record of the Internet sites you have visited, but it stores the actual contents of where you were. This can include html pages, ftp file lists, GIF or JPEG images, text files, or anything else that can be placed on the Internet.

By default, the first time you access an Internet location (or page) its contents are checked against the cache. If you have been there before, the contents of the cached file are used rather than getting the information from the Internet server. You can turn this caching off, or change the size of the cache or its location on the View menu by clicking Options, and then clicking Advanced. The cache is set to 10 percent of your computer's hard disk size by default.

Favorites

One other important file location for the Internet Explorer is the Favorites folder. This folder and any folders within it show up in your list of favorite places on the Favorites menu. The Favorites folder is not located in the Internet folder. Instead, it is located under the Windows folder on the user's computer. The Favorites folder is used as a shared location for favorite items throughout the Windows 95 system including document templates as well as Internet Shortcuts. Again, the information about Internet sites is stored here in shortcut format.

Glossary

A

account *See* user account.

account policy Controls the way passwords must be used by all user accounts in a domain, or in an individual computer.

ACK An acknowledgment signal.

acknowledgment The process used to guarantee reliable end-to-end message delivery.

active window The window in which the user is currently working. An active window is typically at the top of the window order and is dis-tinguished by the color of its title bar.

agent Software that runs on a client computer for use by administrative software running on a server. Agents are typically used to support administrative actions, such as detecting system information or running services.

American National Standards Institute (ANSI) An organization dedicated to the development of trade and communications standards.

amplifier A device that amplifies signals so they can travel on additional cable segments at their original strength.

ANSI *See* American National Standards Institute.

Application layer The top (seventh) layer of the OSI model. This layer serves as the window for application processes to access network services. It represents the services that directly support user programs, such as software for file transfers, for database access, and for electronic mail.

application programming interface (API) A set of routines that an application program uses to request and carry out lower-level services performed by the operating system.

ARC Advanced RISC Computing. A standard developed by a consortium of hardware and software manufacturers. This standard specifies a computer that is similar to a personal computer but is based on a RISC processor.

ArcNet A baseband, token-passing media-access network protocol created by the Datapoint Corporation. ArcNet runs on coaxial cable, twisted-pair cable, and fiber-optic cable, and supports up to 255 nodes.

ASCII file *See* text file.

associate To identify a filename extension as "belonging" to a certain program, so that when a file with that extension is opened, the program starts automatically.

Attachment Unit Interface (AUI) The connector used with standard Ethernet that often includes a cable running off the main, or backbone, coaxial cable. This is also known as a DIX connector.

B

backbone The backbone, or trunk segment, is the main cable from which drop cables are connected to stations, repeaters, and bridges.

back end In a client/server program, back end refers to the part of the program executing on the server.

backup domain controller For Windows NT Server domains, refers to a computer that receives a copy of the domain's security policy and domain database, and authenticates network logons. *See also* primary domain controller.

bandwidth In communications, the difference between the highest and lowest frequencies in a given range; for example, a telephone accommodates a bandwidth of 3000 Hz the difference between the lowest (300 Hz) and highest (3300 Hz) frequencies it can carry. In computer networks, greater bandwidth indicates faster data-transfer capability.

baseband A system used to transmit the encoded signals over cable. Baseband uses digital signaling over a single frequency. Signals flow in the form of discrete pulses of electricity or light. With baseband transmission, the entire communication-channel capacity is used to transmit a single data signal.

base I/O port Specifies a channel through which information is transferred between your computer's hardware (such as your network card) and its CPU.

base memory address Defines the address of the location in your computer's memory (RAM) that is used by the network adapter card. This setting is sometimes called the RAM start address.

batch program An ASCII file (unformatted text file) that contains one or more commands. A batch program's filename has a BAT or CMD extension. When you type the filename at the command prompt, the commands are processed sequentially.

bind To associate two pieces of information with one another.

binding A process that establishes the communication channel between a protocol driver and a network adapter driver.

BIOS enumerator Responsible, in a Plug and Play system, for identifying all hardware devices on the motherboard of the computer. The BIOS supports an API that allows all Plug and Play-compliant computers to be queried in a common manner.

bit Short for binary digit: either 1 or 0 in the binary number system. In processing and storage, a bit is the smallest unit of information handled by a computer. It is represented physically by an element such as a single pulse sent through a circuit or small spot on a magnetic disk capable of storing either a 1 or 0.

bit time The time it takes each station to receive and store a bit.

BNC (British Naval Connector) A connector for coaxial cable that locks when one connector is inserted into another and is routed 90 degrees.

branch A segment of the directory tree, representing a directory and any subdirectories it contains.

bridge A device that allows you to join two local area networks, and allows stations on either network to access resources on the other. The bridge makes connections at the Data-Link layer of the OSI model.

broadband A system used to transmit the encoded signals over cable. A broadband system uses analog signaling and a range of frequencies. With analog transmission, the signals employed are continuous and nondiscrete. Signals flow across the physical medium in the form of electromagnetic or optical waves.

browse To look through lists of directories, files, user accounts, groups, domains, or computers.

buffer A reserved portion of memory in which data is temporarily held, pending an opportunity to complete its transfer to or from a storage device or another location in memory.

buffering The process of using buffers to hold data

that is being transferred, particularly to or from I/O devices such as disk drives and serial ports.

bus enumerator A new type of driver required for each specific bus type, responsible for building ("enumerating") the hardware tree on a Plug and Play system.

bus topology This topology connects each computer, or station, to a single cable. At each end of the cable is a terminating resistor, or terminator. A signal is passed back and forth along the cable, past the stations, and between the two terminators. The bus carries a message from one end of the network to the other. As the bus passes each station, the station checks the destination address on the message. If the address in the message matches the station's address, the station receives the message. If the address doesn't match, the bus carries the message to the next station, and so on.

C

Card Services A system component that is a protected-mode VxD, linked with the PCMCIA bus driver. Card Services passes the event notification from socket services to the PCMCIA bus driver, provides information from the computer's cards to the PCMCIA bus driver, and sets up the configuration for cards in the adapter sockets.

Carrier-Sense Multiple Access with Collision Detection (CSMA/CD)

A type of access control generally used with bus topologies. Using CSMA/CD, a station "listens" to the physical medium to determine whether another station is currently transmitting a data frame. If the medium is "quiet," that is, if no other station is transmitting, the station sends its data. A station "listens" to the medium by testing the medium for the presence of a carrier, a specific level of voltage or light. Thus, the term *carrier-sense*.

cascading menu A menu that is a submenu of a menu item. Also known as a hierarchical menu.

CDFS Compact disc file system, which controls access to the contents of CD-ROM drives.

central file server A network in which specific computers take on the role of a server with other computers on the network sharing the resources. *See also* client/server.

CHAP (Challenge Handshake Authentication Protocol)

The CHAP server sends a random challenge to the client. The client encrypts the challenge with the user's password and sends it back to the server. This prevents someone from gaining access by recording the authentication and playing it back to the server. Because the challenge is different on each call, a recorded sequence would fail.

character mode A mode of operation in which all information is displayed as text characters. This is the mode in which MS-DOS–based programs are displayed in windows in Windows 95. Also called alphanumeric mode or text mode.

check box A small, square box in a dialog box that can be selected or cleared, representing an option that you can turn on or off. When a check box is selected, an X appears in the box.

class 1. For OLE, the definition of a data structure and functions that manipulate that data. Objects are instances of a class; that is, an object must be a member of a given class. 2. For hardware, the manner in which devices and buses are grouped for purposes of installing and managing device drivers and allocating resources. The hardware tree is organized by device class, and Windows 95 uses class installers to install drivers for all hardware classes.

client A computer that accesses shared network resources provided by another computer (called a server). *See also* workstation.

client/server A network in which specific computers take on the role of a server, with other computers on the network sharing the resources. *See also* central file server.

coaxial cable (coax) A conductive center wire surrounded by an insulating layer, a layer of wire mesh (shielding), and a nonconductive outer layer. Coaxial cable is resistant to interference and signal weakening that other cabling, such as unshielded twisted-pair cable, can experience.

codec Compression/decompression technology for digital video and stereo audio.

computer name A unique name of up to 15 characters that identifies a computer to the network. The name cannot be the same as any other computer or domain name in the network, and it cannot contain spaces.

Configuration Manager The central component of a Plug and Play system that drives the process of locating devices, setting up their nodes in the hardware tree, and running the resource allocation process. Each of the three phases of configuration management—boot time (BIOS), real mode, and protected mode—has its own Configuration Manager.

context menu A menu that is displayed at the location of a selected object (sometimes called a pop-up menu or shortcut menu). The menu contains commands that are contextual to the selection.

Control menu *See* context menu.

controller *See* domain controller.

D

data frame Logical, structured packets in which data can be placed. Data that is being transmitted is segmented into small units and combined with control information such as message start and message end. Each package of information is transmitted as a single unit called a frame. The Data-Link layer packages raw bits from the Physical layer into data frames. The exact format of the frame used by the network depends on the topology.

datagram A packet of data and other delivery information that is routed through a packet-switched network or transmitted on a local area network. A datagram is a basic messaging service. It provides connectionless data transfer where no association exists between the sender and receiver when the message is sent. Because the status of the receiver is unknown and no acknowledgments are sent, datagrams are considered unreliable. Datagrams allow messages to be broadcast to many stations at once.

Data-Link layer The second layer in the OSI model. This layer packages raw bits from the Physical layer into data frames.

DDE *See* dynamic data exchange.

default An operation or value that the system assumes, unless the user makes an explicit choice.

desktop The background of your screen, on which windows, icons, and dialog boxes appear.

device A generic term for a computer component, such as a printer, serial port, or disk drive. A device frequently requires its own controlling software called a device driver.

device contention The way Windows 95 allocates access to peripheral devices, such as a modem or a printer, when more than one program is trying to use the same device.

device driver A program that enables a specific piece of hardware (device) to communicate with Windows 95. Although a device may be installed on your computer, Windows 95 cannot recognize the device until you have installed and configured the appropriate driver.

device ID A unique ASCII string created by enumerators to identify a hardware device and used to cross-reference data about the device stored in the registry.

device node The basic data structure for a given device, built by Configuration Manager; sometimes called devnode. Device nodes are built into memory at system startup for each device and enumerator with information about the device, such as currently assigned resources. The complete representation of all device nodes is referred to as the hardware tree.

DHCP *See* Dynamic Host Configuration Protocol.

Dial-Up Networking A service that provides remote networking for telecommuters, mobile workers, and system administrators who monitor and manage servers at multiple branch offices. Users with Dial-Up Networking on a computer running Windows 95 can dial in for remote access to their networks for services such as file and printer sharing, electronic mail, scheduling, and SQL database access.

DIP switch One or more small rocker or sliding type switches contained in a housing of a dual inline package (DIP) connected to a circuit board. Each DIP switch can be set to one of two switches, closed or open, to control options on the circuit board.

directory tree The directories and subdirectories branching out from the root directory in the FAT file system.

disk caching A method used by a file system to improve performance. Instead of reading and writing directly to the disk, frequently used files are temporarily stored in a cache in memory, and reads and writes to those files are performed in memory. Reading and writing to memory is much faster than reading and writing to disk.

diskless workstations Workstations that do not have a hard drive.

DLL *See* dynamic-link library.

DMA channel A channel for direct memory access that does not involve the microprocessor, providing data transfer directly between memory and a disk drive.

DNS *See* Domain Name System.

dock To insert a portable computer into a base unit. Cold docking means the computer must begin from a power-off state and restart before docking. Hot docking means the computer can be docked while running at full power.

docking station The base computer unit into which a user can insert a portable computer, to expand it to a desktop equivalent. A typical dock provides drive bays, expansion slots, all the ports on the desktop computer, and AC power.

domain For Microsoft networking, a collection of computers that share a common domain database and security policy that is stored on a Windows NT Server domain controller. Each domain has a unique name. *See also* workgroup.

domain controller The Windows NT Server-based computer that authenticates domain logons and maintains the security policy and the master database for a domain.

Domain Name System (DNS) Sometimes referred to as the BIND service in BSD UNIX; a static, hierarchical name service for TCP/IP hosts. A DNS server maintains a database for resolving host names and IP addresses, allowing users of computers configured to query the DNS to specify remote computers by host names rather than IP addresses. DNS domains should not be confused with Windows NT networking domains.

dynamic data exchange (DDE) A form of interprocess communication (IPC) implemented in the Microsoft Windows family of operating systems. Two or more programs that support dynamic data exchange (DDE) can exchange information and commands. Most DDE functions have been superseded in later versions of OLE.

Dynamic Host Configuration Protocol (DHCP) A protocol for automatic TCP/IP configuration that provides static and dynamic address allocation and management.

dynamic-link library (DLL) An application programming interface (API) routine that user-mode applications access through ordinary procedure calls. The code for the API routine is not included in the user's executable image. Instead, the operating system automatically modifies the executable image to point to DLL procedures at run time.

E

EISA Enhanced Industry Standard Architecture, a bus design specified by an industry consortium for x86-based computers. An EISA device uses cards that are upwardly compatible from ISA.

encapsulated PostScript (EPS) file A file that prints at the highest possible resolution for your printer. An EPS file may print faster than other graphical representations.

end systems Another name for workstations and servers. This term is often used in the context of wide area networks (WAN).

enumerator A Plug and Play-compliant device driver that detects devices below its own device node, creates unique device IDs, and reports to Configuration Manager during startup. For example, a SCSI adapter provides a SCSI enumerator that detects devices on the SCSI bus.

environment variable A string consisting of environment information, such as a drive, path, or filename, associated with a symbolic name that can be used by Windows 95. Use the System option in Control Panel or the **set** command from the command prompt to define environment variables.

event 1. An action or occurrence to which a program might respond. Examples of events are mouse clicks, key presses, and mouse movements. 2. Any significant occurrence in the system or in a program that requires users to be notified, or an entry to be added to a log.

F

FAT file system A file system based on a file allocation table, maintained by the operating system, to keep track of the status of various segments of disk space used for file storage. The 32-bit implementation in Windows 95 is called the Virtual File Allocation Table (VFAT).

file allocation table (FAT) *See* FAT file system.

file sharing The ability of a Microsoft network computer to share parts (or all) of its local file systems with remote computers. You can share resources if file and printer sharing services are enabled on the computer.

file system In an operating system, the overall structure in which files are named, stored, and organized.

File Transfer Protocol (FTP) A service that supports file transfers between local and remote computers. FTP supports several commands that allow bidirectional transfer of binary and ASCII files between computers. The FTP client is installed with the TCP/IP connectivity utilities.

focus The area of a dialog box which receives input. To find the focus, look for highlighted text (for example, in a list box) or a button enclosed in dotted lines.

folder A type of container of objects (typically files).

font A set of attributes for characters.

frame A package of information transmitted as a single unit. *See also* data frame.

frame preamble Header information, added to the beginning of a data frame in the Physical layer.

free space An unused and unformatted portion of a hard disk that can be partitioned or subpartitioned. Free space within an extended partition is available for the creation of logical drives. Free space that is not within an extended partition is available for the creation of a partition, with a maximum of four partitions allowed.

friendly name A name, typically identifying a network user or a device, intended to be familiar, meaningful, and easily identifiable. A friendly name for a printer might indicate the printer's physical location (for example, "Sales Department Printer").

front end In a client/server program, front end refers to the part of the program executing on the client.

FTP *See* File Transfer Protocol.

G

gateway A computer connected to multiple physical networks, capable of routing or delivering packets between them. It is used to connect dissimilar networks (networks using dissimilar protocols) so that information can be passed from one to the other. A gateway is at the Network layer of the OSI model.

graphics engine The print component that provides WYSIWYG (what you see is what you get) support across devices.

group In User Manager, an account containing other accounts that are called members. The permissions and rights granted to a group are also provided to its members, which makes groups a convenient way to grant common capabilities to collections of user accounts. For Windows NT, groups are managed with User Manager. For Windows NT Server, groups are managed with User Manager for Domains. *See also* user account.

H

handle   1. In the user interface, an interface added to an object that facilitates moving, sizing, reshaping, or other functions pertaining to an object. 2. In programming, a pointer to a pointer—that is, a token that lets a program access a resource identified in another variable. *See also* object handle.

hardware branch   The hardware archive root key in the registry, which is a superset of the memory-resident hardware tree. The name of this key is Hkey_Local_Machine\Hardware.

hardware tree   A record in RAM of the current system configuration, based on the configuration information for all devices in the hardware branch of the registry. The hardware tree is created each time the computer is started or whenever a dynamic change occurs to the system configuration.

hertz (Hz)   The unit of frequency measurement. Frequency measures how often a periodic event occurs, such as the manner a wave's amplitude, changes with time. One hertz equals one cycle per second. Frequency is often measured in kilohertz (kHz, 1000 Hz), megahertz (MHz), gigahertz (GHz, 1000 MHz), or terahertz (THz, 10,000 GHz).

hierarchical menu   *See* cascading menu.

Hkey_Classes_Root   A predefined registry handle that defines OLE and file-class association data. This key is a symbolic link to a subkey of Hkey_Local_Machine\Software.

Hkey_Current_User   A predefined registry handle that defines the current user's preferences, including environment variables, personal program groups, desktop settings, network connections, printers, and program preferences. This key maps to a subkey of Hkey_Users.

Hkey_Local_Machine   A predefined registry handle that defines the hardware and operating system characteristics such as bus type, system memory, installed device drives, and boot control data.

Hkey_Users   A predefined registry handle that defines the default user configuration for users on the local computer and configuration data from user profiles stored on the local computer.

home directory   A directory that is accessible to the user and contains files and programs for that user. A home directory can be assigned to an individual user or can be shared by many users. *See also* machine directory.

host   Any device that is attached to the internetwork and uses TCP/IP.

host table   The HOSTS or LMHOST file that contains lists of known IP addresses mapped to host names or NetBIOS computer names.

HPFS   File system primarily used with the OS/2 operating system version 1.2 or later. It supports long filenames but does not provide security.

hub   A unit that provides a common connection among computers in a star-configured network so that all of the computers can communicate with one another.

I

IETF   *See* Internet Engineering Task Force.

INF file   A file that provides Windows 95 Setup with the information required to set up a device, such as a list of valid logical configurations for the device, the names of driver files associated with the device, and so on. An INF file is typically provided by the device manufacturer on a disk.

INI files Initialization files used by Windows-based programs to store per-user information that controls program startup. In Windows 95, such information is stored in the registry, and INI files are supported for backward compatibility.

Institute of Electrical and Electronics Engineers (IEEE) Project 802 A networking model developed by the Institute of Electrical and Electronics Engineers (IEEE). This project is called 802, for the year and month it began (February 1980). Project 802 defines LAN standards for the Physical and Data-Link layers of the OSI model. The 802 project divides the Data-Link layer into two sublayers: *Media Access Control* (MAC) and *Logical Link Control* (LLC).

intermediate systems Equipment that provides a link, such as bridges, routers, and gateways.

internal command Commands that are stored in the CMD.EXE file and that reside in memory at all times.

International Organization for Standardization (ISO) An international association of member countries, each represented by its leading standard-setting organization—for example, ANSI (American National Standards Institute) for the United States. The ISO works to establish global standards for communications and information exchange.

Internet Engineering Task Force (IETF) A consortium that introduces procedures for new technology on the Internet. IETF specifications are released in documents called Requests for Comments (RFCs).

internet group name In Microsoft networking, a name registered by the domain controller that contains a list of the specific addresses of computers that have registered the name. The name has a 16th character ending in 0x1C.

interrupt (IRQ) An asynchronous operating condition that disrupts normal execution and transfers control to an interrupt handler. Interrupts are usually initiated by I/O devices requiring service from the processor. An electronic signal sent to the computer's central processing unit.

interrupt request lines (IRQ) Hardware lines over which devices can send signals to get the attention of the processor when the device is ready to accept or send information. Typically, each device connected to the computer uses a separate IRQ.

I/O device An input/output device, which is a piece of hardware used for providing information to and receiving information from the computer—for example, a disk drive, which transfers information in one of two directions, depending on the situation. Some input devices, such as keyboards, can be used only for input; some output devices (such as a printer or a monitor) can be used only for output. Most of these devices require installation of device drivers.

I/O request packet (IRP) Data structures that drivers use to communicate with each other.

IP address Used to identify a node on a network and to specify routing information on an internetwork. Each node on the internetwork must be assigned a unique IP address, which is made up of the network ID, plus a unique host ID assigned by the network administrator. In Windows 95, the IP address can be configured statically on the computer or configured dynamically through DHCP.

IP router A computer connected to multiple physical TCP/IP networks that can route or deliver IP packets between the networks. *See also* gateway.

IPXODI.COM The ODI version of the IPX/SPX protocol. Used in place of the standard IPX.COM, IPXODI.COM communicates between the LSL and the programs.

IPX/SPX Transport protocols used in Novell NetWare and other networks. For Windows 95, the NWLINK.VXD module is used to implement the IPX/SPX-compatible protocol.

IRP *See* I/O request packet.

IRQ *See* interrupt request lines.

ISA Industry Standard Architecture bus design of the IBM PC/AT.

ISO *See* International Organization for Standardization.

K

Kernel The portion of Windows 95 that manages the processor.

kernel driver A driver that accesses hardware.

L

legacy Hardware and device cards that don't conform to the Plug and Play standard.

link (v.) To form a connection between two objects. (n.) 1. For OLE, a reference to an object that is linked to another object. 2. For networking, a connection at the LLC layer that is uniquely defined by the adapter's address and the destination service access point (DSAP). The communication system connecting two LANs. Equipment that provides the link, including bridges, routers, and gateways. 3. Also refers to shortcuts.

Link Support Layer (LSL or LSL.COM)
This layer provides a foundation for the MAC driver to communicate with multiple protocols. LSL.COM performs functions similar to the protocol manager in NDIS.

list box In a dialog box, a box that lists available choices—for example, a list of all files in a directory. If all the choices do not fit in the list box, there is a scroll bar.

LLC Logical link control, in the Data-Link layer of the networking model.

LMHOSTS file A local text file that maps IP addresses to the NetBIOS computer names of Microsoft networking computers outside the local subnet. In Windows 95, this file is stored in the Windows directory.

local area network (LAN) Computers connected in a geographically close network, such as in the same building or campus.

localization The process of adapting software for different countries, languages, or cultures.

local printer A printer that is directly connected to one of the ports on your computer.

logical drive A subpartition of an extended partition on a hard disk.

Logical Link Control sublayer The IEEE 802 standards divided the Data-Link layer into two sublayers. The Logical Link Control (LLC) layer is the upper sublayer that manages data link communication and defines the use of logical interface points (called Service Access Points [SAPs]) that other computers can refer to and use to transfer information from the LLC sublayer to the upper OSI layers.

login script A batch file that runs automatically every time the user logs on. It can be used to configure a user's working environment at every logon, and it allows an administrator to control a user's environment without managing all aspects of it.

lost token   Refers to an error condition on a token ring network. This error causes an errant station to stop the token, causing a condition where there is no token on the ring.

M

MAC   Media access control. A layer in the network architecture.

MAC address   The address for a device as it is identified at the Media Access Control layer in the network architecture.

MAC driver   The device driver located at the MAC sublayer. This driver is also known as the network adapter card driver or NIC driver. It provides low-level access to network adapters by providing data transmission support and some basic adapter management functions. These drivers also pass data from the Physical layer to transport protocols at the Network and Transport layers.

machine directory   For shared installations, the directory that contains the required configuration files for a particular computer. The machine directory contains WIN.COM, the registry, and startup configuration files.

management information base (MIB)
A set of objects that represent various types of information about a device, used by SNMP to manage devices. Because different network-management services are used for different types of devices or protocols, each service has its own set of objects. The entire set of objects that any service or protocol uses is referred to as its MIB.

map   To translate one value into another.

MAPI   *See* messaging application program interface.

Media Access Control (MAC)   The IEEE 802 standards divided the Data-Link layer into two sublayers. The Media Access Control (MAC) sublayer communicates directly with the network adapter card and is responsible for delivering error-free data between two computers on the network.

messaging application program interface (MAPI)
A set of calls used to add mail-enabled features to other Windows-based programs.

MIB   *See* management information base.

millions of bits per second (Mbps)
The unit of measure of supported transmission rates on the following physical media: coaxial cable, twisted-pair cable, and fiber-optic cable.

miniport driver   A 32-bit installable driver that allows easy additions. Windows NT was the first operating system to use miniport drivers.

monolithic protocol stack   A protocol driver that manages all functions of the MAC driver through the Transport layer in one protocol driver.

MS-DOS–based program   A program that is designed to run with MS-DOS, and, therefore, may not be able to take full advantage of all Windows 95 features.

Multiple Link Interface Driver (MLID)
The part of the ODI interface that communicates between the adapter and the LSL. This is the hardware dependent code created by the network adapter card manufacturer. This code usually carries the name of the supported adapter.

Multistation Access Unit (MAU)   The name for a token ring wiring concentrator. Also known as a *hub*.

N

name registration The method by which a computer registers its unique name with a name server on the network. In a Microsoft network, a WINS server can provide name registration services.

name resolution The process used on the network for resolving a computer address as a computer name, to support the process of finding and connecting to other computers on the network.

named pipe An interprocess communication (IPC) mechanism that allows one process to communicate with another local or remote process.

NDIS *See* Network Device Interface Specification.

NetBEUI transport NetBIOS (Network Basic Input/Output System) Extended User Interface. A local area network transport protocol provided with Windows 95. *See also* NetBIOS interface.

NetBIOS interface A programming interface that allows I/O requests to be sent to and received from a remote computer. It hides networking hardware from programs.

NetBIOS (network basic input/output system) A software interface for network communication.

NetBIOS over TCP/IP The networking module that provides the functionality to support NetBIOS name registration and resolution.

network Two or more computers that are connected together by cables and that are running software enabling them to communicate with one another.

network adapter card An expansion card or other device used to connect a computer to a local area network (LAN).

network adapter driver Software that coordinates communication between the network adapter and the computer's hardware and other software, controlling the physical function of the network adapters.

Network Device Interface Specification (NDIS) In Windows networking, the interface for network adapter drivers. All transport drivers call the NDIS interface to access network adapters. NDIS is a standard that defines an interface for communication between the MAC sublayer and protocol drivers. It allows for a flexible environment of data exchange and defines the software interface, called the *NDIS interface*. This interface is used by protocol drivers to communicate with the network adapter card.

network directory *See* shared directory.

Network layer The third layer in the OSI model. This layer is responsible for addressing messages and translating logical addresses and names into physical addresses. This layer also determines the route from the source to the destination computer. It determines which path the data should take based on network conditions, priority of service, and other factors. It also manages traffic problems such as switching, routing, and controlling the congestion of data packets on the network.

network provider The component that allows a computer running Windows 95 to communicate with the network. Windows 95 includes providers for Microsoft networking and for Novell NetWare networks; other providers' DLLs are supplied by the respective networks' vendors.

node On a LAN, a device that is connected to the network and is capable of communicating with other network devices. For example, workstations, servers, and repeaters are called nodes.

NTFS Windows NT file system.

O

object 1. An entity or component, identifiable by the user, that may be distinguished by its properties, operations, and relationships. 2. Any piece of information, created by using a Windows-based program with OLE capabilities, that can be linked or embedded into another document.

object handle Code that includes access control information and a pointer to the object itself.

OLE The name that describes the technology and interface for object interaction. A way to transfer and share information between programs.

OLE object A discrete unit of data that has been supplied by an OLE program—for example, a worksheet, module, chart, cell, or range of cells.

Open Datalink Interface (ODI) A specification defined by Novell and Apple to simplify driver development and to provide support for multiple protocols on a single network adapter. Similar to NDIS in many respects, ODI allows Novell NetWare drivers to be written without concern for the protocol that will be used on top of them.

Open Systems Interconnection (OSI) reference model
A seven-layer architecture that standardizes levels of service and types of interaction for computers exchanging information through a communications network. It is used to describe the flow of data between the physical connection to the network and the end-user program. This model is the best known and most widely used model to describe networking environments.

optical fibers Fiber used to carry digital data signals in the form of modulated pulses of light. An optical fiber consists of an extremely thin cylinder of glass, called the *core*, surrounded by a concentric layer of glass, known as the *cladding*.

P

package An icon that represents an embedded or linked object. When you choose the package, the program used to create the object either plays the object (for example, a sound file) or opens and displays the object.

packet A transmission unit of fixed maximum size that consists of binary information representing both data and a header containing an ID number, source and destination addresses, and error-control data.

page In memory, a fixed-size block.

paging file *See* swapfile.

PAM *See* pulse amplitude modulation.

partition A portion of a physical disk that functions as though it were a physically separate unit. *See also* system partition.

password A unique string of characters that must be provided before logon or access to a resource or service is authorized. A password is a security measure used to restrict logons to user accounts and access to computer systems and resources.

path Specifies the location of a file within the directory tree.

PCI The Peripheral Component Interconnect local bus being promoted as the successor to VL. This type of device is used in most Pentium computers and in the Apple PowerPC™ Macintosh.

PCM *See* pulse code modulation.

PCMCIA The Personal Computer Memory Card International Association standard for the credit card-sized interface cards in portables and other small computers.

peer-to-peer network A network configuration in which devices operate on the same communications level. In other words, each station can operate as both a client and a server.

permission A rule associated with an object (usually a directory, file, or printer) in order to regulate which users can have access to the object and in their manner of access.

persistent frame Refers to an error condition on a token ring network. This error prevents a sending station from recognizing an acknowledgment data frame, which would then continue to circulate around the ring.

Physical layer The first (bottommost) layer of the OSI model. This layer addresses the transmission of the unstructured raw bitstream over a physical medium (that is, the networking cable). The Physical layer relates the electrical/optical, mechanical, and functional interfaces to the cable. The Physical layer also carries the signals that transmit data generated by all the higher layers.

piercing tap This is a connector for coaxial cable that pierces through the insulating layer and makes direct contact with the conducting core.

pipe A portion of memory that can be used by one process to pass information along to another. It connects two processes so that the output of one can be used as the input to the other.

plenum The short space in many buildings between the false ceiling and the floor above, used to circulate warm and cold air through the building. Fire codes are very specific on the type of wiring that can be routed through this area.

Plug and Play BIOS A BIOS with responsibility for configuring Plug and Play cards and system board devices during system power-up; provides run-time configuration services for system board devices after startup.

Point-to-Point Protocol (PPP) An industry standard that is part of Windows 95 Dial-Up Networking to ensure interoperability with remote access software from other vendors.

pop-up menu *See* context menu.

port A connection or socket used to connect a device, such as a printer, monitor, or modem, to your computer. Information is sent from your computer to the device through a cable.

port replicators Low-cost docking station substitutes that provide one-step connection to multiple desktop devices.

postoffice A temporary message store, holding the message until the recipient's workstation retrieves it. The postoffice exists as a directory structure on a server and has no programmatic components.

PPP *See* Point-to-Point Protocol.

preemptive multitasking An operating system scheduling technique that allows the operating system to take control of the processor at any instant, regardless of the state of the currently running program. Preemption guarantees better response to the user and higher data throughput.

Presentation layer The sixth layer of the OSI model. It determines the form used to exchange data between networked computers. It can be viewed as the network's translator. At the sending computer, this layer translates data from a format sent down from the Application layer into a commonly recognized intermediary format. At the receiving end, this layer translates the intermediary format into a format useful to that computer's Application layer. The Presentation layer also manages network security issues by providing services such as data encryption. It also provides rules for data transfer as well as data compression to reduce the number of bits that have to be transmitted.

primary domain controller For Windows NT Server domains, refers to the computer that maintains the domain's security policy and domain database, and authenticates network logons. *See also* backup domain controller.

primary partition A portion of a physical disk that can be marked for use by an operating system. There can be up to four primary partitions (or up to three, if there is an extended partition) per physical disk. A primary partition cannot be subpartitioned.

print device Refers to the actual hardware device that produces printed output. *See also* printer.

print monitor The component that receives information from the printer driver by way of the spooler and sends it onto the printer or destination file. The print monitor tracks physical devices so the spooler doesn't have to.

print provider A software component that allows the client to print to the print server's device.

printer Refers to the software interface between the program and the print device. *See also* print device.

printer driver A program that controls how your computer and printer interact.

printer sharing The ability for a computer running Windows 95 to share a locally attached printer for use on the network.

program file A file that starts a program. A program file has an EXE, PIF, COM, or BAT filename extension.

Project 802 topologies

- 802.3 defines standards for bus networks, such as Ethernet, that use a mechanism called Carrier Sense Multiple Access with Collision Detection (CSMA/CD).

- 802.4 defines standards for token-passing bus networks.

- 802.5 defines standards for token-passing ring networks.

IEEE defined functionality for the LLC layer in Standard 802.2 and defined functionality for the MAC and Physical layers in Standards 802.3, 802.4, and 802.5.

properties Attributes or characteristics of an object used to define its state, appearance, or value.

properties dialog box A secondary window that displays the properties of an object.

protocol A set of rules and conventions by which two computers pass messages across a network. Networking software usually implements multiple levels of protocols layered one on top of another. Windows 95 includes NetBEUI, TCP/IP, and IPX/SPX-compatible protocols.

protocol driver The protocol driver is responsible for offering four or five basic services to other layers in the network, "hiding" the details of how the service is actually implemented. The services the protocol driver performs include session management, datagram service, data segmentation and sequencing, acknowledgment, and possibly routing across a wide area network.

pulse amplitude modulation (PAM)

A method of encoding information in a signal by varying the amplitude of pulses. The unmodulated signal consists of a continuous train of pulses of constant frequency, duration, and amplitude. During modulation, the pulse amplitudes are changed to reflect the information being encoded.

pulse code modulation (PCM) A method of encoding information in a signal by varying the amplitude of pulses. Unlike pulse amplitude modulation (PAM) in which pulse amplitude can vary continuously, pulse code modulation limits pulse amplitudes to several predefined values. Because the signal is discrete, or digital, rather than analog, PCM is more immune to noise than PAM.

R

redirector Networking software that accepts I/O requests for remote files, named pipes, or mailslots and then sends (redirects) them to a network service on another computer. Redirectors (also called network clients) are implemented as file system drivers in Windows 95.

registry The database repository for information about a computer's configuration. The registry supersedes use of separate INI files for all system components and programs that know how to store values in the registry.

Registry Editor A program, provided with Windows 95, that is used to view and edit entries in the registry.

remote administration Administration of one computer by an administrator located at another computer and connected to the first computer across the network.

remote procedure call (RPC) A message-passing facility that allows a distributed program to call services available on various computers in a network. Used during remote administration of computers, RPC provides a procedural view, rather than a transport-centered view, of networked operations.

repeater A device that regenerates signals so they can travel on additional cable segments at their original strength.

Request for Comments (RFC) An official document of the Internet Engineering Task Force (IETF) that specifies the details for protocols included in the TCP/IP family.

resource Any part of a computer or a network, such as a disk drive, printer, or memory, that can be allotted to a program or a process while it is running. Users on a network can share computer resources, such as hard drives, printers, modems, CD-ROM drives, and even the processor.

RFC *See* Request for Comments.

RJ-11 An attachment used to join a telephone line to a device such as a modem.

RJ-45 An attachment used to join a telephone line to a device such as a modem. It is similar to an RJ-11 telephone connector but has twice the number of conductors.

root directory *See* directory tree.

router 1. The printing model component that locates the requested printer and sends information from the workstation spooler to the print server's spooler. 2. In network gateways, computers with two or more network adapters that are running some type of routing software, with each adapter connected to a different physical network. Used to connect LANs. Routers allow the two networks to be administered independently, yet to remain accessible to each other when communication is necessary. Routers connect networks at the Network layer of the OSI model.

routing The process of forwarding packets to other gateways until the packet is eventually delivered to a gateway connected to the specified destination.

RPC   *See* remote procedure call.

S

screen buffer   The size reserved in memory for the MS-DOS Prompt display.

scroll   To move through text or graphics (up, down, left, or right) in order to see parts of the file that cannot fit on the screen.

scroll bar   A bar that appears at the right or bottom edge of a window or list box whose contents are not completely visible. Each scroll bar contains two scroll arrows and a scroll box, which enable you to navigate through the contents of the window or list box.

SCSI   Small computer standard interface. This is a multidevice, chained interface used in many devices such as hard disk drives and CD-ROM drives.

segment   A segment is the length of cable between two terminators. A segment can also refer to messages that have been broken up into smaller units by the protocol driver.

sequence information   Enables the protocol driver on the receiving end to get data frames back together in the right order.

Serial Line IP (SLIP)   An industry standard that can be used with Windows 95 Dial-Up Networking to ensure interoperability with remote access software from other vendors.

server   For a LAN, a computer running administrative software that controls access to all or part of the network and its resources. A computer acting as a server makes resources available to computers acting as workstations on the network. *See also* client.

server message block (SMB)   The protocol developed by Microsoft, Intel, and IBM that defines a series of commands used to pass information between network computers. The redirector packages SMB requests into a network control block (NCB) structure that can be sent over the network to a remote device. The network provider listens for SMB messages destined for it and removes the data portion of the SMB request so that it can be processed by a local device.

service   A process that performs a specific system function and often provides an application programming interface (API) for other processes to call. If services are RPC-enabled, their API routines can be called from remote computers.

session   A connection that two programs on different computers establish, use, and end. The Session layer performs name recognition and the functions needed to allow two programs to communicate over the network.

Session layer   The fifth layer of the OSI model. This layer allows two programs on different computers to establish, use, and end a connection called a *session*. This layer performs name recognition and the functions needed to allow two programs to communicate over the network, such as security functions. The Session layer provides synchronization between user tasks. This layer also implements dialog control between communicating processes, regulating which side transmits, the time and duration of transmission, and so on.

session management   Establishing, maintaining, and terminating connections between stations on the network.

share   To make resources, such as directories and printers, available to network users.

share name   The name of a shared resource.

shared directory A directory that network users can connect to.

shared resource Any device, data, or program that is used by more than one other device or program. For Windows 95, refers to any resource that is made available to network users, such as directories, files, printers, and named pipes.

shell A generic term used to refer to the interface supplied by the operating system.

Simple Network Management Protocol (SNMP)
A protocol used by SNMP consoles and agents to communicate.

single server *See* central file server.

SLIP *See* Serial Line IP.

SMB *See* server message block.

SNMP *See* Simple Network Management Protocol.

socket A bidirectional pipe for incoming and outgoing data between networked computers. The Windows Sockets API is a networking API used by programmers creating TCP/IP-based sockets programs.

socket services A protected-mode VxD that manages the PCMCIA adapter hardware. It provides a protected-mode PCMCIA Socket Services 2.*x* interface for use by Card Services. A socket services driver must be implemented for each separate PCMCIA controller that is used.

source directory The directory that contains the file or files you intend to copy or move.

SPAP (Shiva Password Authentication Protocol)
SPAP is a version of PAP implemented by Shiva in their remote client software. SPAP allows you to authenticate with existing Shiva servers. Implementation is a reversible encryption scheme. It is not as secure as CHAP, but it is more secure than PAP.

spooler A scheduler for the printing process. It coordinates activity among other components of the print model and schedules all print jobs arriving at the print server.

static VxD A VxD that is loaded statically during system startup. A static VxD can be loaded in a number of different ways, including a line in SYSTEM.INI, a response to an INT 2F call, or by way of device enumeration by the Plug and Play static device enumerator.

status bar A line of information related to the program in the window. Usually located at the bottom of a window. Not all windows have a status bar.

string A data structure composed of a sequence of characters, usually representing human-readable text.

stubs Nonexecutable placeholders used by calls from the server environment.

subnet On the Internet, refers to any lower network that is part of the logical network identified by the network ID.

subnet mask A 32-bit value that allows the recipient of IP packets to distinguish the network ID portion of the IP address from the host ID.

swapfile A special file on your hard disk. With virtual memory under Windows 95, some of the program code and other information is kept in RAM while other information is temporarily swapped to virtual memory. When that information is required again, Windows 95 pulls it back into RAM and, if necessary, swaps other information to virtual memory. Also called a paging file.

syntax The order in which you must type a command and the elements that follow the command.

system partition The volume that contains the hardware-specific files needed to load Windows 95. *See also* partition.

T

T-connector A T-shaped coax connector that connects two Thinnet Ethernet cables while supplying an additional connector for a network interface card.

tap A connection to a network. Sometimes this refers specifically to a connection to a cable.

TAPI *See* telephony application program interface.

TCP/IP Transmission Control Protocol/Internet Protocol. The primary wide area network (WAN) transport protocol used in Windows 95 to communicate with computers on TCP/IP networks and to participate in UNIX-based bulletin boards and electronic mail services.

telephony application program interface (TAPI) A set of calls that allows applications to control modems and telephones, by routing application function calls to the appropriate "service provider" DLL for a modem.

Telnet service The service that provides basic terminal emulation to remote computers supporting the Telnet protocol over TCP/IP.

terminator A resistor used at each end of an Ethernet cable to ensure that signals do not reflect back and cause errors. It is usually attached to an electrical ground at one end.

text file A file containing only letters, numbers, and symbols. A text file contains no formatting information, except possibly linefeeds and carriage returns. A text file is an ASCII file.

Thicknet (standard Ethernet) A relatively rigid coaxial cable about ½ inch in diameter. Typically, Thicknet is used as a backbone to connect several smaller Thinnet-based networks because of its ability to support data transfer over longer distances. Thicknet can carry a signal for 500 meters (about 1,640 feet) before needing a repeater.

Thinnet (thin-wire Ethernet) RG-58 cabling. It is a flexible coaxial cable about ¼ inch thick. It is used for relatively short distance communication and is fairly flexible to facilitate routing between workstations. Thinnet coaxial cable can carry a signal up to approximately 185 meters (or about 607 feet) before needing a repeater.

thread 1. An executable entity that belongs to a single process, comprising a program counter, a user-mode stack, a kernel-mode stack, and a set of register values. All threads in a process have equal access to the processor's address space, object handles, and other resources. In Windows 95, threads are implemented as objects. 2. A collection of electronic mail messages organized chronologically and hierarchically to reflect the flow of the discussion.

thunking The transformation between 16-bit and 32-bit formats, which is carried out by a separate layer in the VM.

time-out If a device is not performing a task, the amount of time the computer should wait before detecting it as an error.

token passing A media access control method that involves passing a small data frame, called a *token*, from one station to the next around the ring.

token ring network On a token ring network, workstations are situated on a continuous network loop on which a "token" is passed from one workstation to the next. Workstations are centrally connected to a hub called a Multistation Access Unit (MAU) and are wired in a star configuration. Workstations use a token to transmit data and must wait for a free token in order to transfer messages.

toolbar A standard control that provides a frame for a series of shortcut buttons providing quick access to commands. Usually located directly below the menu bar. Not all windows have a toolbar.

transceiver A device that receives and transmits signals.

Transport layer The fourth layer of the OSI model. It ensures that messages are delivered error-free, in sequence, and with no losses or duplications. This layer repackages messages for their efficient transmission over the network. At the receiving end, the Transport layer unpacks the messages, reassembles the original messages, and sends an acknowledgment of receipt.

transport protocol Defines how data should be presented to the next receiving layer in the networking model and packages the data accordingly. It passes data to the network adapter driver through the NDIS interface.

tuple In a database table (relation), a set of related values, one for each attribute (column). A tuple is stored as a row in a relational database management system. It is the analog of a record in a nonrelational file.

twisted-pair cable A cable that consists of two insulated strands of copper wire twisted together. A number of twisted-wire pairs are often grouped together and enclosed in a protective sheath to form a cable. Unshielded twisted-pair cable is commonly used for telephone systems.

U

UNC Universal naming convention. *See also* UNC names.

UNC names Filenames or other resource names that begin with the string \\, indicating that they exist on a remote computer.

Unimodem Name used to refer to the universal modem driver. It is a driver-level component that uses modem description files to control its interaction with the communications driver, VCOMM.

user account Refers to all the information that defines a user to Windows 95. This includes such things as the user name and password required for the user to log on, the groups in which the user account has membership, and the rights and permissions the user has for using the computer and accessing its resources.

user name A unique name identifying a user account to Windows 95. An account's user name cannot be identical to any other group name or user name of its own domain or workgroup. *See also* user account.

V

value entry A parameter under a key or subkey in the registry. A value entry appears as a string with three components: name, type, and value.

virtual machine (VM) A complete MS-DOS environment and a console in which to run an MS-DOS–based program or 16-bit Windows-based programs. A VM establishes a complete virtual x86 (that is, 80386 or higher) computer running MS-DOS. Any number of VMs can run simultaneously. Also known as a virtual DOS machine.

virtual printer memory In a PostScript printer, a part of memory that stores font information. The memory in PostScript printers is divided into banded memory and virtual memory. The banded memory contains graphics and page-layout information needed to print your documents. The virtual memory contains any font information that is sent to your printer either when you print a document or when you download fonts.

visual editing The ability to edit an embedded object in place, without opening it into its own window.

VL The Video Electronic Standards Association (VESA) local bus standard for a bus that allows high-speed connections to peripherals.

VM See *virtual machine*.

volume A partition or collection of partitions that have been formatted for use by a file system.

VxD Virtual device driver. The *x* represents the type of device, so that, for example, a virtual device driver for a display is a VDD and a virtual device driver for a printer is a VPD.

W

WAN *See* wide area network.

wide area network (WAN) Computer networks using long-range telecommunications links, allowing the computers to be networked over long distances.

wildcard A character that represents one or more characters. The question mark (?) wildcard can be used to represent any single character, and the asterisk (*) wildcard can be used to represent any character or group of characters that might match that position in other filenames.

Win32-based API A 32-bit application programming interface for both Windows 95 and Windows NT. It updates earlier versions of the Windows API with sophisticated operating system capabilities, security, and API routines for displaying text-based programs in a window.

Windows Internet Name Service (WINS) A name resolution service that resolves Windows networking computer names to IP addresses in a routed environment. A WINS server, which is a Windows NT Server-based computer, handles name registrations, queries, and releases.

Windows NT The portable, secure, 32-bit, preemptive-multitasking member of the Microsoft Windows operating system family. Windows NT Server provides centralized management and security, advanced fault tolerance, and additional connectivity. Windows NT Workstation provides operating system and networking functionality for computers without centralized management.

Windows NT file system (NTFS) An advanced file system designed for use specifically with the Windows NT operating system. NTFS supports file system recovery and extremely large storage media, in addition to other advantages. It also supports object-oriented programs by treating all files as objects with user-defined and system-defined attributes.

WINS *See* Windows Internet Name Service.

workgroup A collection of computers that are grouped for viewing purposes and for sharing resources. Each workgroup is identified by a unique name. *See also* domain and peer-to-peer network.

workstation 1. In general, a powerful computer having considerable calculating and graphics capability. *See also* domain controller and server. 2. A computer that accesses shared network resources provided by another computer (called a server). *See also* client.

Index

M

WELCOME TO THE WORLD OF WINDOWS® 95

The MICROSOFT® WINDOWS® 95 RESOURCE KIT provides you with all of the information necessary to plan for and implement Windows 95 in your organization.

ISBN 1-55615-678-2
1376 pages, $49.95 ($67.95 Canada)
Three 3.5" disks

Details on how to install, configure, and support Windows 95 will save you hours of time and help ensure that you get the most from your computing investment. This exclusive Microsoft publication, written in cooperation with the Windows 95 development team, is the perfect technical companion for network administrators, support professionals, systems integrators, and computer professionals.

The MICROSOFT WINDOWS 95 RESOURCE KIT contains important information that will help you get the most out of Windows 95. Whether you support Windows 95 in your company or just want to know more about it, the MICROSOFT WINDOWS 95 RESOURCE KIT is a valuable addition to your reference library.

Microsoft Press